# Careers in Focus

# COMPLEMENTARY
# AND
# ALTERNATIVE
# HEALTH CARE

**THIRD EDITION**

Ferguson
*An imprint of Infobase Publishing*

**Careers in Focus: Complementary and Alternative Health Care, Third Edition**

Copyright © 2009 by Infobase Publishing

Ferguson
An imprint of Infobase Publishing
132 West 31st Street
New York NY 10001

**Library of Congress Cataloging-in-Publication Data**

Careers in focus. Complementary and alternative health care.
    p. cm.
  Rev.ed. of: Careers in focus. Alternative health care.
  Includes index.
  ISBN-13: 978-0-8160-7302-3 (hardcover : alk. paper)
  ISBN-10: 0-8160-7302-3 (hardcover : alk. paper) 1. Alternative medicine—
Vocational guidance.
  R733.C365 2009
  610.69—dc22

                              2008055094

Ferguson books are available at special discounts when purchased in bulk quantities for businesses, associations, institutions, or sales promotions. Please call our Special Sales Department in New York at (212) 967-8800 or (800) 322-8755.

You can find Ferguson on the World Wide Web at http://www.fergpubco.com

Text design by David Strelecky
Cover design Alicia Post
Composition by Mary Susan Ryan-Flynn
Cover printed by Maple Press, York, PA
Book printed and bound by Maple Press, York, PA
Date printed: September, 2010
Printed in the United States of America

10 9 8 7 6 5 4 3 2

This book is printed on acid-free paper.

# Table of Contents

# Introduction

The fields of complementary and alternative health care are not part of an established industry, with a defined structure and branches, but rather a diverse collection of approaches to wellness, health care, and medicine. These therapies can be grouped into three broad categories: ancient traditional medical systems, more recent complete medical systems, and individual therapies.

Traditional medical systems, such as Ayurveda (traditional Indian medicine) and Oriental medicine, have been developed and practiced over thousands of years in their cultures of origin. These traditional systems are based upon complete philosophies of the origins and nature of life, human beings, wellness, and medicine. To learn and practice such systems successfully, you must be open to understanding what may be (for you) a different value system and integrating that philosophy into your approach to life and the practice of health care and medicine.

A number of alternative health care approaches are of more recent origin, but these are also complete health care systems. Learning health care systems such as homeopathy and chiropractic does not require that you adopt a different philosophy, but many of these disciplines require an educational process that is as demanding as the study of conventional Western medicine.

Other alternative health care approaches focus on a particular type of therapy. Aromatherapy and massage therapy are examples of this group. These therapies are not complete systems of health care: Many of these practices are incorporated into the work of other health care practitioners, and are labeled complementary, or integrative, treatments. Although the therapies in this category generally have less rigorous education requirements for practitioners, they still provide very meaningful opportunities to help people improve their lives.

The rapid changes that have occurred in health care and medicine in recent years seem to have a life and momentum of their own, and the potential for further change is great. In late 1998, the U.S. government gave additional recognition to the field of complementary and alternative health care when it elevated the Office of Alternative Medicine to the status of a center: the National Center for Complementary and Alternative Medicine (NCCAM). The U.S government has also dramatically increased NCCAM's budget since its inception, from $20 million in 1998 to more than $121 million for fiscal year 2008. The center focuses on conducting clinical trials in a variety of complementary and alternative approaches. These trials may provide scientific data that will help legitimize alternative approaches in the eyes of conventional practitioners and thus pave the way toward more cooperation between alternative and conventional practitioners.

In 2000, the White House Commission on Complementary and Alternative Medicine was established to help access and regulate the methods and practitioners of complementary and alternative medicine (CAM). According to a report from the commission, as much as 43 percent of the U.S. population used some form of CAM in 2002. (Although more recent data is unavailable, this percentage is likely higher today as more people embrace complementary and alternative therapies.) Medical professionals, hospitals, and other health care professionals are also showing a growing interest in CAM. In fact, 27 percent of hospitals offered CAM therapies in 2005, according to *US News & World Report*—an increase of 19 percent since 1998.

With its atmosphere of hope, excitement, and change, complementary and alternative health care is one of the most rapidly growing segments of the field of health care. Significant recent events indicate that the complementary and alternative health care explosion will continue well into the 21st century.

Each article in this book discusses a particular complementary or alternative health care occupation in detail. Many of the articles in *Careers in Focus: Complementary* and *Alternative Health Care* appear in Ferguson's *Encyclopedia of Careers and Vocational Guidance,* but the articles here have been updated and revised with the latest information from the U.S. Department of Labor and other sources. Throughout the book you will find informative sidebars, photos, and interviews with professionals working in complementary and alternative health care, as well as the following sections in each article:

The **Quick Facts** section provides a brief summary of the career including recommended school subjects, personal skills, work environment, minimum educational requirements, salary ranges, certification or licensing requirements, and employment outlook. This section also provides acronyms and identification numbers for the following government classification indexes: the *Dictionary of Occupational Titles* (DOT), the *Guide for Occupational Exploration* (GOE), the National Occupational Classification (NOC) Index, and the Occupational Information Network (O*NET)-Standard Occupational Classification System (SOC) index. The DOT, GOE, and O*NET-SOC indexes have been created by the U.S. government;

the NOC index is Canada's career classification system. Readers can use the identification numbers listed in the Quick Facts section to access further information about a career. Print editions of the DOT (*Dictionary of Occupational Titles*. Indianapolis, Ind.: JIST Works, 1991) and GOE (*Guide for Occupational Exploration*. Indianapolis, Ind.: JIST Works, 2001) are available at libraries. Electronic versions of the NOC (http://www23.hrdc-drhc.gc.ca) and O*NET-SOC (http://online.onetcenter.org) are available on the Internet. When no DOT, GOE, NOC, or O*NET-SOC numbers are present, this means that the U.S. Department of Labor or Human Resources Development Canada have not created a numerical designation for this career. In this instance, you will see the acronym "N/A," or not available.

The **Overview** section is a brief introductory description of the duties and responsibilities involved in this career. Oftentimes, a career may have a variety of job titles. When this is the case, alternative career titles are presented. Employment statistics are also provided, when available. The **History** section describes the history of the particular job as it relates to the overall development of its industry or field. **The Job** describes the primary and secondary duties of the job. **Requirements** discusses high school and postsecondary education and training requirements, any certification or licensing that is necessary, and other personal requirements for success in the job. **Exploring** offers suggestions on how to gain experience in or knowledge of the particular job before making a firm educational and financial commitment. The focus is on what can be done while still in high school (or in the early years of college) to gain a better understanding of the job. The **Employers** section gives an overview of typical places of employment for the job. **Starting Out** discusses the best ways to land that first job, be it through the college career services office, newspaper ads, Internet employment sites, or personal contact. The **Advancement** section describes what kind of career path to expect from the job and how to get there. **Earnings** lists salary ranges and describes the typical fringe benefits. The **Work Environment** section describes the typical surroundings and conditions of employment—whether indoors or outdoors, noisy or quiet, social or independent. Also discussed are typical hours worked, any seasonal fluctuations, and the stresses and strains of the job. The **Outlook** section summarizes the job in terms of the general economy and industry projections. For the most part, Outlook information is obtained from the U.S. Bureau of Labor Statistics and is supplemented by information gathered from professional associations. Job growth terms follow those used in the *Occupational Outlook Hand-*

*book*. Growth described as "much faster than the average" means an increase of 21 percent or more. Growth described as "faster than the average" means an increase of 14 to 20 percent. Growth described as "about as fast as the average" means an increase of 7 to 13 percent. Growth described as "more slowly than the average" means an increase of 3 to 6 percent. "Little or no change" means a decrease of 2 percent to an increase of 2 percent. "Decline" means a decrease of 3 percent or more. Each article ends with **For More Information,** which lists organizations that provide information on training, education, internships, scholarships, and job placement.

Whether you have been curious about complementary and alternative health care for some time or are just starting to think about your career, this book provides you with the most current information on the opportunities available in these innovative and rewarding fields.

# Acupuncturists

## OVERVIEW

*Acupuncturists* are health care professionals who practice the ancient Oriental healing art of acupuncture. Acupuncture is a complete medical system that helps to improve body functioning and promote natural healing. It has been practiced in China for thousands of years to maintain health, prevent disease, treat illness, and alleviate pain. It has been proven to be effective in the treatment of emotional and psychological problems as well as physical ailments.

There are more than 22,000 licensed acupuncturists in the United States, some of whom are licensed medical doctors. Acupuncture is one of the fastest growing health care professions. Most acupuncturists work in private practice, although an increasing number work in clinics and hospitals.

## HISTORY

Acupuncture has been practiced for thousands of years. It is one of the ancient Chinese healing arts. The Chinese believe that acupuncture began during the Stone Age, when ancient people used sharp stone tools to puncture and drain boils. As time passed, primitive needles made of stone or pottery replaced the earlier tools. These crude needles were, in turn, replaced by metal needles, which evolved into the very thin needles acupuncturists use today.

Early metal needles had nine different shapes, and they were used for a variety of purposes. However, they weren't applied to specific points on the body. Through centuries of experience and observation, the Chinese learned that the use of the needles on very specific points on the skin was effective in treating particular ailments. They later grouped specific acupuncture points into a system of channels, or *meridians*. Acupuncturists think that these channels run over and through the body, much like rivers and streams run over and through the earth. They teach that the body has a type of vital energy, called *qi* or *chi* (both are pronounced "chee"), and that this energy flows through the body. The acupuncture points along the channels are thought to influence the flow of the vital energy.

Acupuncture developed virtually uninterrupted over thousands of years until the Portuguese landed in China in 1504. Once China was thus opened to the rest of the world, Western medical concepts gradually began to influence the practice of medicine there. Over centuries, the practice of acupuncture declined, and in 1929, it was outlawed in China. Even so, it remained a part of Chinese folk medicine. When the Communist Party came to power in China in 1949, there were almost no medical services. The communists encouraged the use of traditional Chinese remedies, and acupuncture again began to grow.

Just as Western medicine filtered into China, the concept of acupuncture gradually traveled back to the West. It was probably known and used in Europe as early as the 17th century. The first recorded use was in 1810 at the Paris Medical School, where Dr. Louis Berlioz used it to treat abdominal pain. Acupuncture was also used in England in the early 1800s. Ear acupuncture, one of the newer forms of acupuncture, was largely developed outside of China. In the early 1950s, Dr. Paul Nogier of France developed the detailed map of the ear that most acupuncturists now use.

After President Nixon visited China in 1972, public awareness and use of acupuncture began to grow in North America. Today acupuncture is increasingly used in Europe, North America, and Russia. Over one-third of the world's population relies on acupuncture and Oriental medicine practitioners for prevention and treatment of disease, as well as for the enhancement of health. In the West, acupuncture is most well known for pain relief, but a growing body of research shows that it is effective in health maintenance as well as the treatment of many diseases. In 1979, the World Health Organization, the medical branch of the United Nations, issued a list of more than 40 diseases and other health conditions that acupuncture helps alleviate.

During the last decade of the 20th century, major developments in the perception of health care in the United States and throughout the world brought acupuncture and Oriental medicine to the forefront of health care. In 1996, the Food and Drug Administration reclassified acupuncture needles from "investigational" to "safe and effective" medical devices. This opened the door for acupuncture to be recognized by and covered under insurance programs. A 1997 report sponsored by the National Institutes of Health concluded that acupuncture should be integrated into standard medical practice and included in Medicare. These milestones have paved the way toward greater acceptance of acupuncture by the medical community and by the U.S. public.

## THE JOB

Acupuncture is the best-known component of a larger system of medicine known as Oriental medicine. Oriental medicine encompasses a variety of healing modalities, including acupuncture, Chinese herbology, bodywork, dietary therapy, and exercise. An *Oriental medicine practitioner* may practice them all or specialize in only one or two.

Acupuncturists treat symptoms and disorders by inserting very thin needles into precise acupuncture points on the skin. They believe that the body's qi flows along specific channels in the body. Each channel is related to a particular physiological system and internal organ. Disease, pain, and other physical and emotional conditions result when the body's qi is unbalanced, or when the flow of qi along the channels is blocked or disrupted. Acupuncturists stimulate the acupuncture points to balance the circulation of this vital energy. The purpose of acupuncture and other forms of traditional Oriental medicine is to restore and maintain whole body balance.

Acupuncture has been used for centuries to maintain health and relieve a wide range of common ailments, including asthma, high blood pressure, headache, and back pain. A more recent use of acupuncture is treatment of substance abuse withdrawal. Some areas of medicine that use acupuncture include internal medicine, oncology, obstetrics and gynecology, pediatrics, urology, geriatrics, sports medicine, immunology, infectious diseases, and psychiatric disorders. In the United States, acupuncture is perhaps most frequently used for relief of pain.

Like many other health care professionals, acupuncturists take an initial health history when they meet with a new patient. They need to know about the patient's past and present problems. They listen carefully and sensitively, and they incorporate the patient history into their plan of treatment.

Next, acupuncturists give a physical examination. During the examination, they try to determine if a patient's qi is unbalanced. If it is, they look for the location of the imbalance. They test the quality of the pulses in both of the patient's wrists. They examine the shape and color of the tongue, skin color, body language, and tone of voice.

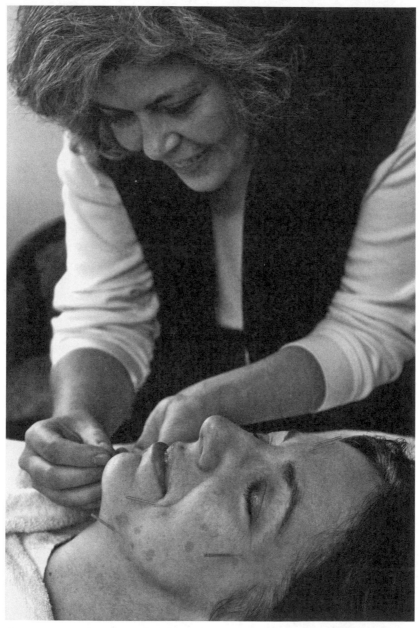

An acupuncturist gives a facial acupuncture treatment to a patient.
(Jim McKnight, AP Photo)

They also check the feel of diagnostic areas of the body, such as the back and the abdomen. Acupuncturists may test for weaknesses in the muscles or along the meridians.

Once acupuncturists identify the source of the qi imbalance, they choose the type of needle to be used. Traditionally, there are nine types of acupuncture needles, ranging in length from just over an inch to as long as seven inches. Each type of needle is used to treat certain conditions. Most acupuncturists in the United States and other Western countries use only three types of needles that range from one to three inches in length. After selecting the type of needle, acupuncturists determine where the needles will be inserted on the patient's body. There are thousands of possible insertion points on the body. Four to 12 needles are typically used in a treatment.

Acupuncture needles are flexible. They are about the diameter of a human hair—much thinner than injection-type needles. They are inserted to a depth of up to an inch. Insertion of the needles is generally painless, although sensitive individuals may feel fleeting discomfort. During treatment, acupuncturists may stimulate the needles to increase the effect. Stimulation is done by twirling the needles or by applying heat or a low electrical current to them.

The first visit usually lasts an hour or more because the history and physical require extra time. Follow-up visits are usually shorter—perhaps 15–45 minutes, although treatments sometimes last an hour or longer. Occasionally only one treatment is required. Other times, the patient may have to return for several sessions.

If acupuncturists incorporate other modalities of Oriental medicine into their practices, they may supplement the acupuncture with the other treatments. They might include herbal therapy, massage, exercise, or nutritional counseling.

In addition to treating patients, acupuncturists have a number of other duties. Most are self-employed, so they have to do their own paperwork. They write reports on their patients' treatments and progress. They bill insurance companies to make sure they get paid. They also have to market their services in order to build their clientele. It is important for them to maintain contacts with other professionals in the medical community, because other professionals may be good sources of referrals. Acupuncturists must also keep up with developments and changes in their profession through continuing education.

## REQUIREMENTS

### High School

If you are interested in a career in acupuncture, take courses that will give you an understanding of the human body. Courses in biology, physiology, and psychology will help you gain an understanding of the body and insight into the mind. Good communication skills are important in all professions, so take English, speech, drama, and debate classes to improve your communication skills.

You are likely to be self-employed if you become an acupuncturist, so math, business, and computer courses will also be helpful. A good, well-rounded education will help prepare you for any career you might choose.

## Postsecondary Training

More than 50 U.S. schools are accredited by the Accreditation Commission for Acupuncture and Oriental Medicine (ACAOM). All of these programs offer master's degrees or master's-level courses. In 2004, the ACAOM approved a doctorate in acupuncture degree, which consists of a 4,000-hour curriculum (minimum 1,200 at the doctoral level) that includes the master's-level training requirements. To be admitted into these programs, virtually every school requires a minimum of two years of undergraduate study. Others require a bachelor's degree in a related field, such as science, nursing, or pre-med.

Most acupuncture programs provide a thorough education in Western sciences, acupuncture techniques, and all aspects of traditional Oriental medicine. See the ACAOM's Web site (http://www.acaom.org) for names, addresses, and descriptions of the programs.

Choosing a school for acupuncture can be complex. One important decision is where you might like to live and practice. Eligibility requirements vary from state to state, so it is important to be sure the school you choose will prepare you to practice in the state in which you wish to live. In some states, only physicians can be licensed to practice acupuncture. In other states, there are no requirements for practicing acupuncture.

Another consideration in making a school choice is the tradition of acupuncture you want to study. There are a number of different types of acupuncture. You will need to find a school that offers the type that interests you. If you need financial assistance, it is important to choose a college that is accredited by the ACAOM. These schools are recognized by the U.S. Department of Education and students may be eligible for federal student loans.

## Certification or Licensing

Acupuncture certification indicates that an individual meets the standards established by a nationally recognized commission. Licensing is a requirement established by a state's governmental body that grants individuals the right to practice within that state.

Licensing requirements vary widely around the country and are changing rapidly.

Certification and licensing are usually achieved by meeting educational requirements and passing an examination. Forty-two states and the District of Columbia use National Certification Commission for Acupuncture and Oriental Medicine (NCCAOM) standards as an integral part of their licensing process. To become nationally board certified in acupuncture, NCCAOM requires applicants to have followed one of the following: a formal education route, apprenticeship route, professional acupuncture practice route, or combination of training and experience. All applicants are required to complete a Clean Needle Technique course and to pass the NCCAOM Acupuncture Examination, which consists of a written examination and the Point Location Examination.

Many states certify only licensed physicians to practice acupuncture, while some states extend this right to chiropractors. In certain states, an acupuncturist is granted the right to practice only after a ruling from the state's board of medical examiners. States that currently have no requirements for practicing acupuncture are considering legislation on the subject.

### Other Requirements
Like other health care practitioners, acupuncturists frequently work with people who are in pain and who have been ill for a long time. Patients often come to acupuncturists after other medical treatments have failed. They may be especially pessimistic about finding relief or cures. Acupuncturists need to be good listeners, patient, and compassionate. Acupuncturists also need to have sensitive hands.

Claudette Baker, Lic. Ac. (licensed acupuncturist), has her office in Evanston, Illinois. She believes that people who become acupuncturists need to have a special perspective on health care. Baker says, "Those who consider a career in acupuncture should be interested in medicine and in healing, but they should also be aware that this profession requires a change in their perception of medicine. Oriental medicine is a science of understanding energetics in the body, and it is a healing art. Students should only consider acupuncture if they have an aptitude for understanding and learning this approach to medicine."

## EXPLORING

If a career in acupuncture interests you, there are many ways to learn more about it. You will find many books at the library. Studying

## Acupuncture and Medical Conditions

The World Health Organization recommends acupuncture as a treatment for the following medical conditions:

**Bronchopulmonary Diseases**
- Acute bronchitis
- Bronchial asthma

**Disorders of the Mouth Cavity**
- Gingivitis
- Pain after tooth extraction
- Pharyngitis
- Toothache

**Eye Disorders**
- Acute conjuctivitis
- Central retinitis
- Myopia

**Gastrointestinal Disorders**
- Acute and chronic colitis
- Acute and chronic gastritis
- Acute bacterial dysentery
- Chronic duodenal ulcer

- Constipation
- Diarrhea
- Hiccups

**Neurologic Disorders**
- Facial paralysis
- Headache
- Low back pain
- Migraine
- Neurogenic bladder dysfunction

**Orthopedic Disorders**
- Rheumatoid arthritis
- Sciatica
- Tennis elbow

**Respiratory Diseases**
- Acute rhinitis
- Acute sinusitis
- Acute tonsillitis
- Common cold

Sources: American Academy of Medical Acupuncture, World Health Organization

Oriental history, thought, and philosophy will help you learn to understand the approach to healing in Oriental medicine.

Health food stores sometimes have books on acupuncture, and they are good places to learn about other alternative or complementary health modalities. Ask the staff if they know acupuncturists in your area. Talk with people who have experienced acupuncture. Find out what it was like and how they felt about it. Make an appointment for a health consultation with an acupuncturist. Find out if this approach to medicine works for you, and if you would like to use it to help others.

Read about or take courses in yoga or t'ai qi (t'ai chi). These are ancient methods for achieving control of the mind and body, and the principles on which they are based are similar to those of acupuncture.

You can also learn more about acupuncture by visiting the Web sites of the national and state professional associations. Some of them offer student memberships and many of them have excellent information online or for purchase.

You could also visit a college of acupuncture to sit in on classes and talk to the students. Ask them about their courseload and what they like and dislike about their programs.

## EMPLOYERS

Most acupuncturists operate private practices. Some form or join partnerships with other acupuncturists or with people skilled in other areas of Oriental medicine. Professionals and clinics in other areas of health care, such as chiropractors, osteopaths, and medical doctors, increasingly count acupuncturists among their ranks.

As acupuncture is finding more acceptance, there are growing opportunities for acupuncturists in hospitals and university medical schools. A few acupuncturists are engaged in medical research. They conduct studies on the effectiveness of acupuncture in treating various health conditions. There is a growing emphasis on research in acupuncture, and this area is likely to employ greater numbers in the future. A small number of acupuncturists work for government agencies, such as the National Institutes of Health.

More than 22,000 licensed acupuncturists are employed in the United States, with about one-third of all practitioners working in California.

## STARTING OUT

To get started as an acupuncturist, one of the most important elements is being sure that you have the proper certification and licensing for your geographical area. This bears repeating, since the requirements for the profession, for each state, and for the nation are changing rapidly.

The career services office of your school may be able to help you find job opportunities. When starting out, some acupuncturists find jobs in clinics with doctors or chiropractors or in wellness centers. This gives them a chance to start practicing without having to equip an office. Some begin working with a more experienced acupuncturist and then later go into private practice. Acupuncturists frequently work in private practice. When starting a new practice, they often have full-time jobs and begin their practices part time.

Networking with professionals in local and national organizations is a good way to learn about job opportunities.

## ADVANCEMENT

Acupuncturists advance in their careers by establishing their own practices and by building large bases of patients. Some start their own clinics. Because acupuncturists receive referrals from physicians and other health care practitioners, relationships with other members of the medical community can be very helpful in building a patient base.

Acupuncturists may eventually wish to teach acupuncture at a school of Oriental medicine. After much experience, an acupuncturist may achieve a supervisory or directorship position in a school. The growing acceptance of acupuncture by the American public and the medical community will lead to an increasing need for research. Acupuncturists can build rewarding careers participating in this effort.

## EARNINGS

Acupuncturists can expect starting earnings that range from $30,000 to $40,000. Experienced acupuncturists earn about $60,000 per year. Physicians who practice acupuncture as part of their medical practices have incomes that can be well over $100,000 per year. As with any other form of self-employment, income is directly related to the number of hours an acupuncturist works and the rates they can charge. Rates increase with experience. Like other self-employed individuals, acupuncturists must provide their own insurance, vacation, and retirement benefits.

## WORK ENVIRONMENT

Acupuncturists usually work indoors in clean, quiet, comfortable offices. Since most are in solo practice, they can choose their surroundings. Private practitioners set their own hours, but many work some evenings and weekends to accommodate their patients' schedules. They usually work without supervision and must have a lot of self-discipline.

For acupuncturists who work in clinics, hospitals, and universities, the surroundings vary. They may work in large hospitals or small colleges. However, wherever they work, acupuncturists need clean, quiet offices. In these larger settings, acupuncturists need to be able to work well in a team environment. They may also need to be able to work well under supervision. Those who are employed in these organizations usually receive salaries and benefits. They may have to follow hours set by the employer.

## OUTLOOK

Acupuncture is growing rapidly as a profession due to increasing public awareness and acceptance. There are more than 22,000 licensed acupuncturists in the United States. The number of certified and licensed acupuncturists is expected to grow as additional states establish legal guidelines for acupuncturists to follow. The recent advances in research, changes in government policy, and interest from the mainstream medical community are strong indicators that the field will continue to expand. As insurance, health maintenance organization (HMO), and other third-party reimbursements increase, acupuncture is expected to grow even more rapidly.

The number of people who receive acupuncture treatments is growing annually. One of the areas of greatest growth is in the treatment of addictions. The United States has provided more than $1 million for research programs to investigate acupuncture's effect on cocaine addiction and alcoholism. Many hospitals and prisons now use acupuncture in their substance abuse programs. Besides the treatment of addictions, other areas of increase in acupuncture include the treatment of chronic pain, bronchial asthma, and premenstrual syndrome.

Despite these factors favoring job growth, much education and research still need to be done to integrate this system of natural healing into the conventional American health care system.

## FOR MORE INFORMATION

*For information on accredited programs, contact*
   **Accreditation Commission for Acupuncture and Oriental
      Medicine**
   Maryland Trade Center #3
   7501 Greenway Center Drive, Suite 760
   Greenbelt, MD 20770-3580
   Tel: 301-313-0855
   Email: coordinator@acaom.org
   http://www.acaom.org

*For information on acupuncture, contact*
**American Academy of Medical Acupuncture**
1970 E. Grand Avenue, Suite 330
El Segundo, CA 90245-5082
Tel: 310-364-0193
Email: administrator@medicalacupuncture.org
http://www.medicalacupuncture.org

*For general information, comprehensive information on the legal status of acupuncture and Oriental medicine in individual states, a list of schools, and a Web site with good links, contact*
**American Association of Acupuncture and Oriental Medicine**
PO Box 162340
Sacramento, CA 95816-2340
Tel: 866-455-7999
http://www.aaaomonline.org

*For information on accredited colleges, contact*
**Council of Colleges of Acupuncture and Oriental Medicine**
3909 National Drive, Suite 125
Burtonsville, MD 20866-6110
Tel: 301-476-7790
http://www.ccaom.org

*For information on certification, contact*
**National Certification Commission for Acupuncture and Oriental Medicine**
76 South Laura Street, Suite 1290
Jacksonville, FL 32202-5410
Tel: 904-598-1005
Email: info@nccaom.org
http://www.nccaom.org

*For answers to frequently asked questions about acupuncture, visit*
**Acupuncture.com**
http://www.acupuncture.com

# Aromatherapists

## OVERVIEW

*Aromatherapists* are health care specialists who use essential plant oils to promote health in their clients. Essential oils are highly concentrated substances that give plants their fragrance. These substances are extracted from various parts of aromatic plants, such as roots, woods, seeds, fruits, leaves, and flowers. Only about 5 percent of all types of plants are used for their essential oils.

Since the early 20th century, the professions of cosmetology, medicine, and psychology have rediscovered the healing powers of essential oils that were known to earlier civilizations. Scientific studies show that inhaling the fragrance of certain essential oils has physiological and psychological effects on the brain. Aromatherapists study the oils and their effects on individuals. They use this knowledge to help improve their clients' quality of life.

Most aromatherapists are licensed in other areas of health care or body care, using aromatherapy as a supplementary tool in their licensed profession. Among these licensed professionals are beauticians, chiropractors, cosmeticians, massage therapists, medical doctors, naturopathic doctors, nurse practitioners, and nurses. A few individuals who specialize in aromatherapy work as chemists, educators, or authors. Others grow plants for the distillation of essential oils, become consultants, or start their own lines of aromatherapy products.

## QUICK FACTS

**School Subjects**
Biology
Chemistry
English

**Personal Skills**
Helping/teaching
Technical/scientific

**Work Environment**
Primarily indoors
Primarily one location

**Minimum Education Level**
Some postsecondary training

**Salary Range**
$13,000 to $45,000 to $80,000+

**Certification or Licensing**
Voluntary

**Outlook**
Faster than the average

**DOT**
N/A

**GOE**
N/A

**NOC**
3232

**O*NET-SOC**
N/A

## HISTORY

Throughout history, civilizations have used essential oils for many purposes—including healing. As an art and science, aromatherapy finds its roots in ancient cultures, dating back 4,000 to 5,000 years. Early Egyptians are often credited with being the first to make an art of the use of essential oils. They used myrrh and frankincense (fragrant resins from trees) in their daily rituals. However, other early cultures also used essential oils. In ancient Africa, people discovered that certain plants provided protection from the sun when they were rubbed on the skin. Chinese, Indian, Persian, and other African cultures used plant oils for incense burning, cooking, cosmetics, mummifying, bathing, perfumery, meditating, and healing.

In the spas of ancient Rome, oils were used in public baths and were applied during massages. The knowledge of oils went along with the spread of Roman culture. Europeans used oils during medieval times to fight disease. During the Middle Ages, the emergence of chemistry and the improvement of distillation helped simplify the process of extracting essential oils from plants. This opened the door to oil trading, which spread the new practices to more people and places.

Until the advent of scientifically derived medicines in the 19th century, Europeans used essential oils both as perfumes and for medicinal purposes. With the growth of newer medical practices, doctors began to choose modern medicine over the tradition of oils. It was not until the 20th century that several individuals "rediscovered" the healing power of essential oils. Once again the use of oils was integrated into Western culture.

In 1928, the French perfumer and chemist René-Maurice Gattefossé experienced the healing power of essential oils. When he severely burned his hand, he stuck it into the nearest liquid, which happened to be lavender oil. He was surprised how quickly the hand healed. His experience caused him to become interested in the therapeutic use of essential oils. It was Gattefossé who coined the term *aromatherapy*.

Dr. Jean Valnet, a French physician, was the first to reintegrate essential oils into Western medical practice. Dr. Valnet served as an army surgeon during World War II. Inspired by the work of Gattefossé, he used essential oils to treat soldiers' burns and wounds. He also successfully treated psychiatric problems with fragrances.

Marguerite Maury, an Austrian biochemist, was also influenced by the work of Gattefossé. She integrated the use of essential oils into cosmetics.

In 1977, Robert Tisserand, an expert in aromatherapy, wrote *The Art of Aromatherapy*. Tisserand was strongly influenced by the work of both Gattefossé and Valnet. His book caught the interest of the American public and made a major contribution to the growth of aromatherapy in this country.

The Western world has rediscovered the uses of essential oils and fragrances through the work of people like Valnet, Maury, and Tisserand. In France, aromatherapy is practiced by medical doctors. Conventional and alternative medicine practitioners in England, Australia, Sweden, Japan, the United States, and other parts of the world are recognizing and utilizing the healing power of essential oils. The world is reawakening to the healing and life-enhancing capabilities of aromatherapy.

## THE JOB

Whether aromatherapists work primarily as beauticians, chiropractors, massage therapists, or doctors, they must possess a strong working knowledge of aromatherapy as a science and an art. They need to understand the components and healing benefits of many essential oils. The quality of essential oils varies greatly depending on the plant, where it is grown, the conditions under which it is grown, and other factors. As a result, aromatherapists must be very careful about choosing the sources from which their oils come. Pure, high-quality, therapeutic grade oils are essential to good aromatherapy. Aromatherapists must even know the differences between the oils of different species of the same plant. Essential oils are very powerful because of their high concentration. It may take well over 100 pounds of plant material to produce just one pound of essential oil.

Because of the powerful concentration of essential oils, aromatherapists use great care in diluting them and in adding them to what are called carrier oils. These are most often high-quality vegetable oils, such as almond, olive, or sesame. Unlike essential oils, carrier oils are fixed, rather than volatile. A small amount of an essential oil is blended into the carrier oil, which "carries" it across the body. Aromatherapists are especially careful when the oils are to be applied to a client's skin or put into a bath. In addition, aromatherapists must know how different essential oils work together because they are often combined to achieve certain results.

Aromatherapists need to know much more than what oils to use. They use the essential oils in three types of aromatherapy: cosmetic, massage, and olfactory. Aromatherapists have to know the differences among the types of therapy. They must decide which type or combination of types to use in a particular situation, and they must be skilled in each type.

Aromatherapists must know how the body, mind, and emotions work together. For example, a client who complains of muscle tension may need physical relief. A massage with relaxing oils that the skin soaks in will relax the client. However, aromatherapists are able to take this treatment a step further. They consider the underlying causes of the condition. Why is the client feeling tense? Is it stress? Anxiety? Strong emotion? Massage therapists who are trained in aromatherapy may inquire about the client's life in order to pinpoint the source of the tension. Once the source is identified, aromatherapists utilize specific oils to produce a certain emotional effect in the client. When the scents of these oils are inhaled, they create a response within the entire body. The oils may be added to a bath or a compress that is applied to the body. (A compress is a towel soaked in water that has a bit of an essential oil added to it.) An aroma may take the client back to happier times, as a reminder of warmth, comfort, and contentment.

An aromatherapist's client may have skin problems due to stress. The aromatherapist may use certain essential oils to help both the skin condition on the surface and the underlying emotional source of the problem. This might be accomplished through olfactory aromatherapy—the inhalation of the oil vapors.

In a hospital, nursing home, or hospice setting, an aromatherapist might choose essential oils that help relieve stress. In England, hospital nursing staffs utilize essential oil massage. This type of therapy has been shown to relieve pain and induce sleep. Essential oil massage has proven effective in relieving the stress that patients experience with general illness, surgery, terminal cancer, and AIDS. Aromatherapists emphasize that these treatments are supplementary and enhancing to medical care—they do not replace medical treatment.

No two clients' problems are the same, and neither are the remedies for those problems. Each client must be treated as an individual. During the first visit, aromatherapists usually take a careful client history. Aromatherapists must listen carefully both for things their clients say and for things they don't say. Aromatherapists need to know if a client is taking any medicine or using any natural healing substances, such as herbs. They must understand the properties of essential oils and how they might interact with any other treatment the client is using. Next, they use the information gathered from the client interview to determine the proper essential oils and the appropriate amounts to blend to serve the client's particular needs.

Aromatherapists are employed in a number of different work environments. Those connected to the beauty industry may work in salons, spas, or hotel resorts, incorporating aromatherapy into facial care, body care, and hair care. In the health care field, many professionals are turning to alternative approaches to care, and some conventional medical practitioners are beginning to implement more holistic approaches. As a result, a growing number of aromatherapists work in the offices of other health care specialists, where their aromatherapy treatments complement the other therapies used. Aromatherapists often give seminars, teach, or serve as consultants. Some who become experts on essential oils buy farms to grow plants for the oils, create

# Top 10 Essential Oils

**Clary Sage**
Reduces pain, encourages relaxation, fights insomnia, balances hormones in females

**Eucalyptus**
Treats respiratory problems, strengthens immune system, relieves muscle tension

**Geranium**
Encourages relaxation, helps fight depression, encourages healthy skin, balances hormones in females

**Lavender**
Treats infections and wounds, encourages relaxation

**Lemon**
Treats infections and wounds, encourages relaxation, mood elevator, deodorizer

**Peppermint**
Treats digestive disorders, headaches, and muscle aches

**Roman Chamomile**
Encourages relaxation, fights insomnia, reduces anxiety, treats muscle aches, infection, and wounds

**Rosemary**
Provides mental stimulation, boosts the immune system, treats muscle aches, aids digestive system

**Tea Tree**
Provides antifungal properties, strengthens immune system

**Ylang Ylang**
Encourages relaxation, reduces muscle tension, helps fight depression

Source: National Association for Holistic Aromatherapy

their own lines of aromatherapy products, or sell essential oils to other aromatherapists.

## REQUIREMENTS
### High School
If you are interested in working with aromatherapy, begin in high school by building up your knowledge of the human body's systems. Biology, anatomy, and physiology will help lay the foundation for a career in aromatherapy. Chemistry courses will familiarize you with laboratory procedures. Aromatherapists need to have an understanding of mixtures and the care involved in using powerful essential oils. Chemistry can help you gain the experience you need to handle delicate or volatile substances. It will also familiarize you with the properties of natural compounds.

Keep in mind that the majority of aromatherapists are self-employed. Math, business, and computer courses will help you develop the skills you need to be successful at running a business. Aromatherapists also need good communication and interpersonal skills to be sensitive to their clients. English, speech, and psychology classes can help you sharpen your ability to interact constructively with other people.

Eva-Marie Lind is an aromatherapist, author, and former dean of the Aromatherapy Department of the Australasian College of Herbal Studies in Portland, Oregon. She has worked in the field of aromatherapy for more than 15 years. According to Lind, "Education is the key to good aromatherapy. There is so much to learn, and it takes real dedication to study."

### Postsecondary Training
In 1999, the National Association for Holistic Aromatherapy (NAHA) established criteria for aromatherapy education that have been voluntarily adopted by a number of schools and education programs. The NAHA guidelines recommend that aromatherapy education include courses on topics such as the history of aromatherapy, physiology, production of essential oils, botany, chemistry, safety and methods of application, and business planning.

While the NAHA provides a listing of schools complying with its guidelines, there are also other schools, seminars, and distance learning courses that offer training in aromatherapy. Be aware, however, that the quality of programs can vary. Take the time to call the schools or organizations that interest you. Ask how their programs are set up. For correspondence courses (or distance courses), ask if you will be able to talk to a teacher. How will you be evaluated? Are there tests? How are the tests taken and graded? Try to talk with current students. Ask how they are treated and what they learn. Ask what you receive when you graduate from the program. Will you receive help with job placement? Access to insurance programs? Other benefits? Depending on the program you pick, the length of study ranges from short workshops to four-year college courses. Vocational schools, major universities, and naturopathic colleges are increasingly offering training in aromatherapy.

Most aromatherapists are also professionals in other fields. Consider whether you would want to combine aromatherapy with a profession such as chiropractic, massage therapy, nursing, or another field. These other fields require additional education and certification as well as licensing. If you decide to add aromatherapy to another profession, learn the requirements for certification or licensing that apply to that profession. Adding aromatherapy to another profession requires a comprehensive understanding of both fields from a scientific standpoint.

## Certification or Licensing

The Aromatherapy Registration Council offers voluntary registration to aromatherapists who meet minimum educational standards from a council-approved academic institution and pass an examination, which focuses on four knowledge areas: Basic Concepts of Aromatherapy, Scientific Principles, Administration, and Professional Issues. Registration must be renewed every five years. Contact the council for more information on registration requirements.

If you choose to combine aromatherapy with another profession, you must meet the national and local requirements for that field in addition to aromatherapy requirements.

## Other Requirements

According to Eva-Marie Lind, "Aromatherapy demands love and passion at its roots. You need to honor, respect, and celebrate the beauty of this field."

You must also enjoy disseminating knowledge because clients often have many questions. More practically, it takes a good nose and a certain sensitivity to successfully treat clients through aromatherapy. It takes good listening skills and immense creativity to understand each client's personal issues and decide on the best means of administering a treatment. Which essential oils or combination of oils should you choose? Should you use a bath, a compress, a massage, or inhalation? What parts of the body are the best avenues for delivering the remedy?

Aromatherapists must be good self-teachers who are interested in continuing education. This is a relatively new field that is developing and changing rapidly. To stay competitive and successful, you need to keep up with the changing trends, products, and technologies that affect the field. Like most healing professions, aromatherapy is a lifelong education process for the practitioner.

## EXPLORING

There are many ways to explore the field of aromatherapy to see if it is for you. For one, there are many books and specialized periodicals available on the subject. These will help you to get a glimpse of the types of knowledge you need for the field. Find out whether it is too scientific or not scientific enough. Look in your local library for books and magazines that show you what a typical student of aromatherapy might be learning.

Visit health food stores. The staff members of health food stores are often very helpful. Most have books, magazines, and newspapers about many kinds of alternative health care, including aromatherapy. Ask about essential oils, and ask for the names of aromatherapists in the area. Find out if there are garden clubs that you can join—particularly ones that specialize in herbs. Consider taking up cooking. This could give you practice in selecting herbs and seasonings and blending them to create different aromas and flavors.

Contact local and national professional organizations. Some offer student memberships or free seminars. Check out their Web sites. They have a lot of valuable information and good links to other alternative health care sites. Join online forums and discussion groups where you can communicate with professionals from all over the country and the world. Some distance learning courses are open to students of all ages. Check into them.

If you find you have a real interest in aromatherapy, another way to explore the field is to seek a mentor, a professional in the field who is willing to help you learn. Tell everyone you know that you are interested in aromatherapy. Someone is bound to have a connection with someone you could call for an information interview. Perhaps you could spend a day "shadowing" an aromatherapist to see what the work is like. If you are unable to find an aromatherapy specialist, you could call spas and salons in search of professionals who use aromatherapy in their work. Someone may be willing to speak to you about their day-to-day work. Make an appointment and experience an aromatherapy treatment. Taking it a step further, you could explore the possibility of getting a part-time job at an establishment that employs aromatherapists.

# EMPLOYERS

Most aromatherapists are self-employed. They run their own small businesses and build their own clientele. Some set up their own offices, but many build their businesses by working in the offices of other professionals and giving aromatherapy treatments as supplements to the treatments provided by the resident professionals. Many different kinds of employers are looking for skilled aromatherapists. In the cosmetic industry, beauticians, cosmeticians, and massage therapists employ aromatherapists to give treatments that complement their own. Spas, athletic clubs, resorts, and cruise ships may hire aromatherapists on a full-time basis. These types of employment may be temporary or seasonal.

In the health care industry, chiropractors, acupuncturists, and other alternative therapy practitioners and clinics may offer aromatherapy in addition to their basic services. Hospitals, nursing homes, hospice centers, and other medical establishments are beginning to recognize the physiological and psychological benefits of aromatherapy for their patients.

# STARTING OUT

Because the practice of aromatherapy may be incorporated into numerous other professions, there are many ways to enter the field. How you enter depends on how you want to use aromatherapy. Is your interest in massage therapy, skin care, or hair care? Do you want to be a nurse, doctor, acupuncturist, or chiropractor? Are you interested in becoming an instructor or writer? Once you are certified in another area, you need to search for clinics, salons, spas, and other establishments that are looking for professionals who use aromatherapy in their treatments. School career services offices are also ways to find work. Classified ads in newspapers and trade magazines list positions in the related fields.

Networking can be an important source of job opportunities. Networking is simply getting to know others and exchanging ideas with them. Go to association meetings and conventions. Talk to people in the field. Job openings are often posted at such gatherings.

# ADVANCEMENT

Aromatherapists can advance to many different levels, depending on their goals and willingness to work. Those who are self-employed can increase their clientele and open their own offices or even a salon. Those who are employed at a spa or salon could become a department director or the director of the entire spa or salon. They might start a private practice or open a spa or salon.

As their skills and knowledge grow, aromatherapists may be sought after to teach and train other aromatherapists in seminars or at schools that offer aromatherapy programs or courses. Others become consultants or write books and articles. A few start their own aromatherapy product lines of esthetic or therapeutic products. Some may become involved in growing the plants that are the sources of essential oils. Still others work in distilling, analyzing, or blending the oils.

This new field is growing so rapidly that the potential for advancement is enormous. The field has so many facets that the directions for growth are as great as your imagination and determination. A public relations representative from the National Association for Holistic Aromatherapy says, "If you are self-motivated, creative, and have a talent for any aspect of aromatherapy, the sky is the limit. It is what you make it."

## EARNINGS

Since aromatherapists work in such a variety of settings, and aromatherapy is often a supplementary therapy added to other professional training, it is particularly difficult to make statements about average earnings in the field. Government agencies do not yet have wage statistics for the field. The national professional associations have not yet developed surveys of their members that give reliable information.

For those who are self-employed in any profession, earnings depend on the amount of time they work and the amount they charge per hour. Experienced professional aromatherapists estimate that hourly rates can range from $25 to $65 for beginning aromatherapists and instructors. Rates increase with experience to between $75 and $100 per hour. Based on those rates, a beginning aromatherapist who charges $25 an hour and averages 10 appointments per week will earn around $13,000. According to the U.S. Department of Labor, in 2007 the median annual salary for people engaged in personal care and service occupations (the category aromatherapy would fall into) was $19,760, with the bottom 10 percent earning $14,190 or less per year and the top 10 percent $38,990 or more. Established aromatherapists who have a solid client base report earning $25,000 to $45,000.

The hourly rate an aromatherapist charges depends on his or her level of expertise, the type of clientele served, and even the area of the country. In many of the larger cities and much of the West

Coast, people are already more aware and accepting of alternative health therapies. In those areas, higher hourly rates will be more accepted. Where such therapies are practically unknown, lower rates will apply. Another consideration for the self-employed is that they must provide their own insurance and retirement plans and pay for their supplies and other business expenses.

An aromatherapist with determination, creativity, and initiative can find jobs that pay well. Some who run exclusive spas or develop their own lines of aromatherapy products are reported to earn $70,000 to $80,000 or more.

Aromatherapists who are primarily employed in other professions, such as massage therapists, chiropractors, cosmetologists, and nurses, can expect to make the salaries that are average for their profession. Those professionals who use aromatherapy as a supportive therapy to their primary profession tend to have higher incomes than those who specialize in aromatherapy. The addition of aromatherapy to their profession will probably enhance their clients' and their own satisfaction, but it may not increase their income.

Self-employed aromatherapists must provide their own benefits, such as health and life insurance and a savings and pension plan.

## WORK ENVIRONMENT

Aromatherapists work in a service-oriented environment, in which the main duty involves understanding and helping their clients. The surroundings are usually clean, peaceful, and pleasant. They work with very potent substances (strong essential oils), but most aromatherapists love the scents and the experience of the oils. They often spend a great deal of time on their feet. They sometimes work long or inconsistent hours, such as weekends and evenings, to accommodate their clients' needs.

Aromatherapists are people-oriented. Those who are self-employed must be highly motivated and able to work alone. Aromatherapists who work in clinics, spas, hospitals, resorts, and other locations need to be able to work well with others.

## OUTLOOK

Aromatherapy has been growing very rapidly and is gathering steam in the United States. Opportunities are increasing rapidly as public awareness of alternative therapies is increasing.

The status of aromatherapy in European and other countries may provide a glimpse of the future of the field in the United States. In Great Britain and France, for example, more doctors have embraced aromatherapy, and these services are covered by major health plans. If the United States follows this lead, new doors will open in this field. In general, the outlook is very good for aromatherapy because of an overwhelming increase in public awareness and interest.

## FOR MORE INFORMATION

*For information regarding state regulations for massage therapists and general information on therapeutic massage, contact*
**American Massage Therapy Association**
500 Davis Street, Suite 900
Evanston, IL 60201-4695
Tel: 877-905-2700
Email: info@amtamassage.org
http://www.amtamassage.org

*For information on registration, contact*
**Aromatherapy Registration Council**
5940 SW Hood Avenue
Portland, OR 97039-3719
Tel: 503-244-0726
Email: info@aromatherapycouncil.org
http://www.aromatherapycouncil.org

*The National Association for Holistic Aromatherapy has developed guidelines for aromatherapy training. See its Web site for a listing of schools in compliance with these guidelines.*
**National Association for Holistic Aromatherapy**
3327 West Indian Trail Road, PMB 144
Spokane, WA 99208-4762
Tel: 509-325-3419
Email: info@naha.org
http://www.naha.org

*For general information about aromatherapy and education options, visit the following Web site:*
**AromaWeb**
http://www.aromaweb.com

# Ayurvedic Doctors and Practitioners

## OVERVIEW

*Ayurvedic doctors and practitioners* use theories and techniques developed thousands of years ago in India to bring people into physical, mental, emotional, and spiritual balance, thereby maintaining health, curing diseases, and promoting happiness and fulfillment. In the West, where Ayurveda is not an officially accepted and licensed form of medicine, only licensed medical doctors who are also thoroughly trained in Ayurveda can legally practice Ayurvedic medicine. These individuals are referred to as Ayurvedic doctors.

Licensed practitioners of paramedical professions, such as nutritionists, psychologists, naturopaths, massage therapists, and acupuncturists, may be called Ayurvedic practitioners if they are also trained in Ayurveda and use Ayurvedic techniques in their professional work. Any non-M.D. who practices the full range of Ayurvedic medicine in the West, however, is seen as practicing medicine without a license, which is illegal.

## HISTORY

The Vedas, which may be up to 5,000 years old, are the oldest and most important scriptures of Hinduism, which is the primary religion in India. The Sanskrit word *veda* means "knowledge," and the Vedas contain the knowledge and beliefs on which Hinduism is based. The Atharvaveda—the Veda that deals primarily with the practical aspects of life—contains chants, rites, and spells that are thought to enable believers to do such things as create love and goodwill among people, defeat enemies, and ensure success in agriculture. Most experts believe that the Atharvaveda is the basis of Ayurveda.

The word *Ayurveda* means "knowledge of life." The oldest of the specifically Ayurvedic texts, the *Charaka Samhita*, was written in approximately 1000 B.C. and deals with internal medicine. This and more recent texts, such as the *Astanga Hridayam,* a compilation of Ayurvedic knowledge written in approximately 1000 A.D., provide Ayurvedic practitioners with the knowledge they need to help their patients.

Ayurvedic medicine is officially accepted in India, where approximately 80 percent of those who seek medical help go to Ayurvedic doctors. In its country of origin, Ayurveda has been substantially modernized, and it now includes many techniques and medications that originated in the West. For example, in addition to ancient herbal formulas, Indian Ayurvedic doctors often prescribe antibiotics. Most Indian doctors have discarded the use of certain older practices that are described in early texts, such as the use of leeches for bloodletting.

## THE JOB

Ayurveda is a way of life rather than simply a system of healing. It is a holistic system, which means that it views physical, mental, and spiritual health as intrinsically connected. An Ayurvedic doctor or practitioner treats the whole person, not simply the symptoms that a patient displays.

Ayurvedic doctors and practitioners base their treatments and recommendations on a complex body of beliefs. One of the most important beliefs holds that everything in the universe is composed of one or more of the five elements: air, fire, earth, water, and ether (space). These elements are concepts or qualities as much as they are actual entities. For example, anything that has the qualities that Ayurveda associates with fire is a manifestation of fire. A person's violent temper demonstrates the existence of fire within that person.

For the purposes of treating people, Ayurveda distills the concept of the five elements to three combinations of two elements. These are the *doshas,* which may be thought of as qualities or energies. The first dosha, Vata, is a combination of air and ether, with air predominating. The second dosha, Pitta, is a combination of fire and water, with fire predominating. The third dosha, Kapha, is a combination of water and earth, with water predominating. Every person is dominated by one or more doshas, although every person contains some element of all three. The unique combination of doshas that appears in a person is that person's *tridosha,* and that combination determines the person's constitution, or *prakriti.*

Because Ayurvedic theory holds that a person's nature and personality are based on his or her doshic makeup, or tridosha, the first thing that an Ayurvedic doctor or practitioner does when seeing a patient is to determine what that doshic makeup is. This is done by various means, including observation of physical qualities such as build, nails, lips, hair color, eye color, and skin type; taking the pulse in various locations; examination of the "nine doors," which are eyes, ears, nostrils, mouth, genitals, and anus; and questioning the patient about past history, present problems, goals, and so forth. After analyzing all this information, the practitioner determines which dosha or combination of doshas predominates in the patient's makeup.

Vata people tend to be extremely tall or extremely short and to have long fingers and toes. They are generally thin and have dark complexions and dry skin. The air element that predominates in their makeup tends to makes light, cold, and dry in various ways. They are often extremely creative, but their minds tend to flit from idea to idea, and they may be spacey and disorganized.

Pitta people, who are dominated by the fire element, are generally of medium build, and their fingers and toes are of medium length. They tend to be fair in complexion, with blond, light brown, or red hair. All redheads are said to have a significant amount of Pitta in their tridoshas. Pittas are quick to anger, can be forceful and domineering, and are highly organized. They make good engineers, accountants, and managers.

Kapha people, who are dominated by the water element, are generally large and well-built, with dark hair and oily skin. Their toes and fingers are short and thick. Kaphas may gain weight easily but have great physical stamina. They are usually calm people who avoid confrontation, but once they are angered, they hold a grudge. They like routine, tend not to be extremely creative, and are reliable.

Once the practitioner has determined the patient's tridosha and has ascertained what the patient's condition, problems, and desires are, the practitioner creates a program that will improve the patient's health and well-being. One of the most important methods that the practitioner will use is diet. If the patient's tridosha is out of balance, controlled to an extreme degree by one of the doshas, the practitioner may put together a diet that will decrease that dosha and/or increase the others, gradually and safely bringing the patient to a state of balance. Ayurvedic practitioners must therefore have a thorough knowledge of foods, traditional nutrition, and cooking.

Proper eating and good digestion are extremely important in Ayurveda, but Ayurvedic practitioners also use many other methods, among which are the techniques of *panchakarma,* which means "five actions." Panchakarma is a powerful set of cleansing practices that is ideally undertaken only under the guidance of an Ayurvedic doctor. The treatment varies by individual, but generally a patient must undergo one to seven days of preparation before the treatment begins. The preparation involves oil massage and steam baths, which sometimes include herbal treatments. After the body is sufficiently cleansed, the panchakarma may begin.

The first of the five practices is *vamana,* which involves removing excess Kapha from the stomach by inducing vomiting by gentle means. The second practice is *virechana,* which involves using laxatives to purge the body of excess Pitta. The third and fourth practices are both forms of *vasti,* or enema therapy, in which herbal preparations are used to remove Vata from the system. One form is relatively mild; the other is stronger. The fifth practice is *nasya,* which involves ingesting liquid or powdered substances through the nose. This practice is generally used to treat illnesses that affect the head and neck. It can take up to 30 days to complete the process of panchakarma.

There are many more aspects of Ayurvedic practice, and one of the most important things that doctors and practitioners do is advise patients regarding their lifestyle. They recommend various practices, such as cleaning the tongue daily, engaging in meditation, practicing yoga, and massaging the body with oils suitable for one's tridosha and the time of year. They may even advise patients regarding what kinds of clothes are best for them and where they will be most comfortable living.

## REQUIREMENTS

### High School

If Ayurvedic medicine interests you, learn as much as possible about health, medicine, science, and anatomy while in high school, just as you would to prepare for a career in Western medicine. Courses in biology and chemistry are important. It will also be important to study the Hindu tradition and become familiar with Sanskrit terms. Studying Sanskrit, the language of the Vedas and the Ayurvedic texts, is a good idea, although it is not absolutely essential. Although Sanskrit is not offered in high schools, correspondence courses are available, and students in large cities may find Sanskrit courses in universities or may find teachers in an Indian community.

## Postsecondary Training

Postsecondary training depends on the path you want to take. To become a full-fledged Ayurvedic doctor in the West, you must be trained as a medical doctor as well as in Ayurveda, which means getting a bachelor's degree, going to medical school, and completing an internship.

According to Scott Gerson, M.D., a fully trained Ayurvedic doctor who runs the National Institute of Ayurvedic Medicine (NIAM), specializing in internal medicine or family practice is usually the best route for those who wish to become Ayurvedic doctors, although it is possible to combine other medical specialties with Ayurvedic practice in a beneficial way. Those who wish to combine Ayurveda with careers as nutritionists, psychologists, naturopaths, and so forth must complete the educational and training requirements for those specialties as well as study Ayurveda. It is not a good idea to go into business in a Western country simply as an expert in Ayurveda, since no licensing is available and doing so may leave you open to charges of practicing medicine without a license.

The single most important part of a doctor's or practitioner's Ayurvedic training is the completion of a rigorous course of study and practice. Naturally, a student who wishes to practice should select the most comprehensive course available. An excellent way to learn Ayurveda is to study at a good Indian institution and become a full-fledged Ayurvedic doctor in India. That kind of program typically takes five years to complete and also involves supervised practice afterward. Remember, though, that being licensed in India does not make it legal to practice as a doctor in the West. Alternatively, a student may study in the West, where various institutions offer Ayurvedic training. The NIAM offers a three-year program in Ayurvedic medicine (see contact information at the end of this article).

## Other Requirements

Ayurvedic practitioners and doctors work closely with their clients, so it is essential that they be able to gain their clients' or patients' trust, make them comfortable and relaxed, and communicate effectively enough with them to gather the information that they need in order to treat them effectively. It is unlikely that an uncommunicative person who is uncomfortable with people will be able to build a successful Ayurvedic practice. In addition, a practitioner must be comfortable making decisions and working alone.

Although some jobs are available in alternative health practices, most Ayurvedic doctors and practitioners have their own practices, and anyone who sets up shop will need to deal with the basic tasks and problems that all business owners face: advertising, accounting, taxes, legal requirements, and so forth. In addition, because Ayurveda is rooted in Hinduism, people whose religious beliefs are in conflict with Hinduism or who are uncomfortable with organized religion may be unwilling or unable to practice Ayurveda effectively.

## EXPLORING

The best way to learn about Ayurveda is to speak with those who practice it. Call practitioners and ask to interview them. Find practitioners in your area if you can, but do not hesitate to contact people in other areas. There is no substitute for learning from those who actually do the work. Although many practitioners run one-person practices, it may be possible to find work of some kind with a successful practitioner or a clinic in your area, especially if you live in a large city.

You should also do as much reading as you can on the subject. Many books on Ayurveda are available. Also look for information on Ayurveda in magazines that deal with alternative medicine or Hinduism. You may also wish to read about traditional Oriental medicine, which is similar to Ayurveda in many ways.

## EMPLOYERS

For the most part, Ayurvedic practitioners work for themselves, although some teach in institutions and others work for alternative clinics.

## STARTING OUT

In addition to receiving training in medicine or in another professional field of your choice, you should begin by taking a comprehensive Ayurvedic course of study. After that, if you have not found an organization that you can work for, you should begin to practice on your own. You may rent an office or set up shop at home. Be sure to investigate the state and local laws that affect you.

A practitioner who runs his or her own business must be well versed in basic business skills. Take courses in business or get advice from the local office of the Small Business Administration. Seek advice from people you know who run their own businesses. Your financial survival will depend on your business skills, so be sure that you are as well prepared as possible.

## ADVANCEMENT

Because most Ayurvedic doctors and practitioners work for themselves, advancement in the field is directly related to the quality of treatment they provide and their business skills. Ayurvedic practitioners can advance in their field by proving to the members of their community that they are skilled, honest, professional, and effective. Before they can be financially successful, there must be a strong demand for their services.

## EARNINGS

Generally, Ayurvedic doctors earn what most doctors in their fields of specialty earn. The situation is the same for practitioners, who generally earn what other people in their fields earn. It is probably safe to say that Ayurvedic practitioners on the low end make $20,000 per year and up, practitioners in more lucrative fields make between $35,000 and $60,000. Ayurvedic doctors earn amounts up to—and in some cases even more than—$150,000.

Self-employed Ayurvedic doctors and practitioners must provide their own benefits. Those who are employed by academic institutions and alternative clinics receive benefits such as vacation days, sick leave, health and life insurance, and a savings and pension program.

### Books to Read

Balch, Phyllis A. *Prescription for Nutritional Healing.* 4th ed. New York: Avery, 2006.

Bratman, Steven. *Collins Alternative Health Guide.* New York: Collins, 2007.

Ernst, Edzard, Max H. Pittler, and Barbara Wider, eds. *The Desktop Guide to Complementary and Alternative Medicine: An Evidence-Based Approach.* 2d ed. St. Louis: Mosby, 2006.

Lake, James, and David Spiegel. *Complementary and Alternative Treatments in Mental Health Care.* Arlington, Va.: American Psychiatric Publishing, 2006.

Strozier, Anne L., and Joyce E. Carpenter. *Introduction to Alternative and Complementary Therapies.* Binghamton, N.Y.: Haworth Press, 2006.

Tierney, Gillian. *Opportunities in Holistic Health Care Careers.* New York: McGraw-Hill, 2006.

## WORK ENVIRONMENT

Ayurvedic practitioners usually work in their own homes or offices. Some practitioners may have office help, while others work alone. For this reason, they must be independent enough to work effectively on their own. Because they must make their clients comfortable in order to provide effective treatment, they generally try to make their workplaces as pleasant and relaxing as possible.

## OUTLOOK

Although no official government analysis of the future of Ayurveda has yet been conducted, it seems safe to say that the field is expanding more rapidly than the average for all fields. Although science still views it with skepticism, Ayurveda has become relatively popular in a short period of time, largely because of the popularity of Deepak Chopra, an Ayurvedic expert who is also an M.D. It has certainly benefited from the popular acceptance of alternative medicine and therapies in recent years, particularly because it is a holistic practice that aims to treat the whole person rather than the symptoms of disease or discomfort. Because Western medicine is too often mechanical and dehumanizing, many people are looking for alternative forms of medicine.

## FOR MORE INFORMATION

*The AIVS provides on-site and correspondence training in Ayurveda, as well as courses in Sanskrit and other subjects of interest to Ayurvedic practitioners. It should be noted that correspondence courses do not qualify one as a practitioner, but they do prepare one for more in-depth training.*

**American Institute of Vedic Studies (AIVS)**
PO Box 8357
Santa Fe, NM 87504-8357
Tel: 505-983-9385
Email: vedicinst@aol.com
http://www.vedanet.com

*The Ayurvedic Institute offers both on-site and correspondence courses in Ayurveda. Some of the organization's resources are available only to those who pay a membership fee.*

**Ayurvedic Institute**
11311 Menaul Boulevard, NE
Albuquerque, NM 87112-2438
Tel: 505-291-9698

Email: info@ayurveda.com
http://www.ayurveda.com

*Deepak Chopra's Center does not offer training for practitioners, but it does offer courses for those who are interested in using Ayurveda in their own lives.*
**Chopra Center at La Costa Resort and Spa**
2013 Costa del Mar Road
Carlsbad, CA 92009-6801
Tel: 888-424-6772
Email: info@chopra.com
http://www.chopra.com

*The NIAM offers on-site training, sells correspondence courses, and sells Ayurvedic books and supplies. It offers a three-year training program in Ayurveda.*
**National Institute of Ayurvedic Medicine (NIAM)**
584 Milltown Road
Brewster, NY 10509
Tel: 845-278-8700
Email: ayurveda@niam.com
http://www.niam.com

# Biofeedback Therapists

## OVERVIEW

Biofeedback training is a process that helps patients gain control of their responses to stress, anxiety, physical strain, and emotional stimuli. Special instruments monitor a variety of physiological conditions, including heart rate, skin temperature, muscle tension, and blood pressure. *Biofeedback therapists* assist patients in interpreting the information gathered through monitoring. They help them learn to control individual body functions and reactions in ways that can decrease stress and alleviate the effects of a wide range of disorders, such as migraine headaches, gastrointestinal concerns, and epilepsy.

## HISTORY

Biofeedback therapy has a relatively short history. The term itself did not come into widespread use until roughly 1969, when the results of four separate lines of research converged into a new approach to the treatment of a variety of medical and psychological conditions.

Until the early 1960s, psychologists generally accepted the premise that biological responses typically thought to be "involuntary," or under the control of the autonomic nervous system (such as heart rate, stomach acid secretion, blood pressure, or skin resistance), could not be modified or influenced using measurable instrumental means. Instead, this form of conditioned learning was thought possible only for responses that were under "voluntary" control, such as skeletal muscle responses. A definitive statement of this collective assumption appeared in a 1961 textbook, prompting a number of scientists to begin studies to refute it.

Four areas of study in particular yielded notable results. One approach employed a shock-avoidance technique in which subjects could avoid mild electrical shocks by making appropriate adjustments in heart rate. These studies demonstrated that statistically significant increases and decreases in heart rate could be obtained using instrument-based conditioning techniques. Other work achieved similar results using positive reinforcement rather than shock avoidance.

About the same time, several other researchers showed that galvanic skin response, the ability of the body to conduct minute amounts of naturally occurring electrical current across the skin, could also be controlled by individuals.

As these reports surfaced, critics began to appear. They pointed to the fact that some voluntary responses can elicit a response that appears to be autonomic or involuntary. For instance, changes in heart rate can be initiated by altering respiration patterns or tensing certain muscle groups—both responses under voluntary control. If changes in heart rate, an autonomically mediated response, were "caused" by changes in responses under voluntary control, critics argued, such a demonstration would not prove that heart rate itself could be changed by voluntary control.

A third line of research sought to address this concern, removing the effect of voluntary responses from the equation. Laboratory rats were injected with curare, a drug that paralyzes all skeletal muscles (including those that enable the animals to breathe). They then were maintained on artificial respiration, which kept them alive and exactly regulated their breathing. Finally, an electrode was implanted in the hypothalamus, the part of the brain that regulates body temperature, certain metabolic processes, and other involuntary activities, so the researchers could control its actions. With this preparation, scientists showed that several involuntary responses could be spontaneously conditioned—not only heart rate, but blood pressure and urine formation, among others. This demonstration of large magnitude changes in the responses of the internal organs in animals encouraged researchers to speculate on the wide range of human psychosomatic disorders that might be treatable with biofeedback.

Eventually, a fourth avenue of research emerged in the field of electroencephalography (EEG), the study of electrical activity in the brain. Several scientists began to study whether subjects could "voluntarily" produce certain EEG patterns—particularly the *alpha rhythm,* a distinctive rhythm associated with deep relaxation. Because of the similarity in the subjective experience of a "high alpha state" with that reported for meditation, self-control of EEG patterns attracted much attention beyond the scientific community, helping the entire field to grow.

# THE JOB

Biofeedback therapy is a treatment that over the last three decades has shown considerable promise for patients with a wide range of conditions and disorders. Because it can be adapted to so many uses, it has developed more as a complementary skill than as a separate career. Biofeedback therapists come from a variety of backgrounds—physicians, social workers, psychologists, physical therapists, chiropractors, speech pathologists, and dental hygienists, among others. These professionals incorporate biofeedback learning techniques into the more traditional treatments they regularly provide. While it is not impossible to have a career in biofeedback without underlying training in a different field, few people are trained only as biofeedback therapists. It is true, however, that many therapists with experience in other disciplines choose to focus their practices largely on biofeedback.

An understanding of the uses of biofeedback begins with an understanding of the effects of stress. Stress often arises from major life changes, such as divorce, the death of a loved one, a move to a new home, or even celebrating holidays with family. In such high-stress times, a person's body undergoes "fight-or-flight" reactions. The body reacts physiologically to a person's mental and emotional concerns.

The effects of a typical fight-or-flight situation, such as a mugging or assault, may be considerable. A person reacting to such a potentially life-threatening situation will experience physiological changes. But much smaller stresses to a person's system, such as anxiety the night before an important exam, can also have lingering negative effects. An exam is not a life-threatening situation, but if someone perceives it that way, these perceptions can cause the same types of physiological changes.

Some people are terrified to speak in front of a group. There is no physical danger, but the speaker feels threatened in nonphysical ways—he or she may trip, forget lines, mispronounce words, fail at getting a message across, or be ridiculed. The speaker becomes nervous and tense, activating the fight-or-flight response when there is no real reason to do so.

Scientists believe that if people can learn to make themselves ill in this way, by moving their body systems out of balance, they might very well be able to learn to reverse the process and make themselves well. Biofeedback training teaches patients to restore balance to their body systems by voluntarily controlling generally involuntary reactions to various forms of stress.

There are three primary forms of biofeedback therapy; they involve the measurement of skin temperature, muscle tension, and brain waves. Each form is useful in a different range of disorders and conditions, and the list continues to grow.

*Skin temperature biofeedback* is often used with a therapeutic technique called autogenic training. Skin temperature is affected by blood flow, which is affected by stress. When a person is tense, blood vessels narrow, limiting the flow of blood in the body and causing skin temperature to drop. Biofeedback therapists place sensors on the hands or feet to determine blood flow. *Autogenic training* involves mastering passive concentration and, when properly practiced, helps the patient relax deeply through a number of repeated formula phrases. ("My right arm is heavy. My right arm is heavy. My right arm is heavy. My left arm is heavy....") The relaxation improves blood flow and raises skin temperature. These techniques have been shown to aid patients suffering from severe migraine headaches, Raynaud's disease (a disorder of the blood vessels in the extremities characterized by extreme sensitivity to cold), and hypertension or high blood pressure, among other complaints.

*Muscle tension biofeedback,* or *electromyograph (EMG) biofeedback training,* involves using sensitive electrodes to detect the amount of electrical activity in muscles. Auditory and visual feedback helps patients learn to control the pace and intensity of this activity. Autogenic training may be used in these situations as well to encourage relaxation. Many disorders respond to EMG biofeedback therapy, including tension headaches, anxieties, phobias, and psychoses.

The last line of research is the study of brain waves using *electroencephalograph (EEG),* or *neurobiofeedback.* Brain waves display certain characteristic rhythmic patterns. *Beta rhythms* are fast and have small amplitude; they predominate when you are awake or mentally aroused. *Alpha rhythms,* the first to be identified in EEG biofeedback therapy, are extraordinarily symmetrical, have large amplitude, and increase in most patients when they close their eyes and relax their bodies. *Theta rhythms* continue the slide toward sleep and increase as a person becomes drowsy, corresponding to early dreaming states. *Delta rhythms* are irregular and occur in heavy, dreamless sleep. Biofeedback training that teaches patients to seek the alpha state has been shown to be helpful in the treatment of epilepsy, attention deficit disorder, autism, and obsessive-compulsive disorders, among other maladies. Scientists currently are exploring the use of EEG training in enhancing creativity and improving learning.

A biofeedback therapist's approach depends on his or her primary training. Physicians use biofeedback to complement medical remedies. Social workers use biofeedback to help patients cope with the social and emotional effects of chronic and sometimes debilitating problems. Music therapists use music and rhythm in conjunction with biofeedback to help patients understand and control physiological and emotional reactions. Other professionals who might use biofeedback therapy include nurses, psychiatrists, physical therapists, and anyone involved in health care or counseling work.

## REQUIREMENTS

### High School

To enter this range of careers you will need to take science courses, such as biology and anatomy. Physical education and health will give you some understanding of the physical aspects of biofeedback. Since counseling skills are also important, classes in psychology and sociology can be helpful.

Biofeedback currently is a rapidly expanding field. The marriages of art and biofeedback (as in an art therapy practice) or sports and biofeedback (as in the development of specialized training programs for top athletes) are just two of the many more unusual applications of this discipline.

### Postsecondary Training

Most people who practice biofeedback therapy first become licensed in some other area of health care. Biofeedback then becomes an area of specialization within their practices. A biofeedback therapist may have a master's degree in social work, a Ph.D. in psychology, a nursing or medical degree, or some other professional designation. After receiving this professional degree (which may take 10 or more years, in the case of a medical degree), you then take courses in biofeedback from schools or other educational providers.

### Certification or Licensing

The Biofeedback Certification Institute of America (BCIA) was created to establish and maintain standards for practitioners who use biofeedback and to certify practitioners who meet those standards. BCIA certification requires you to complete a comprehensive course in human anatomy, human biology, or human biology and have a minimum of a bachelor's degree granted by a regionally accredited academic institution in one of the following approved health care fields: counseling, chiropractic, dental hygiene, dentistry, exercise physiology, medicine, nursing (licensed RNs are accepted with an associate's degree), occupational therapy, physical therapy, physician's assistant, psychology, recreational therapy, rehabilitation, respiratory therapy, social work, speech pathology, and sports medicine. Those who do not have a degree in one of these fields may be eligible for certification through a special review.

Candidates must complete training at an accredited biofeedback training program. This involves coursework as well as hands-on experience. Class work covers topics such as neuromuscular intervention, the autonomic nervous system, and professional conduct. The clinical training involves working directly with patients while under careful supervision and using a variety of biofeedback techniques. Candidates must also receive biofeedback, have supervised patient case conferences, and complete a comprehensive course in human anatomy, human biology, or human physiology. Once all of these requirements are fulfilled candidates are eligible to take the rigorous written certification exam.

At this time, BCIA certification is not mandatory, but it is recommended. In addition to its general program, the BCIA offers specialty certifications in EEG biofeedback and pelvic muscle dysfunction biofeedback.

## Other Requirements

The practice of biofeedback therapy involves a great deal of personal interaction. As a result, you must enjoy being around a variety of people. Biofeedback practitioners also need excellent communication skills and must be careful listeners, able to pay attention to details. A genuine empathy for patients is important as well. Because biofeedback is a growing but still fairly new field, business and management skills will be important. Therapists generally are responsible for building their own practices and, like most other health care professionals, typically spend many hours dealing with insurance, managed care, and financial issues.

# EXPLORING

You can begin exploring this field by contacting and interviewing biofeedback therapists in your area to gain a more specific understanding of their day-to-day activities.

If your school participates in an annual science fair, consider using the opportunity to develop a presentation on biofeedback. Many simple experiments are possible and appropriate for this setting. (Consider a sophisticated take on mood rings, for instance.)

Outside school, you can practice a number of forms of noninstrumental biofeedback. Yoga and Zen meditation both will help you become more attuned to your own body and its rhythms—an important skill to have as a biofeedback therapist. Learning either of these disciplines will give you a taste of how body systems can be trained to respond to intention and outside control and will teach you how to recognize some of your own body's feedback patterns.

## EMPLOYERS

Biofeedback therapy has been shown to be useful in the treatment of such a wide variety of conditions and disorders that therapists can be found in a number of background specialties, from medicine and psychology to occupational therapy and dentistry. This means that biofeedback therapists are employed by many different types of institutions. They often have private practices as well. If you can envision ways in which biofeedback can assist people in whatever career field you might find yourself, chances are you can build a practice around it, either alone, or working with a group or for an institutional employer. Medical centers are the most common place of employment for biofeedback therapists, but more and more corporations are finding applications for biofeedback in the workplace.

## STARTING OUT

Most biofeedback therapists come to the discipline with established practices in other fields. Once you have received the minimum of a bachelor's degree in your primary field, you can begin to think about specific training in biofeedback therapy. (A master's or sometimes even a doctorate is preferred to a bachelor's, depending on your areas of study.)

BCIA certification may be the most appropriate first goal for beginning therapists as it will lend credibility to your training and help you build your practice. Therapist candidates can earn BCIA certification concurrently with training, and they offer the option of taking courses on a part-time basis.

## ADVANCEMENT

Advancement opportunities are dependent on the main specialty a therapist has chosen and the environment in which he or she is working. Continuing education is important to any health care professional, so biofeedback therapists advance within their practices by developing their skills and learning about new methods of treatment. In some cases, such as in academic medical centers, the addition of biofeedback therapy to a practice may assist the therapist in reaching promotion goals.

## EARNINGS

Biofeedback therapists generally charge from $50 to $150 per session. Depending on the level of their experience, the size of their client base, and their level of training, biofeedback therapists can have substantial earnings. Because biofeedback therapists come from different professional backgrounds, however, it is difficult to give a salary range for them as a group. For example, a clinical psychologist with a Ph.D. is going to make more money practicing biofeedback than will a social worker with a master's degree. Therapists working in more urban areas generally make more money than those in smaller communities. A therapist just starting out may have annual earnings in the $30,000s. More established therapists, even in rural areas, may make around $50,000, while those working in larger communities, often handling many patients, may make up to $200,000 a year.

Biofeedback therapists who work for a medical institution usually receive benefits such as vacation days, sick leave, health and life insurance, and a savings and pension program. Self-employed therapists must provide their own benefits.

## WORK ENVIRONMENT
Biofeedback therapists typically spend much of their time working one-on-one with patients. As with most health care practices, they may work in any number of environments, from solo private practices to larger medical centers or corporate complexes. Their responsibilities run the gamut from one-on-one patient visits to collaborative efforts with physicians and diagnosticians tackling difficult cases. Therapists primarily work in an office, although the increasing portability of computers means this may eventually change as well, allowing biofeedback practitioners even to consider house calls on a regular basis.

## OUTLOOK
The employment outlook for biofeedback therapists is good. According to the U.S. Department of Labor, overall employment in health care will grow much faster than the average for all industries through 2016. While the department does not provide specific projections for biofeedback therapists, it is logical to conclude they will be in demand for several reasons. One reason is the growing population of Americans aged 65 and over. People in this age group are more likely to need and seek out treatments for many different conditions. This will increase the demand for most health care industry workers, including biofeedback therapists. Also, because most individuals have some sort of medical insurance, the costs of care, including nontraditional courses of treatment such as biofeedback therapy, have become more affordable. According to EEG Spectrum International, many insurance plans cover biofeedback therapy for treatment of certain conditions.

In many cases, patients seek the assistance of biofeedback therapists after more traditional medical treatment has failed. On the other hand, some people choose to look first to alternative forms of health care to avoid medications or invasive surgery.

In addition, continued research within the field of biofeedback should allow for the treatment of more disorders. Subspecialties like neurobiofeedback are increasing dramatically. The study of brain waves in cases involving alcoholism, attention deficit disorder, insomnia, epilepsy, and traumatic brain injury point to new biofeedback treatment methods.

Some conditions, such as chronic headaches, are often better treated through biofeedback therapy than through more invasive medical treatment.

## FOR MORE INFORMATION

*The AAPB is dedicated to the promotion of biofeedback as a means of improving health. Its Web site is a good place to begin to gather more information about the field.*

**Association for Applied Psychophysiology and Biofeedback (AAPB)**
10200 West 44th Avenue, Suite 304
Wheat Ridge, CO 80033-2840
Tel: 303-422-8436
Email: AAPB@resourcenter.com
http://www.aapb.org

*For more information about biofeedback, certification, and approved programs, contact*
**Biofeedback Certification Institute of America**
10200 West 44th Avenue, Suite 310
Wheat Ridge, CO 80033-2840
Tel: 303-420-2902
Email: info@bcia.org
http://www.bcia.org

*For more on neurofeedback, including training, research, news, and practitioners, contact*
**EEG Spectrum International**
21601 Vanowen Street, Suite 100
Canoga Park, CA 91303-2752
Tel: 818-789-3456
http://www.eegspectrum.com

# Chiropractors

## OVERVIEW

*Chiropractors,* or *doctors of chiropractic* (DCs), are health care professionals who emphasize health maintenance and disease prevention through proper nutrition, exercise, posture, stress management, and care of the spine and the nervous system. Approximately 53,000 chiropractors practice in the United States. Most work in solo practice; other work settings include group practices, health care clinics, and teaching institutions.

Because of its emphasis on health maintenance, the whole person, and natural healing, chiropractic is considered an alternative health care approach. At the same time, chiropractic has more of the advantages enjoyed by the medical profession than does any other alternative health care field: Chiropractic has licensure requirements, accredited training institutions, a growing scientific research base, and insurance reimbursement.

## HISTORY

Although chiropractic as we know it is just over 100 years old, spinal manipulation dates back to ancient civilizations. Reports of manipulative therapy were recorded in China as early as 2700 B.C. Hippocrates used spinal manipulation around the fourth century B.C. to reposition vertebrae and to heal other ailments. Galen, a renowned Greek physician who practiced in Rome during the second century A.D., used spinal manipulation. Ambroise Paré, an important figure in surgical history, used it in France in the 16th century. These "bone-setting" techniques were passed down through the centuries through family tradition. They can be found in the folk medicine of many countries. In 1843, Dr. J. Evans Riadore, a physician, studied the irritation of spinal nerves and recommended spinal manipulation as a treatment.

Daniel D. Palmer, an American, founded the system of chiropractic in 1895. He also coined the term *chiropractic*. Palmer believed that deviations of the spinal column, or subluxations, were the cause of practically all disease and that chiropractic adjustment was the cure. Like many others who have tried to change the practice of medicine, Dr. Palmer encountered strong opposition from the medical establishment. He and other early chiropractors were imprisoned for practicing medicine without a license. In spite of the hardships, he and his followers persevered because of the success of their treatments in alleviating pain and promoting health. Their treatments sometimes had exceptionally positive results.

In spite of their successful work and a growing number of supporters, chiropractors were attacked by the medical establishment because they had little scientific research to support their claims. In the 1970s, Dr. Chang Ha Suh, a Korean immigrant who was working at the University of Colorado, had the courage to conduct studies that provided extensive scientific research related to chiropractic. Since then, numerous important studies have added to the research and to the credibility of chiropractic.

Today, chiropractic is the third largest primary health care profession in the United States. Many quality schools of chiropractic exist, and doctors of chiropractic are licensed in all 50 states and the District of Columbia. Chiropractic is one of the fastest growing health care professions in the country.

## THE JOB

Chiropractors are trained primary health care providers, much like medical physicians. Chiropractors focus on the maintenance of health and disease prevention. In addition to symptoms, they consider each patient's nutrition, work, stress levels, exercise habits, posture, and so on. Chiropractors treat people of all ages—from children to senior citizens. They see both women and men. Doctors of chiropractic most frequently treat conditions such as backache, disk problems, sciatica, and whiplash. They also care for people with headaches, respiratory disorders, allergies, digestive disturbances, elevated blood pressure, and many other common ailments. Some specialize in areas such as sports medicine or nutrition. Chiropractors do not use drugs or surgery. If they determine that drugs or surgery are needed, they refer the individual to another professional who can meet those needs.

Doctors of chiropractic look for causes of disorders of the spine. They consider the spine and the nervous system to be vitally important to the health of the individual. Chiropractic teaches that problems in the spinal column (backbone) affect the nervous system and the body's natural defense mechanisms and are the underlying causes of many diseases. Chiropractors use a special procedure called a "spinal adjustment" to try to restore the spine to its natural healthy state. They believe this will also have an effect on the individual's total health and well-being.

On the initial visit, doctors of chiropractic meet with the patient and take a complete medical history before beginning treatment. They ask questions about all aspects of the person's life to help determine the nature of the illness. Events in the individual's past that may seem unrelated or unimportant may be significant to the chiropractor.

After the consultation and the case history, chiropractors perform a careful physical examination, sometimes including laboratory tests. When necessary, they use X rays to help locate the source of patients' difficulties. Doctors of chiropractic study the X rays for more than just bone fractures or signs of disease. X rays are the only means of seeing the outline of the spinal column. Chiropractors are trained to observe whether the structural alignment of the spinal column is normal or abnormal.

Once they have made a diagnosis, chiropractic physicians use a variety of natural approaches to help restore the individual to health. The spinal adjustment is the treatment for which chiropractic is most known. During this procedure, patients usually lie on a specially designed adjusting table. Chiropractic physicians generally use their hands to manipulate the spine. They apply pressure and use specialized techniques of manipulation that are designed to help the affected areas of the spine. Doctors of chiropractic must know many sophisticated techniques of manipulation, and they spend countless hours learning to properly administer spinal adjustments. Chiropractic treatments must often be repeated over the course of several visits. The number of treatments needed varies greatly.

In addition to the spinal adjustment, chiropractic physicians may use "physiologic therapeutics" to relieve symptoms. These are drugless natural therapies, such as light, water, electrical stimulation, massage, heat, ultrasound, and biofeedback. Chiropractors also make suggestions about diet, rest, exercise, and support of the afflicted body part. They may recommend routines for the patient to do at home to maintain and improve the results of the manipulation.

Chiropractors pay special attention to lifestyle factors, such as nutrition and exercise. They believe the body has an innate ability

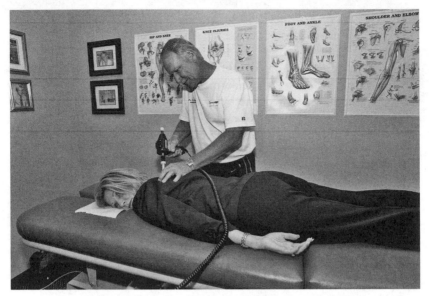

A chiropractor provides back therapy to a patient. *(Rob Crandall, The Image Works)*

to remain healthy if it has the proper ingredients. Doctors of chiropractic propose that the essential ingredients include clean air, water, proper nutrition, rest, and a properly functioning nervous system. Their goal is to maintain the health and well-being of the whole person. In this respect they have been practicing for many years what has recently become known as "health maintenance."

Chiropractors who are in private practice and some who work as group practitioners also have responsibility for running their businesses. They must promote their practices and develop their patient base. They are responsible for keeping records on their patients and for general bookkeeping. Sometimes they hire and train employees. In larger practices or clinics, chiropractic assistants or office managers usually perform these duties.

## REQUIREMENTS

### High School

To become a doctor of chiropractic, you will have to study a minimum of six to seven years after high school. Preparing for this profession is just as demanding as preparing to be a medical doctor, and the types of courses you will need are also similar. Science classes, such as biology, chemistry, physics, and psychology, will prepare you for medical courses in college. English, speech, drama, and debate can sharpen the communication skills that are essential for this profession. Math, business, and computer classes can help you get ready to run a private practice.

## Postsecondary Training

Most chiropractic colleges require at least two years of undergraduate study before you can enroll. Some require a bachelor's degree. Currently, 15 chiropractic programs in the United States are accredited by the Council on Chiropractic Education (CCE). Find out which chiropractic colleges interest you and learn about their requirements. Selecting chiropractic schools while in high school or college will allow you to structure your undergraduate study to meet the requirements of the schools of your choice. Some chiropractic colleges provide opportunities for prechiropractic study and bachelor's degree programs. In general, you need course work in biology, communications, English, chemistry, physics, psychology, and social sciences or humanities. Contact the national professional associations listed at the end of this article for information about schools and their requirements.

Upon completing the required undergraduate work and enrolling in a chiropractic college, you can expect to take an array of science and medical courses, such as anatomy, pathology, and microbiology. During the first two years of most chiropractic programs you will spend a majority of your time in the classroom or the laboratory. The last two years generally focus on courses in spinal adjustments. During this time, potential chiropractors also train in outpatient clinics affiliated with the college. Upon successful completion of the six- or seven-year professional degree program, you will receive the DC degree.

## Certification or Licensing

All 50 states and the District of Columbia require that chiropractors pass a state board examination to obtain a license to practice. Educational requirements and types of practice for which a chiropractor may be licensed vary from state to state. Most state boards recognize academic training only in chiropractic colleges accredited by the CCE. Most states will accept all or part of the National Board of Chiropractic Examiners' test given to fourth-year chiropractic students in place of a state exam. Most states require that chiropractors take continuing education courses each year to keep their licenses.

## Other Requirements

Perhaps the most important personal requirement for any health care professional is the desire to help people and to promote wholeness and health. To be a successful chiropractor, you need good listening skills, empathy, and understanding. As a doctor of chiropractic, you will also need a good business sense and the ability to work independently. Especially sharp observational skills are essential in order for you to recognize physical abnormalities. Good hand dexterity is necessary to perform the spinal adjustments and other manipulations. However, you do not need unusual strength.

## EXPLORING

If you are interested in becoming a chiropractor, there are many ways to start preparing right now. Join all the science clubs you can, design projects, and participate in science fairs. To develop interviewing and communication skills, you might join the school newspaper staff and ask for interview assignments. Learn to play chess, take up fencing, or study art history to increase your powers of observation. Take up an instrument, such as the piano, guitar, or violin, to improve your manual dexterity. Learning to give massages is another way to increase manual dexterity and learn the human body. Be sure to stay in shape and maintain your own health, and learn all you can about homeopathy, yoga, the Alexander technique, Rolfing, and other systems of mind/body wholeness.

Contact the chiropractic professional associations and ask about their student programs. Check the Internet for bulletin boards or forums related to chiropractic and other areas of health care. Volunteer at a hospital or nursing home to gain experience working with those in need of medical care.

If there is a doctor of chiropractic or a clinic in your area, ask to visit and talk to a chiropractor. Make an appointment for a chiropractic examination so you can experience what it is like. You may even find a part-time or summer job in a chiropractic office.

## Earnings for Chiropractors by Industry, 2007

| Field | Mean Annual Earnings |
| --- | --- |
| Offices of Physicians | $93,930 |
| Offices of Other Health Practitioners | $81,040 |
| Outpatient Care Centers | $76,780 |
| General Medical and Surgical Hospitals | $66,440 |

Source: U.S. Department of Labor

## EMPLOYERS

There are approximately 53,000 chiropractors employed in the United States. A newly licensed doctor of chiropractic might find a salaried position in a chiropractic clinic or with an experienced chiropractor. Other salaried positions can be found in traditional hospitals, in hospitals that specialize in chiropractic treatment, or in alternative health care centers and clinics. More than 50 percent of the doctors of chiropractic in the United States are in private practice. Most maintain offices in a professional building with other specialists or at their own clinics.

Chiropractors practice throughout the United States. Jobs in clinics, hospitals, and alternative health care centers may be easier to find in larger cities that have the population to support them. However, most doctors of chiropractic choose to work in small communities. Chiropractors tend to remain near chiropractic institutions, and this has resulted in higher concentrations of chiropractic practices in those geographical areas.

## STARTING OUT

Career services offices of chiropractic colleges have information about job openings, and they may be able to help with job placement. As a newly licensed chiropractor, you might begin working in a clinic or in an established practice with another chiropractor on a salary or income-sharing basis. This would give you a chance to start practicing without the major financial investment of equipping an office. It is sometimes possible to purchase the practice of a chiropractor who is retiring or moving. This is usually easier than starting a new solo practice because the purchased practice will already have patients. However, some newly licensed practitioners do go straight into private practice.

National chiropractic associations and professional publications may also list job openings. Attend an association meeting to get to know professionals in the field. Networking is an important way to learn about job openings.

## ADVANCEMENT

As with many other professions, advancement in chiropractic usually means building a larger practice. A chiropractor who starts out as a salaried employee in a large practice may eventually become a partner in the practice. Chiropractors also advance their careers by building their clientele and setting up their own group practices.

They sometimes buy the practices of retiring practitioners to add to their own practices.

Another avenue for advancement is specialization. Chiropractors specialize in areas such as neurology, sports medicine, or diagnostic imaging (X-ray). As the demand for chiropractors is growing, more are advancing their careers through teaching at chiropractic institutions or conducting research. A few doctors of chiropractic become executives with state or national organizations.

## EARNINGS

Self-employed chiropractors usually earn more than salaried chiropractors, such as those working as an associate with another chiropractor or doctor. Chiropractors running their own office, however, must pay such expenses as equipment costs, staff salaries, and health insurance.

According to the U.S. Department of Labor, the median annual income for chiropractors working on a salary basis was $65,890 in 2007. The lowest 10 percent earned $32,530 that same year, while the top 25 percent earned more than $97,880 per year. According to a survey conducted by *Chiropractic Economics* magazine, the mean income for chiropractors was $104,363 in 2005.

Self-employed chiropractors must provide for their own benefits. Chiropractors who are salaried employees usually receive benefits including health insurance and retirement plans.

## WORK ENVIRONMENT

Chiropractic physicians work in clean, quiet, comfortable offices. Most solo practitioners and group practices have an office suite. The suite generally has a reception area. In clinics, several professionals may share this area. The suite also contains examining rooms and treatment rooms. In a clinic where several professionals work, there are sometimes separate offices for the individual professionals. Most chiropractors have chiropractic assistants and a secretary or office manager. Those who are in private practice or partnerships need to have good business skills and self-discipline to be successful.

Doctors of chiropractic who work in clinics, hospitals, universities, or professional associations need to work well in a group environment. They will frequently work under supervision or in a team with other professionals. Chiropractors may have offices of their own, or they may share offices with team members, depending on their work and the facility. In these organizations, the physical work environment varies, but it will generally be clean and comfortable. Because they are larger, these settings may be noisier than the smaller practices.

Most chiropractors work about 40 hours per week, although many put in longer hours. Larger organizations may determine the hours of work, but chiropractors in private practice can set their own. Evening and weekend hours are often scheduled to accommodate patients' needs.

## OUTLOOK

Employment for doctors of chiropractic is expected to grow faster than the average for all occupations through 2016, according to the U.S. Department of Labor. Many areas have a shortage of chiropractors. Public interest in alternative health care is growing. Many health-conscious individuals are attracted to chiropractic because it is natural, drugless, and surgery-free. Because of their holistic, personal approach to health care, chiropractors are increasingly seen as primary physicians, especially in rural areas. The average life span is increasing, and so are the numbers of older people in this country. The elderly frequently have more structural and mechanical difficulties, and the growth of this segment of the population will increase the demand for doctors of chiropractic.

More insurance policies and health maintenance organizations (HMOs) now cover chiropractic services, but this still varies according to the insurer. As a result of these developments in HMO and insurance coverage, chiropractors receive more referrals for treatment of injuries that result from accidents.

While the demand for chiropractic is increasing, college enrollments are also growing. New chiropractors may find increasing competition in geographic areas where other practitioners are already located. Because of the high cost of equipment such as X-ray and other diagnostic tools, group practices with other chiropractors or related health care professionals are likely to provide more opportunity for employment or for purchasing a share of a practice.

## FOR MORE INFORMATION

*For general information and a career kit, contact*
   **American Chiropractic Association**
   1701 Clarendon Boulevard
   Arlington, VA 22209-2799
   Tel: 703-276-8800
   http://www.amerchiro.org

*For information on educational requirements and accredited colleges, contact*
**Council on Chiropractic Education**
8049 North 85th Way
Scottsdale, AZ 85258-4321
Tel: 480-443-8877
Email: cce@cce-usa.org
http://www.cce-usa.org

*For information on student membership and member chiropractors in your area, contact*
**International Chiropractors Association**
1110 North Glebe Road, Suite 650
Arlington, VA 22201-4795
Tel: 800-423-4690
http://www.chiropractic.org

*For information on licensure, contact*
**National Board of Chiropractic Examiners**
901 54th Avenue
Greeley, CO 80634-4405
Tel: 970-356-9100
Email: nbce@nbce.org
http://www.nbce.org

# Creative Arts Therapists

## OVERVIEW

*Creative arts therapists* treat and rehabilitate people with mental, physical, and emotional disabilities. They use the creative processes of music, art, dance/movement, drama, psychodrama, and poetry in their therapy sessions to determine the underlying causes of problems and to help patients achieve therapeutic goals. Creative arts therapists usually specialize in one particular type of therapeutic activity. The specific objectives of the therapeutic activities vary according to the needs of the patient and the setting of the therapy program.

## HISTORY

Creative arts therapy programs are fairly recent additions to the health care field. Although many theories of mental and physical therapy have existed for centuries, it has been only in the last 75 years or so that health care professionals have truly realized the healing powers of music, art, dance, and other forms of artistic self-expression.

Art therapy is based on the idea that people who cannot discuss their problems with words must have another outlet for self-expression. In the early 1900s, psychiatrists began to look more closely at their patients' artwork, realizing that there could be links between the emotional or psychological illness and the art. Sigmund Freud even did some preliminary research into the artistic expression of his patients.

## QUICK FACTS

**School Subjects**
Art
Music
Theater/dance

**Personal Skills**
Artistic
Helping/teaching

**Work Environment**
Primarily indoors
Primarily one location

**Minimum Education Level**
Master's degree

**Salary Range**
$15,000 to $35,000 to
  $100,000

**Certification or Licensing**
Recommended (certification)
Required by certain states
  (licensing)

**Outlook**
About as fast as the average

**DOT**
076

**GOE**
14.06.01

**NOC**
3144

**O*NET-SOC**
N/A

In the 1930s, art educators discovered that children often expressed their thoughts better with pictures and role-playing than they did through verbalization. Children often do not know the words they need to explain how they feel or how to make their needs known to adults. Researchers began to look into art as a way to treat children who were traumatized by abuse, neglect, illness, or other physical or emotional disabilities.

During and after World War II, the Department of Veterans Affairs (VA) developed and organized various art, music, and dance activities for patients in VA hospitals. These activities had a dramatic effect on the physical and mental well-being of World War II veterans, and creative arts therapists began to help treat and rehabilitate patients in other health care settings.

Because of early breakthroughs with children and veterans, the number of arts therapists has increased greatly over the past few decades, and the field has expanded to include drama, psychodrama, and poetry, in addition to the original areas of music, art, and dance. Today, creative arts therapists work with diverse populations of patients in a wide range of facilities, and they focus on the specific needs of a vast spectrum of disorders and disabilities. Colleges and universities offer degree programs in many types of therapies. National associations for registering and certifying creative arts therapists work to monitor training programs and to ensure the professional integrity of the therapists working in the various fields.

## THE JOB

Creative arts therapy taps into the subconscious and gives people a mode of expression in an uncensored environment. This is important because before patients can begin to heal, they must first identify their feelings. Once they recognize their feelings, they can begin to develop an understanding of the relationship between their feelings and their behavior.

The main goal of a creative arts therapist is to improve the client's physical, mental, and emotional health. Before therapists begin any treatment, they meet with a team of other health care professionals. After determining the strength, limitations, and interests of their client, they create a program to promote positive change and growth. The creative arts therapist continues to confer with the other health care workers as the program progresses and alters the program according to the client's progress. How these goals are reached depends on the unique specialty of the therapist in question.

"It's like sitting in the woods waiting for a fawn to come out." That is how Barbara Fish, former director of activity therapy for the Illinois Department of Mental Health and Developmental Disabilities, Chicago Metropolitan and Adolescent Services, describes her experience as she waits patiently for a sexually abused patient to begin to trust her. The patient is extraordinarily frightened because of the traumatic abuse she has suffered. This may be the first time in the patient's life that she is in an environment of acceptance and support. It may take months or even years before the patient begins to trust the therapist, "come out of the woods," and begin to heal.

In some cases, especially when the clients are adolescents, they may have become so detached from their feelings that they can physically act out without consciously knowing the reasons for their behavior. This detachment from their emotions creates a great deal of psychological pain. With the help of a creative arts therapist, clients can begin to communicate their subconscious feelings both verbally and nonverbally. They can express their emotions in a variety of ways without having to name them.

Creative arts therapists work with all age groups: young children, adolescents, adults, and senior citizens. They can work in individual, group, or family sessions. The approach of the therapist, however, depends on the specific needs of the client or group. For example, if an individual is feeling overwhelmed by too many options or stimuli, the therapist may give him or her only a plain piece of paper and a pencil to work with that day.

Fish has three ground rules for her art therapy sessions with disturbed adolescents: respect yourself, respect other people, and respect property. The therapy groups are limited to five patients per group. She begins the session by asking each person in the group how he or she is feeling that day. By carefully listening to their responses, a theme may emerge that will determine the direction of the therapy. For example, if anger is reoccurring in their statements, Fish may ask them to draw a line down the center of a piece of paper. On one side, she will ask them to draw how anger looks and on the other side how feeling sad looks. Then, once the drawing is complete, she will ask them to compare the two pictures and see that their anger may be masking their feelings of sadness, loneliness, and disappointment. As patients begin to recognize their true feelings, they develop better control of their behavior.

To reach their patients, creative arts therapists can use a variety of mediums, including visual art, music, dance, drama, or poetry or other kinds of creative writing. Creative arts therapists usually specialize in a specific medium, becoming a music therapist, drama therapist, dance therapist, art therapist, or poetry therapist. "In my groups we use poetry and creative writing," Fish explains. "We do all kinds of things to get at what is going on at an unconscious level."

*Music therapists* use musical lessons and activities to improve a patient's self-confidence and self-awareness, to relieve states of depression, and to improve physical dexterity. For example, a music therapist treating a patient with Alzheimer's might play songs from the patient's past in order to stimulate long- and short-term memory, soothe feelings of agitation, and increase a sense of reality.

*Art therapists* use art in much the same manner. The art therapist may encourage and teach patients to express their thoughts, feelings, and anxieties via sketching, drawing, painting, or sculpting. Art therapy is especially helpful in revealing patterns of domestic abuse in families. Children involved in such a situation may depict scenes of family life with violent details or portray a certain family member as especially frightening or threatening.

*Dance/movement therapists* develop and conduct dance/movement sessions to help improve the physical, mental, and emotional health of their patients. Dance and movement therapy is also used as a way of assessing a patient's progress toward reaching therapeutic goals.

There are other types of creative arts therapists as well. *Drama therapists* use role-playing, pantomime (telling a story through expressive body or facial movements), puppetry, improvisation, and

## Typical Employment Settings for Creative Arts Therapists

- Medical and psychiatric hospitals and clinics
- Outpatient mental health agencies and day treatment facilities
- Residential treatment centers
- Pain and stress management clinics
- Elder care settings
- Halfway houses
- Community agencies and nonprofit settings
- Schools at all levels
- Prisons
- Domestic violence and homeless shelters
- Private practice

Sources: American Art Therapy Association, American Dance Therapy Association, American Music Therapy Association, National Association for Drama Therapy

original scripted dramatization to evaluate and treat patients. *Poetry therapists* and *bibliotherapists* use the written and spoken word to treat patients.

## REQUIREMENTS
### High School
To become a creative arts therapist, you will need a bachelor's degree, so take a college preparatory curriculum while in high school. You should become as proficient as possible with the methods and tools related to the type of creative arts therapy you wish to pursue. When therapists work with patients they must be able to concentrate completely on the patient rather than on learning how to use tools or techniques. For example, if you want to become involved in art therapy, you need to be familiar with art tools (such as brushes, palette knives, etc.) as well as artistic techniques.

In addition to courses such as drama, art, music, and English, you should consider taking an introductory class in psychology. Also, a communication class will give you an understanding of the various ways people communicate, both verbally and nonverbally.

### Postsecondary Training
To become a creative arts therapist you must earn at least a bachelor's degree, usually in the area in which you wish to specialize. For example, those studying to be art therapists typically have undergraduate degrees in studio art, art education, or psychology with a strong emphasis on art courses as well.

In most cases, however, you will also need a graduate degree before you can gain certification as a professional or advance in your chosen field. Requirements for admission to graduate schools vary by program, so you should contact the graduate programs you are interested in to find out about their admissions policies. For some fields you may be required to submit a portfolio of your work along with the written application. Professional organizations can be a good source of information regarding high-quality programs. For example, both the American Art Therapy Association and the American Music Therapy Association provide lists of schools that meet their standards for approval. (Contact information for both associations is listed at the end of this article.)

In graduate school, you will conduct in-depth study of psychology and the arts field you choose. Classes for someone seeking a master's in art therapy, for example, may include group psychotherapy, foundation of creativity theory, assessment and treatment planning, and art therapy presentation. In addition to classroom study you will also complete an internship or supervised practicum (that is, work with clients). Depending on your program, you may also need to write a thesis or present a final artistic project before receiving your degree.

### Certification or Licensing

Typically, the nationally recognized association or certification board specific to your field of choice offers registration and certification. For example, the Art Therapy Credentials Board (ATCB) offers registration and certification to art therapists, and the American Dance Therapy Association offers registration to dance therapists. In general, requirements for registration include completing an approved therapy program and having a certain amount of experience working with clients. Requirements for higher levels of registration or certification generally involve having additional work experience and passing a written exam.

For a specific example, consider the certification process for an art therapist: An art therapist may receive the designation art therapist registered from the ATCB after completing a graduate program and having some experience working with clients. The next level,

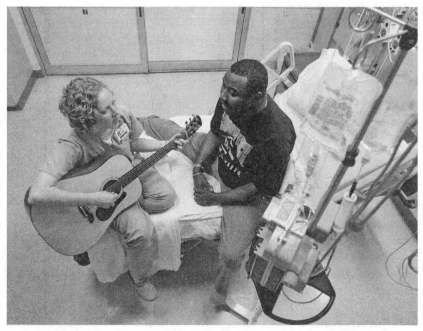

A music therapist plays the guitar for a patient who has recently undergone a heart transplant. *(Dave Martin, AP Photo)*

then, is to become a board-certified art therapist by passing a written exam. To retain certification status, therapists must complete a certain amount of continuing education.

Many registered creative arts therapists also hold additional licenses in other fields, such as social work, education, mental health, or marriage and family therapy. In some states, creative arts therapists need licensing depending on their place of work. For specific information on licensing in your field, you will need to check with your state's licensing board. Creative arts therapists are also often members of other professional associations, including the American Psychological Association, the American Association for Marriage and Family Therapy, and the American Counseling Association.

### Other Requirements

To succeed in this line of work, you should have a strong desire to help others seek positive change in their lives. All types of creative arts therapists must be able to work well with other people—both patients and other health professionals—in the development and implementation of therapy programs. You must have the patience and the stamina to teach and practice therapy with patients for whom progress is often very slow because of their various physical and emotional disorders. A therapist must always keep in mind that even a tiny amount of progress might be extremely significant for some patients and their families. A good sense of humor is also a valuable trait.

## EXPLORING

There are many ways to explore the possibility of a career as a creative arts therapist. Contact professional associations for information on therapy careers. Talk with people working in the creative arts therapy field and perhaps arrange to observe a creative arts therapy session. Look for part-time or summer jobs or volunteer at a hospital, clinic, nursing home, or any of a number of health care facilities.

A summer job as an aide at a camp for disabled children, for example, may help provide insight into the nature of creative arts therapy, including both its rewards and demands. Such experience can be very valuable in deciding if you are suited to the inherent frustrations of a therapy career.

## EMPLOYERS

Creative arts therapists usually work as members of an interdisciplinary health care team that may include physicians, nurses, social workers, psychiatrists, and psychologists. Although often employed in hospitals, therapists also work in rehabilitation centers, nursing homes, day treatment facilities, shelters for battered women, pain and stress management clinics, substance abuse programs, hospices, and correctional facilities. Others maintain private practices. Many creative arts therapists work with children in grammar and high schools, either as therapists or art teachers. Some arts therapists teach or conduct research in the creative arts at colleges and universities.

## STARTING OUT

After earning a bachelor's degree in a particular field, you should complete your certification, which may include an internship or assistantship. Unpaid training internships often can lead to a first job in the field. Graduates can use the career services office at their college or university to help them find positions in the creative arts therapy field. Many professional associations also compile lists of job openings to assist their members.

Creative arts therapists who are new to the field might consider doing volunteer work at a nonprofit community organization, correctional facility, or neighborhood association to gain some practical experience. Therapists who want to start their own practice can host group therapy sessions in their homes. Creative arts therapists may also wish to associate with other members of the alternative health care field in order to gain experience and build a client base.

## ADVANCEMENT

With more experience, therapists can move into supervisory, administrative, and teaching positions. Often, the supervision of interns can resemble a therapy session. The interns will discuss their feelings and ask questions they may have regarding their work with clients. How did they handle their clients? What were the reactions to what their clients said or did? What could they be doing to help more? The supervising therapist helps the interns become competent creative arts therapists.

Many therapists have represented the profession internationally. Barbara Fish was invited to present her paper, "Art Therapy with Children and Adolescents," at the University of Helsinki. Additionally, Fish spoke in Finland at a three-day workshop exploring the use and effectiveness of arts therapy with children and adolescents. Raising the public and professional awareness of creative arts therapy is an important concern for many therapists.

# EARNINGS

A therapist's annual salary depends on experience, level of training, education, and specialty. Working on a hospital staff or being self-employed also affects annual income. According to the American Art Therapy Association (AATA), entry-level art therapists earn annual salaries of approximately $32,000. Median annual salaries are about $45,000, and AATA reports that top earnings for salaried administrators ranged from $50,000 and $100,000 annually. Those who have Ph.D.s and are licensed for private practice can earn between $75 and $150 per hour, according to AATA. However those in private practice must pay professional expenses such as insurance and office rental.

Salaries for music therapists vary based on experience, level of training, and education. Music therapists earned average annual salaries of $42,000 in 2004, according to the AMTA. The average annual starting salary for music therapists was $34,500. According to MENC: The National Association for Music Education, music therapists earn the following annual salaries based on employment setting: hospital-psychiatric facility, $20,000 to $62,000; special education facility, $22,000 to $42,000; clinic for disabled children, $15,000 to $70,000; mental health center, $21,000 to $65,000; nursing home, $17,000 to $65,000; correctional facility, $23,000 to $58,000; and private practice, $18,000 to $77,000.

Benefits depend on the employer but generally include paid vacation time, health insurance, and paid sick days. Those who are in private practice must provide their own benefits.

# WORK ENVIRONMENT

Most creative arts therapists work a typical 40-hour, five-day workweek; at times, however, they may have to work extra hours. The number of patients under a therapist's care depends on the specific employment setting. Although many therapists work in hospitals, they may also be employed in such facilities as clinics, rehabilitation centers, children's homes, schools, and nursing homes. Some therapists maintain service contracts with several facilities. For instance, a therapist might work two days a week at a hospital, one day at a nursing home, and the rest of the week at a rehabilitation center.

Most buildings are pleasant, comfortable, and clean places in which to work. Experienced creative arts therapists might choose to be self-employed, working with patients in their own studios. In such a case, the therapist might work more irregular hours to accommodate patient schedules. Other therapists might maintain a combination of service contract work with one or more facilities in addition to a private caseload of clients referred to them by other health care professionals. Whether therapists work on service contracts with various facilities or maintain private practices, they must deal with all of the business and administrative details and worries that go along with being self-employed.

## OUTLOOK

The American Art Therapy Association notes that art therapy is a growing field. Demand for new therapists is created as medical professionals and the general public become aware of the benefits gained through art therapies. Although enrollment in college therapy programs is increasing, new graduates are usually able to find jobs. In cases where an individual is unable to find a full-time position, a therapist might obtain service contracts for part-time work at several facilities.

The American Music Therapy Association predicts a promising future for the field of music therapy. Demand for music therapists will grow as medical professionals and the general public become aware of the benefits gained through music therapy.

Job openings in facilities such as nursing homes should continue to increase as the elderly population grows over the next few decades. Advances in medical technology and the recent practice of early discharge from hospitals should also create new opportunities in managed care facilities, chronic pain clinics, and cancer care facilities. The demand for therapists of all types should continue to increase as more people become aware of the need to help disabled patients in creative ways. Some drama therapists and psychodramatists are also finding employment opportunities outside of the usual health care field. Such therapists might conduct therapy sessions at corporate sites to enhance the personal effectiveness and growth of employees.

## FOR MORE INFORMATION

*For more detailed information about your field of interest, contact the following organizations:*

**American Art Therapy Association**
11160-C1 South Lakes Drive, Suite 813
Reston, VA 20191-4327
Tel: 888-290-0878
Email: info@arttherapy.org
http://www.arttherapy.org

**American Dance Therapy Association**
10632 Little Patuxent Parkway, Suite 108
Columbia, MD 21044-6258

Tel: 410-997-4040
Email: info@adta.org
http://www.adta.org

**American Music Therapy Association**
8455 Colesville Road, Suite 1000
Silver Spring, MD 20910-3392
Tel: 301-589-3300
Email: info@musictherapy.org
http://www.musictherapy.org

**American Society of Group Psychotherapy and Psychodrama**
301 North Harrison Street, Suite 508
Princeton, NJ 08540-3508
Tel: 609-452-1339
Email: asgpp@asgpp.org
http://www.asgpp.org

**National Association for Drama Therapy**
15 Post Side Lane
Pittsford, NY 14534-9410
Tel: 585-381-5618
Email: answers@nadt.org
http://www.nadt.org

**National Association for Poetry Therapy**
c/o Center for Education, Training & Holistic Approaches
777 East Atlantic Avenue, #243
Delray Beach, FL 33483-5360
Tel: 866-844-NAPT
Email: info@poetrytherapy.org
http://www.poetrytherapy.org

*For an overview of the various types of art therapy, visit the NCCATA's Web site*
**National Coalition of Creative Arts Therapies Associations (NCCATA)**
c/o AMTA
8455 Colesville Road, Suite 1000
Silver Spring, MD 20910-3392
Tel: 201-224-9146
http://www.nccata.org

# Dietitians and Nutritionists

## QUICK FACTS

**School Subjects**
Chemistry
Family and consumer
 science
Health

**Personal Skills**
Helping/teaching
Technical/scientific

**Work Environment**
Primarily indoors
Primarily one location

**Minimum Education Level**
Bachelor's degree

**Salary Range**
$31,830 to $49,010 to
 $72,000+

**Certification or
Licensing**
Required by some states

**Outlook**
About as fast as the
 average

**DOT**
077

**GOE**
14.08.01

**NOC**
3132

**O*NET-SOC**
29-1031.00

## OVERVIEW

*Registered dietitians* (RDs) are professionals who have met certain educational requirements and passed a national certification exam. For the purposes of this article, the terms *dietitian* and *registered dietitian* will be used interchangeably. RDs provide people with foods and dietary advice that will improve or maintain their health. They may be self-employed or work for institutions, such as hospitals, schools, restaurants, and nursing homes—any place where food is served or nutritional counseling is required. *Hospital dietitians,* for example, may ensure that the food served in the cafeteria is nourishing or create special diets for patients with particular nutritional problems and needs.

Regulation of those using the professional title nutritionist varies by state. For example, in some states a person without any specialized training may be able to call himself or herself a nutritionist and offer dietary advice. For the purposes of this article, however, the term *nutritionist* refers to *certified clinical nutritionists* (CCNs), who have received specialized training and passed a certification exam. CCNs usually work in private practice and are concerned with the biochemical aspects of nutrition.

There are approximately 57,000 dietitians and nutritionists working in the United States.

# HISTORY

Nutrition has been an important concern to people throughout the world for millennia, and the use of food as medicine has been recognized throughout recorded history. In India, the form of medicine known as Ayurveda, which tailors diets to individuals to cure or to maintain health, has been practiced for as long as 5,000 years. Traditional Chinese medicine, which is approximately as old as Ayurveda, makes use of many dietary recommendations and proscriptions. Both forms of medicine are still widely used in their countries of origin, and both have spread to other parts of the world.

In ancient Greece, philosophers and healers noted the connection between diet and health, and ultimately it was the Greek practice of careful observation and research that gave rise to the scientific method, on which modern Western nutrition is based. It should be understood, however, that observation and research were also important parts of virtually all other medical traditions.

A major breakthrough in nutrition occurred in the 18th century, when the French chemist Antoine-Laurent Lavoisier began to study the way the body uses food energy, or calories. He also examined the relationship between heat production and the use of energy, and his work has caused him to be known as the "father of nutrition."

By the early 20th century, vitamins had been studied, and the relationship between diets and certain illnesses came to be understood. By 1940, most vitamins and minerals had been discovered and studied, and the field of nutrition had made tremendous strides. Since that time, advances in technology have enabled scientists to learn far more about nutrition than was possible earlier. At present, much is known, but much remains to be learned. It often happens that one study contradicts another regarding the benefits or dangers of certain foods.

# THE JOB

Registered dietitians have a broad-based knowledge of foods, dietetics, and food service. They have at least a bachelor's degree in food science or related field from a school accredited by the Commission on Accreditation for Dietetics Education (CADE); they have completed a CADE-accredited internship; and they have passed a registration exam. CCNs have the same core educational and internship backgrounds as RDs. In addition, CCNs are specialists who have completed a certain amount of post-graduate education that focuses on the biochemical and physiological aspects of nutrition science.

There are many areas of practice within the rapidly growing and changing field of nutrition. One reason for this growth is that the public has become more aware of the importance of nutrition in recent years, and this development has opened up new areas for dietitians and nutritionists. The list of specialties that follows is by no means exhaustive.

*Clinical dietitians* are in charge of planning and supervising the preparation of diets designed for specific patients, and they work for such institutions as hospitals and retirement homes. In many cases, their patients cannot eat certain foods for medical reasons, such as diabetes or liver failure, and the dietitians must see that these patients receive nourishing meals. Clinical dietitians work closely with doctors, who advise them regarding the patients' health and the foods that the patients cannot eat. It is often part of a clinical dietitian's job to educate patients about nutritional principles.

*Community dietitians* usually work for clinics, government health programs, social service agencies, or similar organizations. They counsel individuals or advise the members of certain groups—such as the elderly, families, and pregnant women—regarding nutritional problems, proper eating, and sensible grocery shopping.

Although most dietitians do some kind of teaching in the course of their work, *teaching dietitians* specialize in education. They usually work for hospitals, and they may teach full time or part time. Sometimes teaching dietitians also perform other tasks, such as running a food-service operation, especially in small colleges. In larger institutions, however, different people may perform those tasks. In some cases, teaching dietitians also perform research.

There are many kinds of *consultant dietitians,* who work for such organizations as schools, restaurants, grocery store chains, manufacturers of food-service equipment, pharmaceutical companies, and private companies of various kinds. Some of these organizations have home economics departments that need the services of dietitians. Some consultants spend much of their time advising individuals rather than organizations. One lucrative area for consultants is working with athletes and sports teams, helping to maximize athletes' performance and extend the length of their careers.

*Administrative dietitians,* also known as *management dietitians,* combine management skills with people skills to organize and run large-scale food operations. They may work for food-service companies, oversee the cafeterias of large corporations, be employed by prisons, or work at long-term-care facilities—basically they work for any organization that provides food services to a large number of people. In addition to planning menus, these dietitians are responsible for such things as creating budgets, drawing up work policies, and enforcing institutional and government regulations related to safety and sanitation.

*Research dietitians* typically work for government organizations, universities, hospitals, pharmaceutical companies, and manufacturers, and they may specialize in any of a vast number of research subjects. They often work on improving existing food products or finding alternatives to foods that are unhealthy when eaten in substantial portions.

Certified clinical nutritionists typically work in private practice for themselves, as part of a group of health care professionals, or for a doctor or doctors in private practice. CCNs are specialists who have completed at least some post-graduate training in nutrition science. They work with clients to correct imbalances in the clients' biochemistry and improve their physiological function. Through lab tests, consultations with doctors, and discussions with the clients themselves, CCNs review the clients' overall health and lifestyle and determine what nutrients the clients have too little or too much of. They then come up with plans to enable their clients to get the correct nutrition in order to get their bodies back into balance. Their clients may range from people who are slightly ill, for example, or those who feel run down all the time but do not know why, to people with serious diseases, such as heart disease or cancers. No matter what problem brings a client to a CCN, though, the CCN's goal is to correct that client's biochemistry in order to help that person feel better.

## REQUIREMENTS

### High School

If you want to be a dietitian or a nutritionist, you should take as many courses as possible in health, biology, chemistry, family and consumer science, and mathematics. If you are not sufficiently prepared in high school, you are likely to struggle with college courses in mathematics and biochemistry. Communication skills are also important, since dietitians and nutritionists must interact effectively with clients, employers, and colleagues. Even researchers who spend most of their time in the lab must cooperate with colleagues and write clear, accurate reports on the results of their work. For this reason, dietitians and nutritionists must be well versed in spoken and written English. Psychology, which generally is taught in college nutrition programs, is an important aspect of the work of many dietitians and nutritionists.

## Postsecondary Training

There are a couple different educational routes you can choose from to become a dietitian. The first is to complete a bachelor's or master's level CADE-accredited coordinated program that combines classroom work with 900 hours of supervised internship experience. Currently there are more than 50 programs of this type. Once you have graduated, you are eligible to take the registration exam. Another option is to get at least your bachelor's degree from a CADE-accredited program that provides only classroom instruction. As of 2007, there were about 303 bachelor's and master's degree programs with CADE accreditation. After receiving your degree you then need to get 900 hours of hands-on experience through a CADE-accredited practice program or internship. Currently there are 265 accredited internship programs, which take six to 24 months to complete (depending on whether you are on a full- or part-time schedule). Once you have completed both of these steps, you are eligible to take the registration exam. The American Dietetic Association (ADA) notes that there is no list of courses all would-be dietitians should take. However, the ADA does provide the *Directory of Dietetic Programs* of selected programs that meet CADE standards. In addition, the ADA's Web site (http://www.eatright.org/cade) also provides a listing of these schools. Those who enter this field typically get degrees in food and nutrition science, dietetics, food service, or other related areas. Course work may include classes in economics, business management, culinary arts, biochemistry, physiology, and food science. If you want to teach, do research, or work in public health, you should get a bachelor's degree and one or more advanced degrees.

Nutritionists complete the same type of undergraduate education as dietitians, including fulfilling the 900 hours of a supervised internship. They must also complete at minimum a certain number of courses at the master's degree level to be eligible to sit for the clinical nutritionist certification exam. Many actually complete a master's or Ph.D. in nutrition science.

## Certification or Licensing

Currently 48 states have laws regulating the practice of dietitians and nutritionists through licensure, certification, or registration. Of these states, 35 require licensure, 12 require certification, and one requires registration.

The registered dietitian (RD) credential is awarded by the Commission on Dietetic Registration of the ADA. To receive this designa-

A school dietitian uses a tennis ball to illustrate a point about portion size while teaching a class about nutrition. *(Suzanne Carr-Rossi, AP Photo)*

tion, dietitians must have completed CADE-approved education and training and pass the registration exam. To maintain their standing, registered dietitians must also complete continuing education on a regular basis. Some specialty certifications, such as board certified specialist in pediatric nutrition and board certified specialist in sports dietetics, are also available through the ADA.

The certified clinical nutritionist (CCN) credential is awarded by the Clinical Nutrition Certification Board of the International and American Associations of Clinical Nutritionists. To receive this designation, nutritionists must have completed a bachelor's degree (which includes certain classes in the sciences and nutrition), done post-graduate studies in clinical nutrition, finished an internship, and passed the written examination. Recertification is required every five years.

### Other Requirements

Because there are so many technical requirements in the field of nutrition, dietitians and nutritionists must be detail oriented and able to think analytically. Math and science are a major part of both training and work. Dietitians and nutritionists must be comfortable making decisions and acting on them. Even those who do not work as consultants have to be disciplined and decisive.

For most dietitians, flexibility is crucial. Karen Petty, RD, an administrator who began her career as a clinical dietitian, says about working in institutional food service: "You will never be able to please everyone, because everyone has different tastes in food. You learn to be able to take criticism and go on to try to please the majority."

People who want to become administrators must have people skills. On that subject, Petty says: "When I'm asked what is the hardest part of my job, I never hesitate to say it's personnel management." For administrators, the ability to communicate clearly and effectively is particularly important.

## EXPLORING

You can start exploring this type of work right in your own kitchen. Learn healthy ways to cook and bake. Plan and prepare meals for your family; do your own grocery shopping and learn to pick out the best produce, meats, fish, and other ingredients. And, in addition to taking family and consumer science classes at school, take cooking classes offered by other organizations in your community. Supermarkets, for example, frequently offer classes on topics such as how to prepare low cholesterol meals. Another option is to contact dietitians and nutritionists and ask them about their work. The school cafeteria, the local hospital, or a nursing home are all places to look for those who would be willing to participate in an information interview with you. And, of course, one of the best ways to learn about nutrition is to get a job in a food-related business such as a restaurant or a hospital cafeteria. In such a setting, you will be able to observe and interact with dietitians as they work.

## EMPLOYERS

Approximately 57,000 dietitians and nutritionists are employed in the United States. Many kinds of government and private organizations hire dietitians, and the kinds of available opportunities continue to increase. There are opportunities in hospitals, schools of all levels, community health programs, day care centers, correctional facilities, health clubs, weight-management clinics, health management organizations, nursing homes, government organizations, food-service companies, food equipment manufacturers, sports teams, pharmaceutical companies, and grocery store chains, to name a few. Among the large organizations that need dietitians are the armed forces, which have to feed their personnel as well and as inexpensively as possible. In addition, dietitians and nutritionists can work in private practice, running their own consulting businesses or working in a group practice.

## STARTING OUT

Because dietitians and nutritionists are trained extensively and have some practical experience before they look for their first job, they tend to know the type of organization they want to work for. Most colleges and universities provide placement services, and people often find work through connections they make at school or in practice programs. For this reason, it is wise to make as many professional connections as possible.

Some parts of the country have more dietitians and nutritionists than others, and beginning dietitians should consider taking positions out of their areas in order to get started in the business. Jobs can be found via trade journals, national and state conventions, Web sites, classified ads, and specialized employment agencies. Although it is possible to call organizations to learn about job opportunities, the most effective way to find work is through personal contacts.

## ADVANCEMENT

There are various ways to advance in the business. One of the best is further education. RDs with only a bachelor's degree may wish to obtain an advanced degree, which will enable them to apply for research, teaching, or public health positions that are not otherwise open to them. For example, a dietitian interested in working in community dietetics may get an advanced degree in public health; someone wanting to move into management may get a master's in business administration. RDs can also advance by getting further education that leads to specialty certification, such as the CCN. Often advancement depends upon the goals of the individual, as he or she decides where to go with this career.

In the field of nutrition, as in most others, seniority, reliability, expertise, and experience count. An experienced clinical dietitian might ultimately become an administrative dietitian, for example, and a research dietitian might take charge of a research department.

## EARNINGS

Salaries vary by practice area, years of experience, educational level, and location. In general, administrative, self-employed, and business dietitians earn more than their clinical and community counterparts.

According to the U.S. Department of Labor, the median annual salary for dietitians and nutritionists was $49,010 in 2007. The lowest paid 10 percent earned less than $31,830; the highest paid 10 percent earned more than $71,130 a year.

## Earnings for Dietitians and Nutritionists by Industry, 2007

| Field | Mean Annual Earnings |
| --- | --- |
| Federal Executive Branch | $62,480 |
| Home Health Care Services | $58,200 |
| Medical and Diagnostic Laboratories | $55,490 |
| Outpatient Care Centers | $52,170 |
| General Medical and Surgical Hospitals | $50,500 |
| Nursing Care Facilities | $50,060 |
| Local Government | $46,950 |
| Special Food Services | $46,420 |

Source: U.S. Department of Labor

The ADA reports findings from its membership indicate that of dietitians employed for five years or less, 50 percent had yearly earnings of $35,000 to $46,000. The ADA also found that RDs in business, private practice, and consulting earned more than $72,000 per year.

Benefits such as health insurance, sick pay, paid vacations and holidays, and 401(k) plans are as prevalent in the field of nutrition as they are in other fields. Naturally, dietitians who run their own businesses must make their own arrangements in these areas.

## WORK ENVIRONMENT

Nutritionists usually work in medical office settings that are clean, well lit, and organized. Dietitians generally work in offices or kitchens. Such environments are usually clean and well lit, although some kitchens may be hot and stifling. Some dietitians and nutritionists sit much of the time, while others spend all day on their feet. Most work 40-hour weeks, but some—especially dietitians who work for hospitals and restaurants—are required to work on weekends and at odd hours. Part-time positions are also common.

Some hospitals offer dietitians room, board, and laundry services for a nominal fee, but this arrangement is becoming less common. In the past, many college dietitians lived in apartments provided by the school, but this arrangement is also becoming a thing of the past, except where dietitians run food-service operations in residence halls.

## OUTLOOK

According to the U.S. Department of Labor, employment of dietitians and nutritionists will grow about as fast as the average for all occupations through 2016. One contributing factor to continued growth is the public's increasing awareness of the importance of nutrition. Another is the fact that the average age of the population is increasing rapidly, which will bring about a growing need for nutritional counseling and planning in hospitals, residential care facilities, schools, prisons, community health programs, and home health care agencies. Opportunities will also be good for dietitians and nutritionists who work for contract providers of food services, in outpatient care centers, and in offices of physicians and other health care professionals. Workers who are employed in hospitals and nursing homes that hire contractors to handle food-service operations will have less promising employment prospects.

# FOR MORE INFORMATION

*The ADA is the single best source of information about careers in dietetics. Its Web site is an excellent resource that provides detailed information and links to other organizations and resources.*

**American Dietetic Association (ADA)**
120 South Riverside Plaza, Suite 2000
Chicago, IL 60606-6995
Tel: 800-877-1600
Email: education@eatright.org
http://www.eatright.org

*The goal of the ASN is to improve people's quality of life through the nutritional sciences. It is a good source of educational and career information.*

**American Society for Nutrition (ASN)**
9650 Rockville Pike
Bethesda, MD 20814-3998
Tel: 301-634-7050
Email: info@nutrition.org
http://www.nutrition.org

*For information on dietitian certification, contact*
**Commission on Dietetic Registration**
120 South Riverside Plaza, Suite 2000
Chicago, IL 60606-6995
Tel: 800-877-1600, ext. 5500
Email: cdr@eatright.org
http://www.cdrnet.org

*For more information on becoming a certified clinical nutritionist, contact*
**International and American Associations of Clinical Nutritionists**
15280 Addison Road, Suite 130
Addison, TX 75001-4551
Tel: 972-407-9089
Email: ddc@clinicalnutrition.com
http://www.iaacn.org

# Ergonomists

## OVERVIEW

*Ergonomists* help business, industry, government, and academic institutions use technology responsibly by considering human capabilities and limitations in the workplace. Their goal is to increase human productivity, comfort, safety, and health, and to decrease injury and illness by designing human-centered equipment, furniture, work methods, and techniques. Ergonomists combine knowledge from various sciences and apply it to jobs, systems, products, and environments. They are also known as *human factors engineers* or *human factors specialists*.

## HISTORY

The term "ergonomics" comes from the Greek word *ergon*, meaning "work." The study of people at work began about 100 years ago as employers and employees began to realize that job productivity was tied to job satisfaction and the nature of the work environment. The concerns of many of the early ergonomists centered around increasing industrial production while maintaining safety on the job. They began to design machines and other equipment that improved production and also reduced the number of job-related accidents. As it became clear that improved working conditions increased productivity and safety and improved workers' morale, ergonomists began investigating other physical and psychological factors that influenced people at work.

Increased use of computers and automation have changed the nature of many businesses and workplaces. There is a need for professionals to help adapt the workplace to these changes. The Occupational Safety and Health Administration reports that musculoskeletal disorders caused by ergonomic problems in the workplace affect 1.8

## QUICK FACTS

**School Subjects**
Health
Mathematics
Physical education

**Personal Skills**
Helping/teaching
Mechanical/manipulative

**Minimum Education Level**
Master's degree

**Salary Range**
$42,200 to $69,580 to
$103,300+

**Certification or Licensing**
Voluntary

**Outlook**
About as fast as the average

**DOT**
045

**GOE**
02.07.04

**NOC**
4161

**O*NET-SOC**
17-2111.00

million workers a year. This costs businesses billions in lost workdays, workers compensation, and related costs. Most major insurance carriers today have ergonomics departments. The ergonomist can help businesses develop methods that will more humanely adapt the workplace to technological changes and also prepare the workplace for the different types of jobs and other changes that are sure to come.

## THE JOB

Ergonomists are concerned with the relationship between people and work, studying and dealing with the limitations and possibilities of the human body. They deal with organizational structure, worker productivity, and job satisfaction. Ergonomists are important consultants on many levels: They help employees work in safer environments, they allow employers to achieve higher levels of productivity, and they educate workers. Ergonomists adapt environments to the tasking order to decrease the number of work-related illnesses and injuries.

Ergonomists work to ensure that people can perform their work in the safest manner possible. To be ergonomically sound, a task should allow for three basic principles: It should be able to be completed in several different and safe manners; the largest appropriate muscle groups should be used; and joints should be at approximately the middle of their range of movement.

This first principle implies that a task shouldn't be so repetitive that the worker is limited to only one set of movements to complete it. Over time, repetitive actions can lead to muscle and joint trauma. Ergonomists help people avoid repetitive strain injuries. For instance, ergonomists often are called to an assembly line to study the workers' motions. They may suggest different ways for the employees to complete their tasks while still being safe and efficient.

The second principle of ergonomics has to do with muscle work. Larger muscle groups are often better suited to a task than smaller ones. For instance, when lifting a heavy box from the ground, many people tend to bend at the waist and lift the box using the strength in their arms. But this approach can lead to muscle strain in the arms and the back. A better approach is to bend at the knees, grip the box to the chest, and lift up slowly, using leg power. By using the longer, stronger leg muscles to lift items, you can reduce your risk of injury. In the workplace, ergonomists study how much weight employees have to lift during the day and suggest alternate ways to use their bodies or distribute the weight onto different muscle groups.

Proper ergonomic form requires joints to be as close to the middle of their range as possible, which means employees shouldn't hyper- or hypo-extend their arms or legs. Joints perform best when they aren't too straight and aren't too bent. An ergonomist might be called on to help an employee who works at a computer terminal all day. The ergonomist might watch the person at work for a little while, and then determine that the worker's arm and shoulder pain may be caused by the mouse and keyboard placement. If the worker has to extend his arm fully to reach the mouse, he locks his elbow and moves his arm at an unnatural and uncomfortable angle.

Guided by these basic principles, ergonomists work with ideas, processes, and people to help make the workplace safer and more comfortable. An ergonomist who deals primarily in design creates machines and other materials that are both usable and comfortable to the user. This may include physiological research on how certain types of work-related injuries, such as carpal tunnel syndrome, occur. These professionals study mathematics and physics, in conjunction with the human form, in order to gain a better understanding of how people can avoid performing unsafe and repetitive motions that lead to injury.

Other ergonomists adopt a more hands-on approach by going out in the field to study a workplace and ascertain the needs of particular employees in specific work situations. Their clients may be as varied as secretaries working in front of the computer, factory workers installing headlights in new automobiles, and travel agents working with telephones propped on their shoulders all day. These ergonomists may study assembly-line procedures and suggest changes to reduce monotony and make it easier for workers to load or unload materials, thereby obtaining optimum efficiency in terms of human capabilities. They may also investigate environmental factors such as lighting and room temperature, which might influence workers' behavior and productivity. In an office setting, an ergonomist is likely to make suggestions about keyboard placement and monitor height to help alleviate injuries. Rearrangement of furniture is often one of the easiest ways to make a workplace safer and more comfortable.

Ergonomists usually work as part of a team, with different specialists focusing on a particular aspect of the work environment. For example, one ergonomist may deal with the safety aspects of machinery, and another may specialize in environmental issues, such as the volume of noise and the layout of the surroundings. After analyzing relevant data and observing how workers interact in the work environment, ergonomists submit a written report of their findings and make recommendations to company executives or representatives for changes or adaptations in the workplace. Their suggestions might be as simple as moving a desk closer to the window to allow for more natural light or installing task lighting to reduce eyestrain. They may make proposals for new machinery or suggest a revised design for machinery already in place. They may also suggest environmental changes, like painting walls or soundproofing a noisy work area, so employees can better enjoy the work environment.

Ergonomists may focus on something as large as redesigning the computer terminals for a large multinational corporation, or they may design more comfortable chairs or easier-to-use telephones at a local family-owned business. They may work as consultants for government agencies and manufacturing companies or engage in research at colleges or universities. Often, an ergonomist will specialize in one particular system or application.

Ergonomists are also concerned with the social work environment. They are involved with personnel training and development as well as with the interaction between people and machines. Ergonomists may, for example, plan various kinds of tests that will help screen applicants for employment with the firms. They assist engineers and technicians in designing systems that require people and machines to interact. Ergonomists may also develop aids for training people to use those systems.

## REQUIREMENTS

### High School
High school is not too early to begin preparing for a career in ergonomics. You should follow a broad college-preparatory curriculum with a concentration in the sciences. Courses in the life and physical sciences (biology, anatomy, health, and physics) will be particularly helpful, as will classes in research methods, writing and speech, mathematics, and computer science. Business courses will also help you learn more about the business world and the opportunities available for ergonomists. Any classes that broaden your knowledge of people and how they work, and those that sharpen your skills in communication, will be very important. Knowledge of modern foreign languages may also increase opportunities as global, multicultural economies are developing rapidly.

### Postsecondary Training
Ergonomists need solid skills in three basic areas: business administration, science and technology, and communications. A career in ergonomics begins with an undergraduate degree in one of the behavioral, biomedical, health, social, or computer sciences or engineering. Potential ergonomists take whichever courses are needed to complete a degree in their chosen field. Most science-based degrees require courses in anatomy, psychology, physiology, statistics, mathematics, and education. If a concentration in ergonomics is available at your college or university, you might take additional courses

such as operations research, demographics, biomechanics, kinesiology, psychology, work analysis and measurement, safety and health analysis techniques, and design methodologies.

Additional courses in business, writing, and communications will help you communicate your ideas and suggestions to the people with whom you will be working. Again, knowledge of foreign languages will allow you to work more globally.

Most ergonomists also earn a master's degree in industrial engineering or psychology, along with a concentration in ergonomics/human factors. A doctoral degree is an advantage for those who want to pursue research and teaching at the university level or for those who want to develop specialized methodologies for ergonomics in advanced technologies.

### Certification or Licensing
Although certification is not mandatory, industry is increasingly recognizing board certification in ergonomics as a standard of professional achievement and skill, and it is recommended that ergonomists earn their credentials to be eligible for higher positions. Because ergonomics is a rapidly evolving career field and tied to advances in scientific knowledge and technology, it is especially important to keep up-to-date on the latest developments.

The Board of Certification in Professional Ergonomics offers the designations certified professional ergonomist (CPE) and certified human factors professional (CHFP). To receive either certification, you must have a master's degree in ergonomics, human factors, or equivalent educational experience; three years of professional experience working with ergonomics; documentation of education, work, and project involvement; and a passing score on a written exam. The board also offers the designations associate ergonomics professional, associate human factors professional, and certified ergonomics associate for those who are working on completing their three years of work experience to get the CPE or CHFP.

### Other Requirements
If you are interested in becoming an ergonomist, you should be able to understand the relationships between actions and their results. An analytic mind is essential, and most ergonomists have good problem-solving skills. If you are interested in the research and design side of ergonomics, you should have good research skills and be able to apply research techniques to practical application. If you prefer to work directly with clients, you should enjoy working with people and be able to illustrate proper ergonomic techniques to them. Finally, empathy is an important trait, since many ergonomists are called on site after an

accident or injury has already happened. The ergonomist should be able to investigate the mishap and make recommendations on how to avoid a recurrence and ensure the safety and comfort of the workers.

## EXPLORING

Only those with the required educational credentials can get hands-on experience, so the most practical way to explore career opportunities is to talk with those already working in the field. A great deal of career information can also be found in professional journals. Students may also want to check out some online sources. Many organizations offer electronic newsgroups for people in the industry to discuss news and information about the field. You may wish to subscribe to such a newsgroup or consult Web sites that focus on ergonomics.

After researching the field of ergonomics through published and electronic sources, you may consider trying your hand at setting up an ergonomically sound work area. If you have a computer, you could make sure that the monitor distance, mouse and keyboard placement, and chair height are in accord with accepted ergonomic standards. At school, you might also make sure your desk and locker are put to proper ergonomic use. Place heavy books at the bottom of your locker and bend at the knees to lift them and carry your backpack close to your body with both straps over your shoulders.

Finally, learn to listen to your own body for signs of ergonomic distress. Do your thumbs cramp up after a few hours of video games? That could be an early sign of repetitive stress syndrome and could lead to more serious problems. Before you move on to the next level in a game, press "pause" and stretch out your hands to get the blood flowing again. Does your back hurt after a long day at school? Try to make a conscious effort to sit up straight, with your back straight and lower back flush against the chair. Do your eyeballs get blurry from reading too much? Put down the magazine, put on some good sneakers, and go for a walk.

## EMPLOYERS

Ergonomists are employed by various organizations: hospitals, factories, communications industries, and other businesses. They may be part of the regular staff at a large corporation, or they may work on an as-needed, or contract, basis. Many ergonomists work as consultants for one or many companies. Ergonomists may practice in tandem with physical therapists, sports medicine practitioners, chiropractors, kinesiologists, and physicians. Those who work in research and design may work with engineers, architects, interior decorators, contractors, and builders.

Because ergonomics is a somewhat new occupation, most positions available will be in larger, more urban areas. Since the government also hires ergonomists to work in various organizations, one of the largest concentrations of ergonomists is in Washington, D.C. The field is evolving at a rapid pace, and skilled ergonomists will be able to forge their own way in the profession.

## STARTING OUT

Since it's a relatively new profession, people looking to enter the ergonomic field have many ways to get started. Some complete their undergraduate and graduate degrees prior to getting a job in the profession. Others prefer to work full time while earning their credentials part time. Still others work on the fringes of ergonomics before earning certification. They may have expertise in other areas, such as sports medicine, architecture, or engineering. Often, an interest in preventing injuries rather than treating them leads many people from the medical field to a career in ergonomics. In any case, most certification programs require some professional experience in the field prior to certification.

Your first job in ergonomics can let you shape your own career. If you are interested in using ergonomics in a sport setting, for instance, you could try getting a job as a consultant to a minor league sports team in your community. If you think you would prefer working in a more businesslike environment, you should get a job with an established ergonomic service. Professional organizations usually have job listings and career assistance, and many colleges and universities offer career guidance to their graduates. If you plan on using ergonomics training for your own consultation business, it's often a good idea to do an internship or assistantship with an established ergonomist or group of ergonomists in order to practice your skills and build a client base.

## ADVANCEMENT

Because ergonomics is still rapidly evolving, advancement opportunities should be plentiful for the near future. There are not that many people involved in the field and, therefore, there are many opportunities for qualified individuals, especially those who have a special area of expertise. Many ergonomists develop skills at a first job and then either use that experience to find higher paid work at a different company or to get increased responsibility in their current position.

Qualified ergonomists often are promoted to management positions, with an accompanying increase in earnings and responsibility. They can also start their own consulting firms or branch off into teaching or research. Those in government work may choose to move to the private sector, where salaries are higher. But others may opt for the security and job responsibilities of a government position.

## EARNINGS

The Human Factors and Ergonomics Society reports that the average salary of ergonomists is $44,162. The U.S. Department of Labor reports that the median annual earnings of health and safety engineers (which includes human factors engineers) were $69,580 in 2007. The lowest paid 10 percent earned less than $42,200; the highest paid 10 percent earned more than $103,300.

Individuals with certification, advanced education, and work experience can expect to have the highest earnings. Full-time employees receive benefit packages such as vacation, health insurance, and retirement plans. Private consultants, including self-employed ergonomists, charge a wide range of hourly fees, from $100 to more than $200, depending on skill level, type of job, and the market in which they are competing.

## WORK ENVIRONMENT

Ergonomists encounter various working conditions, depending on specific duties and responsibilities. An ergonomist may work in a typical office environment, with computer and data processing equipment close at hand. The ergonomist may also work in a factory, investigating production problems. Usually, ergonomists do both: They work in an office setting and make frequent visits to a factory or other location to work out particular production issues. Although the majority of the work is not strenuous, ergonomists may occasionally assemble or revamp machinery or work processes. They also spend much of their time explaining procedures and techniques to their clients.

Ergonomists often work as part of a team, but they may also work on an individual research project, spending much time alone, doing research at the library or online, or working out a production schedule on the computer. They usually work a 40-hour week, although overtime and odd hours are not uncommon, especially if a particular project is on deadline or there are urgent safety issues at hand. There may be occasional weekend and evening work, depending on the industry and project. Those involved with research or teaching may only work 10 months a year, although many of these ergonomists work as consultants when not employed full time.

## OUTLOOK

The employment outlook for ergonomists is good. As the public has gained an increased understanding of and appreciation for ergonomy and as numerous work environments have become more complex because of technology advances, ergonomists have found a steady demand for their services. Businesses will continue to use ergonomy to reduce worker injury, raise levels of production, and increase profits. Employment should increase about as fast as the average because of the numerous areas of specialization, the opportunities to combine the practice of ergonomy with fields such as industrial engineering or psychology, and the relatively low number of ergonomists in the field. The rise of technology has created a need for people who can make that technology easy, safe, and effective to use.

## FOR MORE INFORMATION

*For details about the certification process for ergonomists, contact*
**Board of Certification in Professional Ergonomics**
PO Box 2811
Bellingham, WA 98227-2811
Tel: 888-856-4685
Email: bcpehq@bcpe.org
http://www.bcpe.org

*For information on careers and educational programs in human factors and ergonomics, contact*
**Human Factors and Ergonomics Society**
PO Box 1369
Santa Monica, CA 90406-1369
Tel: 310-394-1811
Email: info@hfes.org
http://www.hfes.org

*For general information on ergonomics, contact the following organizations:*
**Institute of Industrial Engineers**
3577 Parkway Lane, Suite 200
Norcross, GA 30092-2833
Tel: 800-494-0460
Email: cs@iienet.org
http://www.iienet.org

**National Society of Professional Engineers**
1420 King Street
Alexandria, VA 22314-2794
Tel: 703-684-2800
http://www.nspe.org

# Herbalists

## QUICK FACTS

**School Subjects**
Biology
Chemistry
Earth science

**Personal Skills**
Helping/teaching
Technical/scientific

**Work Environment**
Primarily indoors
Primarily one location

**Minimum Education Level**
Bachelor's degree

**Salary Range**
$13,000 to $70,000 to
$200,000+

**Certification or Licensing**
Required by certain states

**Outlook**
Faster than the average

**DOT**
N/A

**GOE**
N/A

**NOC**
3232

**O*NET-SOC**
N/A

## OVERVIEW

*Herbalists* are health care professionals who practice healing through the use of herbs. The same term applies to individuals who grow and collect herbs. Herbs are plants or plant parts—roots, bark, leaves, flowers, or berries—that are used for their aromatic, savory, or medicinal qualities. Herbs are sometimes called *botanicals*. They are the fastest growing category in drugstores because of the public's steadily increasing interest in herbal preparations.

The field of herbalism is expanding and changing rapidly. Professional herbalists work in a variety of places. They may work as primary health care providers, as consultants in health care settings, or as clerks or assistants in health food stores. Others assist in the planting, harvesting, or manufacturing of herbs. There are roughly 15,000 professional herbalists in the United States.

## HISTORY

Long before recorded history, early humans undoubtedly used plants and plant products not only for food but also for medicine. Between 8000 and 5000 B.C., people gathered or cultivated more than 200 plants. A number of those plants had medicinal qualities.

The folk medicine traditions of all cultures include the use of plants and plant products. Knowledge of herbs and herbal remedies has been handed down from generation to generation and from culture to culture. Ancient cultures—such as the Babylonian, Chinese, Egyptian, and Syrian—developed detailed pharmacopoeias (books describing medical preparations) that included many commonly used herbs.

In the Orient, the Chinese developed a complete system of herbal medicine called Chinese herbology. The earliest work, the Yellow Emperor's *Classic of Internal Medicine* (Huang Di Nei Ching) was recorded around 2,300 years ago. Like other aspects of traditional Chinese medicine, Chinese herbology is based upon the principle of restoring balance to the individual's vital energy, which is called *qi* (pronounced "chee"). Chinese herbology remains a distinct form of herbalism today.

In the West, the Egyptians developed and recorded herbal medicinal systems. The *Kahun Medical Papyrus* dates back to 1900 B.C. Hippocrates and other early Greek physicians used herbs and other natural remedies to heal their patients. Some of their knowledge was based on early Egyptian herbal medicine. The work of the early Egyptian and Greek healers evolved into what is now considered Western herbalism.

European settlers brought their herbs and herbal remedies with them to this country. They also brought *herbals*—books on herbal medicine. The settlers learned about the herbs of the New World from the Native Americans and through their own observations. In 1751, John Bartram, one of the most respected botanists of the colonial era, published a list of indigenous North American plants and their uses.

Even into the early 20th century, much of the pharmacopoeia of conventional medical practitioners was based on the herbal lore of native peoples. Many of the drugs we commonly use today are of herbal origin. It is estimated that 75 percent of modern drugs were originally derived from plants and that about 20 percent still are. With the rise of modern medicine, herbal and other natural remedies fell out of popularity for a time.

With the immense popular interest in alternative medicine over the last three decades, interest in and demand for herbal products has skyrocketed. In Europe (especially England, Germany, and Switzerland), botanicals have long been considered important complements to conventional drugs. Herbal remedies are also more generally accepted and used in Australia, Japan, India, China, and some African countries. The United States is just beginning to catch up with the rest of the world in recognizing the value of the medicinal use of herbs.

Throughout the history of humanity, men and women have practiced herbalism on a daily basis. The World Health Organization (WHO), which is the medical branch of the United Nations, estimates that 80 percent of the world's population presently uses traditional healing practices that include herbal medicine in some way in primary health care.

# THE JOB

There are several kinds of herbalists in the United States. Their job descriptions vary widely depending upon the area of the herbal industry in which they work. According to Roy Upton, vice-president of the American Herbalists Guild, herbalists who want to practice primarily as health care professionals have two options. They can become primary health care providers or they can work as allied health professionals, working more as consultants than as practitioners. In the United States at this time, there are two officially recognized forms of training for herbalists: Oriental medicine and naturopathy.

*Oriental medicine practitioners* are trained in Chinese herbology. They study approximately 300 herbs and 125 herbal formulas, including their actions, indications, contraindications, side effects, and standard formulas. *Chinese herbalists* practice herbal science according to the philosophy and principals of Oriental medicine. First, they perform a careful evaluation and diagnosis of the client's situation. Next, they consider all of the person's characteristics and symptoms to determine what is out of balance in the person's qi. Oriental medicine practitioners believe that the body's energy flows along specific channels, called meridians, in the body. Each meridian relates to a particular physiological system and internal organ. When qi is unbalanced, or when its flow along the channels is blocked or disrupted, disease, pain, and other physical and emotional conditions result. Finally, Chinese herbalists select the proper herb or combination of herbs to use in a strategy for restoring balance to the individual's qi. Chinese herbalists sometimes develop special herbal formulas based upon their diagnosis of the unique combination of the individual's characteristics, symptoms, and primary complaints. For more information on this career, see the article "Oriental Medicine Practitioners."

*Naturopaths* are trained for many years in a distinct system of health care called naturopathy. They use a variety of natural approaches to health and healing, including herbal medicine. Like Chinese herbalists, naturopaths recognize the integrity of the whole person, and they consider all of the patient's characteristics and symptoms in planning a course of treatment. If they select an herbal remedy as the appropriate approach, they may use Chinese herbs or Western herbs. Naturopathic physicians study approximately 100 herbs. Unlike Chinese herbalists, they do not base their choice of herbs on the philosophy and principles of Oriental medicine. Compared to Chinese herbalists, naturopaths learn few standard herbal formulas, and they do not usually develop their own formulas. Naturopaths take a more Western approach to the use of herbal medicine, and they are more likely to prescribe a particular herbal medicine based upon a particular diagnosis. For more information see the article, "Naturopaths."

Many *professional herbalists* have studied herbalism extensively but are not certified as Oriental medicine practitioners or licensed as naturopathic physicians. Some of them use their knowledge of herbal therapeutics to help their clients improve their health and their lives. They usually describe their services very carefully in order to avoid being charged with practicing medicine without a license. According to Upton, "In rare instances, herbalists have been integrated into managed care programs as herbalist consultants, much as registered dietitians have been integrated into the fabric of the health care delivery system. Their scope of practice is limited."

With the surge of interest in alternative health care and natural approaches to medicine, the demand for botanicals increased dramatically during the 1990s. As a result, a growing number of herbalists work in health food stores, drugstores, and other retail stores. There they decide which botanicals to order, monitor the stock, and help customers understand the myriad of products available.

A few herbalists become *wildcrafters*, individuals who collect herbs that grow naturally outdoors. They may need permission or permits to take herbs from particular areas. They follow very detailed guidelines about which herbs to harvest, and exactly when and how to collect them. Wildcrafters need to be trained to know which species are sensitive or endangered and how to avoid harming them.

Some herbalists grow herbs for sale. They must know exactly the right conditions for growing herbs, how to select good plants, and how to harvest, store, and ship them properly.

Other herbalists work in the manufacturing and distribution of botanicals. Their duties include quality control, literature review, and development of technical, educational, and promotional materials for products. They give educational seminars for health professionals, retailers, and consumers. They may also be called upon to provide technical support to consumers and health professionals and to conduct market analyses.

Herbalists also become teachers. Those who are certified in Oriental medicine or licensed as naturopathic physicians work in colleges and universities that teach the approaches in which they are trained. A few professional herbalists run their own schools. They offer a variety of programs, and some offer certificates of completion. Some also become writers.

Many who work in the various areas of herbalism run their own businesses. Like all business owners, they recruit, hire, and train staff. To be successful, they must maintain detailed records about their businesses.

## REQUIREMENTS

### High School

To prepare yourself for a career as an herbalist, take classes in agriculture, botany, ecology, and horticulture so you can learn about plants and how they are grown. Biology, chemistry, and physics will

A Chinese herbalist prepares a herbal formula. *(David R. Frazier, The Image Works)*

help prepare you to study the properties of herbs and their therapeutic uses. If you want to become a health care practitioner, you will be taking a lot of medical courses in college, so pre-med classes will be especially helpful. Nearly all health care professions involve interacting with people. Classes in psychology, English, debate, and drama can help you develop good communication skills. If you become an herbalist, business and computer skills will be important because you are likely to have your own business.

## Postsecondary Training

If Chinese herbology will be your path toward a career as an herbalist, you will study six to eight years after high school. Oriental medicine schools offer specialties in Chinese herbology. Most are master's level programs. For admission, you need two years of undergraduate study or a bachelor's degree in a related field, such as science, nursing, or premed. Most programs provide a thorough education in Chinese herbology, other aspects of traditional Oriental medicine, and Western sciences.

More than 50 schools in the United States offer courses in Chinese herbology. State requirements to practice Oriental medicine and Chinese herbology vary, so be sure the school you choose will prepare you to practice in your state. The Oriental medicine associations listed at the end of this article have information on school programs and obtaining financial assistance.

If you choose the Western approach to herbalism, you will study naturopathic medicine. Becoming a naturopathic physician requires eight years of study after high school. First, you complete a pre-med undergraduate program including courses in herbal sciences, chemistry, other basic medical sciences, nutrition, and psychology.

The naturopathic doctoral degree is a four-year program. It includes courses in botanical medicine and other basic medical sciences, as well as courses in nutrition, homeopathy, and minor surgery. In addition to course instruction, there is extensive clinical training. When you finish, you will have a Doctor of Naturopathic Medicine degree (ND, or sometimes NMD).

Contact the accredited naturopathic colleges as early as possible to ensure that you complete the prerequisite courses. Accredited schools offer the Doctor of Naturopathic Medicine degree. Schools without accreditation offer correspondence courses and may offer certificates. Only a degree from an accredited school will prepare you to become a licensed naturopath. Currently there are only five U.S. and Canadian schools that are accredited: Bastyr University in Kenmore, Washington; National College of Naturopathic Medicine in Portland, Oregon; Southwest College of Naturopathic Medicine and Health Sciences in Tempe, Arizona; Canadian College of Natural Medicine, Toronto, Ontario, Canada; and the University of Bridgeport College of Naturopathic Medicine in Bridgeport, Connecticut. The Boucher Institute of Naturopathic Medicine, New Westminster, British Columbia, Canada, and the National University of Health Sciences, Lombard, Illinois, have been granted candidacy status. Candidacy status does not ensure accreditation, but it is an important initial step toward it. The professional naturopathic associations listed at the end of this article can help you learn more about accredited schools and their requirements.

At this time, no colleges or universities offer specific programs in herbalism for those who are interested in becoming professional herbalists without following either of the career paths detailed above. Individually run herbal schools generally accept those who have a genuine interest in the field. Some offer certificates of completion, but there is no established career path to follow.

## Certification or Licensing

Certification indicates that an individual meets the standards established by a professional organization. Licensing is a requirement established by a government body that grants individuals the right to practice within the state.

For Chinese herbalists, the National Certification Commission for Acupuncture and Oriental Medicine (NCCAOM) provides certification and promotes nationally recognized standards for Chinese herbology and Oriental medicine. In order to qualify to take the NCCAOM exam, you must meet educational and/or practice requirements. Licensing requirements vary widely from state to state. Most states use the NCCAOM certification as their standard for licensure. Other states seek certification and additional educational requirements. Check with the licensing board of the state in which you intend to practice.

For herbalists who are naturopaths, to practice medicine as a naturopathic physician, you must be licensed in the state in which you practice. Licensing is available in Puerto Rico, the Virgin Islands, and the District of Columbia and in 14 states: Alaska, Arizona, California, Connecticut, Hawaii, Idaho, Kansas, Maine, Montana, New Hampshire, Oregon, Utah, Vermont, and Washington. To become licensed, you must pass the Naturopathic Physicians Licensing Examinations (NPLEX), a standardized test for all naturopathic physicians in North America.

Naturopaths who practice in unlicensed states are not allowed to practice as physicians, but they can still use their skills and knowledge to help people improve their lives.

The American Herbalists Guild (AHG) offers peer review for professional herbalists who specialize in the medicinal use of plants. Members voluntarily submit to a peer-review process that is designed to promote and maintain excellence in herbalism. They also adhere to a code of ethics developed by the AHG. There is no other recognized certification or licensing for professional herbalists at this time.

## Other Requirements

To be a successful herbalist, you need a profound respect for and enjoyment of nature. Like other health care practitioners, herbalists often work with people who may be ill or in pain. You need compassion and understanding for your clients and a strong desire to help them improve their lives. Good listening skills and a reassuring manner are helpful. Strong intuition, careful observation, and good problem-solving skills are also valuable. Idealism, the courage of your convictions, and willingness to stand up for your beliefs are essential. Herbalism and other alternative health care approaches have become much more respected and accepted in recent years, but they are still misunderstood by many people.

## EXPLORING

Numerous opportunities to learn about the field of herbalism are available. Go to health food stores and Chinese herb shops. Look through the books and periodicals they offer. Talk to the people who run the shops—they may be professional herbalists. Ask them about their field and how they like it. Perhaps you can get a part-time job there to learn more.

Join a local horticulture society. Plant a garden or grow plants in containers or a window garden. The professional associations listed at the end of this chapter have many programs and workshops that are available to everyone. Some have student memberships.

The Internet has a wealth of information. Some Web sites have chat groups and searchable herbal databases. If you find that you are seriously interested in this career, consider taking a seminar or a correspondence course from one of the privately run herbal schools.

## EMPLOYERS

Most Chinese herbalists and naturopaths operate private practices. Some form or join partnerships with other alternative health care practitioners. Professionals and clinics in other areas of health care, such as chiropractors, osteopaths, and MDs, may employ herbalists as consultants. As Oriental medicine and naturopathy are becoming more accepted, there are growing opportunities with universities and within government agencies for research into herbal medicine.

Major employers of professional herbalists are dietary supplement manufacturers, health food retailers, pharmaceutical companies, and educational organizations. The largest concentration of manufacturers is in California. Other employers can be found throughout the country. Herbalists who work as consultants, wildcrafters, manufacturers, educators, and writers are usually self-employed.

## STARTING OUT

Herbalists who study naturopathy and Chinese herbology frequently get help from their schools for initial placement. When starting out, some herbalists find jobs in clinics with doctors or chiropractors or in wellness centers. This gives them a chance to start practicing in a setting where they can work with and learn from others. Some begin working with more experienced practitioners and later go into private practice. Both Chinese herbalists and naturopaths frequently work in private practice.

When you start out as a Chinese herbal therapist or as a naturopath, one of the most important considerations is having the proper certification and licensing for your geographical area. This is essential because the requirements for the professions, for each state, and for the nation are changing so rapidly.

For other herbalists, there are no formal career pathways. Networking is a major way to make the connections that lead to jobs. You can get to know people in the herbal community through the Internet, by joining associations, and by attending meetings.

For a career in retailing, identify health food stores and other retailers that offer herbal products, and talk to the store manager. If you are interested in the manufacturing and distribution areas, attend trade shows and send your resume to manufacturers. As in many other fields, finding a mentor can be extremely helpful.

## ADVANCEMENT

Because most naturopaths and Chinese herbalists work in private or group practice, advancement frequently depends on their dedication to building up a client base. As an herbalist in private practice, you will need a general sense of how to run a successful business. You will need to promote your practice within the community and develop a network of contacts with conventional medical doctors or other alternative practitioners who may refer clients to you.

Other herbalists advance through increasing their knowledge of the part of the industry in which they work. An individual who works in retail could become the manager of the department or store. An herb grower or wildcrafter might employ others and expand the business. Those in manufacturing and distribution may have opportunities for foreign travel. Some advance by starting their own businesses.

Herbalists who become distinguished in their fields can become self-employed and consult, write, or teach. With the growing government interest in research into natural health care, more naturopathic physicians and Chinese herbalists will find opportunities for advancement as researchers.

## EARNINGS

Earnings vary according to an herbalist's specialty. For self-employed herbalists, income is usually closely related to the number of hours worked and the rates charged.

Starting pay for a private Oriental medicine practitioner specializing in Chinese herbology may be $13,000 to $20,000 until the practice builds. Rates increase with experience. Clinics might offer $15,000 to $20,000 to start. The average income for full-time Oriental medicine practitioners is $35,000 to $50,000. A very experienced Oriental medicine practitioner with a well-established practice can sometimes net $200,000 or more.

A beginning naturopath earns around $20,000 to $30,000 a year, according to the Association of Accredited Naturopathic Medical Colleges. After some years of practice, N.D.'s generally average $60,000 to $80,000 per year. Although a well-established naturopath can potentially make up to $200,000 a year, most earn much less.

In manufacturing and retail positions, beginning earnings range from $35,000 to $40,000. Mid-level wages are generally from $40,000 to $70,000, and highly skilled, experienced individuals earn from $70,000 to $200,000.

Like other self-employed individuals, herbalists in private practice must provide their own insurance, vacation, and retirement benefits. Herbalists who are employed in industry, at universities, or as researchers generally receive some benefits, such as health insurance, sick pay and vacation pay, and contributions to retirement funds.

## WORK ENVIRONMENT

Herbalists who specialize in Oriental herbal medicine or naturopathy usually work indoors in clean, quiet, comfortable offices. Since most are in private practice, they define their own surroundings. Private practitioners set their own hours, but many work some evenings and weekends to accommodate their patients' schedules. They usually work without supervision and must have a lot of self-discipline.

For herbalists who work in clinics, research settings, and universities, the surroundings vary. Wherever they work, health care practitioners need clean, quiet offices. In these larger settings, herbalists must be good team players. They may also need to work well under supervision.

Herbalists who are employed in retail, manufacturing, or distribution may find themselves in a variety of settings; however, most of their work is indoors. Their jobs may involve travel within the United States or even abroad. They must work well in a group environment, enjoy working with people, and work well under pressure. Wildcrafters and herb growers spend time both indoors and outdoors. They work with plants, soil, and equipment. They may work alone or with others.

## OUTLOOK

With the American public's rapidly increasing interest in alternative health care and natural health remedies, herbalists will remain in demand in the 21st century. Mainstream magazines and newspapers, television, and the Internet are full of articles and advertisements telling of the virtues and successes of herbal therapies.

Sales of herbal supplements have increased dramatically in the last 10 years. Some respected sources report increases in herb sales as high as 35 percent in the mass market and as high as 20 percent for the industry as a whole. Roy Upton of the American Herbalists Guild projects that the employment outlook will be excellent for those who pursue an herbal education with a strong science background, or the reverse.

Both naturopathic physicians and Oriental medicine practitioners are expected to be in demand, so herbalists trained in those fields should have good employment opportunities. Demands for naturopaths and all aspects of Oriental medicine are growing rapidly due to increasing public awareness and acceptance. Interest from the mainstream medical community, recent advances in research, and favorable changes in government policy are strong indicators that these areas will continue to expand.

## FOR MORE INFORMATION

*This association offers information on alternative health care practices.*

American Association of Acupuncture and Oriental Medicine
PO Box 162340
Sacramento, CA 95816-2340
Tel: 866-455-7999
http://www.aaaomonline.org

*For information about naturopathic medicine, accredited schools, and state licensing status, contact*

**American Association of Naturopathic Physicians**
4435 Wisconsin Avenue, NW, Suite 403
Washington, DC 20016-1851
Tel: 202-237-8150
Email: member.services@naturopathic.org
http://www.naturopathic.org

*This national education association is dedicated to educating the public about beneficial herbs and plants and to promoting safe use of medicinal plants.*

**American Botanical Council**
6200 Manor Road
Austin, TX 78723-3754
Tel: 512-926-4900
Email: abc@herbalgram.org
http://www.herbalgram.org

*This national educational organization promotes excellence in herbalism and provides peer review for professional herbalists.*

**American Herbalists Guild**
141 Nob Hill Road
Cheshire, CT 06410-1710
Tel: 203-272-6731
Email: ahgoffice@earthlink.net
http://www.americanherbalistsguild.com

*This national trade association represents the herbal and herbal products industry. Visit its Web site for answers to frequently asked questions about herbs.*

**American Herbal Products Association**
8630 Fenton Street, Suite 918
Silver Spring, MD 20910-3806
Tel: 301-588-1171
Email: ahpa@ahpa.org
http://www.ahpa.org

*This research and educational organization provides information on herbs to the public and to professionals.*

**Herb Research Foundation**
4140 15th Street
Boulder, CO 80304-1123
Tel: 303-449-2265
http://www.herbs.org

*This organization is open to anyone interested in herbs and is dedicated to promoting the use of herbs.*

**The Herb Society of America**
9019 Kirtland Chardon Road
Kirtland, OH 44094-5156
Tel: 440-256-0514
Email: herbs@herbsociety.org
http://www.herbsociety.org

*For information on certification, contact*

**National Certification Commission for Acupuncture and**
    **Oriental Medicine**
76 South Laura Street, Suite 1290
Jacksonville, FL 32202-5410
Tel: 904-598-1005
Email: info@nccaom.org
http://www.nccaom.org

# Holistic Dentists

## OVERVIEW

*Holistic dentists* are health care professionals who use an approach to the practice of dentistry that considers the patient as a whole person—including mind, body, and spirit. They consider the potential effects any dental procedure may have on the entire individual.

Holistic dentists represent a small but steadily growing number of dentists in the United States. More dentists are incorporating holistic approaches into their practices without necessarily declaring themselves to be holistic dentists. At this time, the American Dental Association (ADA) does not recognize holistic dentistry as a specialty. Like most other dentists, the majority of holistic dentists work in private practice.

## HISTORY

As long as 5,000 years ago, healing traditions of India, China, and other ancient cultures promoted living a healthy life in harmony with nature—a concept that is central to a holistic approach to dentistry. The earliest texts of ancient civilizations, such as China, India, and Egypt, detail treatments for toothache.

Hippocrates, who is sometimes considered to be the founder of Western medicine, taught his students to assess the living environment of their patients in order to understand their illnesses. Hippocrates is known to have developed natural dentifrice and mouthwash.

For centuries, healers, surgeons, and even barbers practiced dentistry. It was not until the 16th and 17th centuries that dentistry emerged as a specialty with its own literature. In 1728, Pierre

## QUICK FACTS

**School Subjects**
Biology
Business
Chemistry

**Personal Skills**
Mechanical/manipulative
Technical/scientific

**Work Environment**
Primarily indoors
Primarily one location

**Minimum Education Level**
Medical degree

**Salary Range**
$50,000 to $137,630 to
  $200,000+

**Certification or Licensing**
Required

**Outlook**
About as fast as the average

**DOT**
072

**GOE**
14.03.01

**NOC**
3113

**O\*NET-SOC**
29-1021.00

Fauchard, a French dentist, published the textbook *The Surgeon Dentist*. His writings encouraged a broader education for dentists and elevated dental treatment to a more scientific level. As a result of his work, Fauchard is sometimes considered the father of modern dentistry.

Between 1844 and 1846, Horace Wells and William Morton—both dentists—introduced general anesthesia to medicine. Their efforts (and the efforts of others who tried to find ways to make dental procedures less traumatic for the patient) showed an understanding of the effects dental treatment has on the entire person.

In 1910, two Englishmen, Sir William Hunter and Sir Kenneth Goodby, pointed out that infected teeth could cause infection to spread throughout the entire body.

The modern term "holism" was first used in 1926 by Jan Smuts in his book *Holism and Evolution*. Smuts championed the idea that living things are much more than just the sum of their parts. He challenged modern medical science, which denied the complexity of the human experience by reducing the individual to a collection of body parts and diseases.

During the middle of the 20th century, scientific medical advances focused on germs—outside sources of disease. Being healthy became a matter of overcoming disease, and people looked to modern doctors and dentists to fix their ills. For a time, holistic health concepts fell out of favor in the United States.

However, in the last decades of the 20th century, the general public became increasingly aware that modern medicine did not have all the answers. By the 1970s, "holistic" had become a common term. Today, holistic principles are increasingly incorporated into individual lifestyles and into the practice of medicine and dentistry.

## THE JOB

Holistic dentistry is as much a philosophy as it is a particular set of practices. Holistic dentists consider the ramifications of dental care on the whole person, and they consider the patient to be a partner in the healing process.

In many ways, the primary duties of holistic dentists are very similar to those of other dentists. They examine patients' teeth, diagnose problem areas, fill cavities, treat areas with gum disease, repair broken teeth, and extract teeth when necessary. Some perform corrective surgery to treat gum disease. They administer anesthetics for the relief or prevention of pain during dental procedures, and they prescribe medications. They instruct patients on how to care for their teeth—including proper diet, brushing, flossing, and other aspects of preventive maintenance.

The main difference between holistic dentists and more conventional dentists is in their approach to the client–dentist relationship. Holistic dentists consider themselves to be partners with their patients in the process of helping to enhance the health and well-being of the whole individual, including the body, mind, and spirit. They consider the effects that any procedure may have on the entire person, not just on the physical being. They emphasize prevention and their clients' responsibility for taking an active role in their own health care.

Some holistic dentists use alternative therapies. They take special care to use aromatherapy in their offices to create an environment in which clients can feel comfortable and at ease. They may also use aromatherapies known for their germicidal properties. Homeopathic remedies may be given to relieve pain or to dissipate the effects of anesthesia more quickly. Holistic dentists use nutritional counseling to encourage their patients to take a more active role in improving their health and wellness. They may refer individuals who have special needs to homeopaths or nutritionists.

Holistic dentists use an interdisciplinary approach to health care to facilitate the body's innate ability to heal itself. They differ widely in the methods they use to accomplish that goal. While many incorporate other alternative therapies into their practices, others do not.

In keeping with their philosophy of considering the effects of a treatment on the entire person, holistic dentists minimize or avoid the use of some common dental procedures that they consider potentially harmful. Once again, they vary greatly in their determinations of what is harmful. Some avoid X rays, mercury-based fillings, and fluoride treatments.

Holistic dentists range from those who use mostly conventional methods and incorporate a few alternative ideas to those who use mostly unconventional approaches. While the methods they choose may vary greatly, their approaches to patients have more in common.

In order to understand the whole person, holistic dentists generally spend much more time with their patients than conventional dentists. They discuss possible courses of treatment and involve their patients in decisions about which procedures and materials to use, and they encourage questions. An initial appointment may take an hour and a half, and a routine appointment usually takes 45 minutes to an hour.

In addition to their regular duties as health care providers, holistic dentists must complete an enormous amount of paperwork. Whether they work in clinics or in private practice, they keep accurate patient records. More and more insurance companies are covering dental services. Holistic dental practitioners must frequently submit records to insurance companies in order to be paid for their services.

According to the American Dental Association, approximately 80 percent of dentists are in private practice. All dentists are responsible for setting up, advertising, promoting, and running their own businesses. They have to recruit, hire, and train staff. They also oversee the purchase and care of dental equipment and supplies. Holistic dentists in private practice may spend a large percentage of their time on business matters.

To maintain their licenses, dentists must take continuing education courses. Holistic dentists usually take many more hours than required to maintain their licenses because they want to maintain the skills they need for this interdisciplinary approach to health care.

## REQUIREMENTS

### High School

If you are interested in a career in holistic dentistry, take as many science classes as possible, especially chemistry, biology, and physics. Science classes will help you learn the type of thinking process you need for dentistry, and they will help prepare you for dentistry courses. Art classes can also be helpful because dentists need to have good manual dexterity and excellent judgment of space and shape.

Holistic dentists need to communicate well and compassionately with their patients. Psychology, English, speech, and debate can help you sharpen your communication skills. Business, mathematics, and computer courses will help you gain the skills you need to be a successful businessperson.

### Postsecondary Training

Dental schools require at least two years of college-level pre-dental education, with emphasis on science. However, most students entering dental school have at least a bachelor's degree. To prepare for college, take as many science courses as possible—especially chemistry.

Since holistic dentistry is not yet taught as a specialty, you have the opportunity to create your own course plan. As an undergraduate, you will have more freedom to choose your classes, so take advantage of the opportunity. Courses in nutrition, homeopathy, and psychology will give you some of the background you need to develop your own holistic dentistry specialty.

In addition to educational preparation, all dental schools require that you pass the Dental Admissions Test (DAT). In selecting students, the schools consider your DAT score, overall grade point average (GPA), science course GPA, and any recommendations. You will also have a personal interview at the school to which you apply, which will count in the selection process.

Dental school usually takes four years. During the first two years, you will have classroom instruction and laboratory work. Your courses will include anatomy, biochemistry, microbiology, and physiology and beginning classes in clinical sciences. During the last two years, you will treat patients under the supervision of licensed dentists. When you finish, you will have the degree of Doctor of Dental Surgery (DDS) or Doctor of Dental Medicine (DMD), depending on the school you attend.

## Certification or Licensing

Like conventional dentists, holistic dentists in all 50 states and the District of Columbia must be licensed. In most states, in order to take the test, you must graduate from a dental school accredited by the American Dental Association's Commission on Dental Accreditation and pass written and practical examinations. Holistic dentistry is not presently considered a specialty, so only a general license is necessary for holistic dental practitioners.

Holistic dentistry requires even more continual learning than conventional dentistry. All dentists are required to take 36 hours of continuing education every two years. Some holistic dentists may take as many as 125 hours per year to keep up on developments in areas such as homeopathy, aromatherapy, or nutrition in addition to conventional dental education.

## Other Requirements

To be a successful holistic dentist, you need to enjoy people, have a caring attitude, and have a sincere desire to help others improve their lives. Communication with patients is central to holistic dentistry, so excellent listening and communication skills are important.

Idealism, strong convictions, and high ethical standards are essential. Alternative health care approaches have become more respected within the dental community in recent years, but many dentists still do not accept them. It helps to be a bit of a crusader.

Attention to detail and strong powers of observation are crucial to accurate dental assessment. You also need to be an innovative thinker and good mystery solver. When one approach to a situation doesn't work, you need to be able to quickly think of another. Dentists should have a high degree of manual dexterity. They also need good visual memory and excellent judgment of space and shape.

Most dentists work in private practice, so you will need good business sense and a lot of self-discipline.

## EXPLORING

To find out if a career as a holistic dentist is for you, you can explore the field in a variety of ways. Join science clubs to see if a career in a scientific field really interests you.

Visit your local health food stores and explore the nutrition, homeopathic, herbal, and aromatherapy sections. Talk with the staff; you may find some very knowledgeable, helpful people. Many of these stores also offer alternative newspapers and magazines that will help you learn more.

Contact the professional associations listed at the end of this article for information. The Internet has a wealth of information. Some Web sites have chat groups; others have searchable databases.

Go to a holistic dentist for a dental exam. Experience how the dentist works, and think about whether you would like to practice dentistry this way. Talk with the dentist about the field. Perhaps that person would be willing to hire you for a summer or part-time position or become your mentor.

## EMPLOYERS

The main employers of holistic dentists are other dentists who have similar beliefs about dentistry and have large practices or group practices. A number of holistic dentists become salaried employees of group practices and work as associate dentists. Working for other dentists is usually less expensive initially but also less financially rewarding. A few holistic dentists may work in private and public hospitals, in clinics, or in dental research.

Most holistic dentists practice on their own or with a partner. Working with a partner makes practicing easier because the costs of running an office are shared. Other tasks, such as bookkeeping and record keeping can also be shared. However, the American Dental Association reports that eight out of 10 dentists are in private practice.

## STARTING OUT

The dental school you attend will have listings for job openings for dentists. Professional dental journals, daily newspapers, and Internet job sites also have listings.

Networking is always one of the best ways to find employment. Join professional organizations, attend meetings, and get to know people in the field. By networking, you have a better chance of meeting dentists who share some of your philosophies about holistic dentistry.

Working in the practice or clinic of another physician who shares your beliefs about the practice of dentistry is one of the best ways to get started as a holistic dentist. It is hard to learn in isolation. When you interview potential employers, learn about their approaches to dentistry. Be sure the setting will help you apply the skills you have learned without compromising what you believe about good dental practices.

Most recent dental graduates go into private practice right away. Some set up a new practice. Dental schools have resources to help you learn how to set up your own practice. Some recent graduates purchase an established practice from a dentist who is retiring or moving.

## ADVANCEMENT

As with many professions, advancement in the holistic dental profession usually means building a larger practice. A holistic dentist who starts out as a salaried employee in a large practice may eventually become a partner in the practice. Dentists also advance their careers by building their clientele and setting up their own group practices. They sometimes buy the practices of retiring practitioners to add to their own.

Specialization is another way to advance. Holistic dentists might specialize in pediatric dentistry, geriatric dentistry, or another area.

## EARNINGS

Holistic dentists can generally earn about as much as conventional dentists who work in the same settings. Some holistic dentists may earn less because they spend more time with their patients, so they can see fewer in a day. Some make up the difference by charging more per visit.

According to the Bureau of Labor Statistics, the median net income of dentists in general practice was approximately $137,630 per year in 2007. Those just starting their careers may earn closer to $50,000. The American Dental Association reports that specialty practitioners can earn more than $200,000 a year.

Since most holistic dentists are self-employed, they must arrange for their own benefits. Those who work for other dentists or in clinics or research may receive insurance, paid sick days and holidays, and other benefits.

## WORK ENVIRONMENT

Holistic dentists work in particularly clean, quiet, comfortable offices. Making the office healthful, comfortable, and pleasant is of particular importance to many holistic dentists. Some use air filtration systems and aromatherapy. They may also use distilled water instead of tap water. They choose ergonomically appropriate furniture and work stations.

Most solo practitioners and group practices have an office suite. The suite generally has a reception area. In clinics, several professionals may share this area. Most dentists have a secretary or office staff. Some employ dental assistants and dental hygienists to handle routine services.

Holistic dentists who work in large practices or clinics need to work well in a group environment. They may work under supervision or in a team with other professionals.

Most holistic dentists work four to five days a week. Most work around 40 hours a week, although some put in longer hours. Larger practices and clinics may determine the hours of work, but holistic dentists in private practice can set their own hours. Evening and weekend hours may be scheduled to accommodate patients.

## OUTLOOK

According to the *Occupational Outlook Handbook* (OOH), the employment of dentists in general is expected to grow about as fast as the average for all occupations through 2016. Practicing holistic dentists project that employment for holistic dentists will also grow at least about as fast as the average due to its increasing acceptance by the general public. The national movement toward alternative health care therapies is likely to bring an even greater demand for holistic dentists.

Jobs should remain plentiful as long as dental school enrollments remain steady. The largest segment of the population—baby boomers—will likely need complicated dental work as they advance into middle age. People are living longer, and the elderly are more likely than earlier generations to retain their teeth. That means they will continue to need dental care.

## FOR MORE INFORMATION

*For comprehensive general information about the practice of dentistry in the United States, information on state and local dental organizations, and on the American Student Dental Association, contact*

American Dental Association
211 East Chicago Avenue
Chicago, IL 60611-2678
Tel: 312-440-2500
http://www.ada.org

*For articles on holistic health, self-help resources in the United States,
and a searchable database of practitioner members, contact*
American Holistic Health Association
PO Box 17400
Anaheim, CA 92817-7400
Tel: 714-779-6152
Email: mail@ahha.org
http://www.ahha.org

*For an introduction to the field and philosophy of holistic dentistry
and a searchable database of members, visit*
Holistic Dental Association
PO Box 151444
San Diego, CA 92175-1444
Tel: 619-923-3120
http://www.holisticdental.org

## ━━━━━━ INTERVIEW ━━━━━━

*Charles Martinez, DDS, MS, PC, is a holistic dentist in Barrington,
Illinois. He discussed his career and holistic dentistry with the editors
of* Careers in Focus: Complementary and Alternative Health Care.

**Q.  What made you want to specialize in holistic dentistry?**
**A.**  In the early '90s one of my sons was diagnosed with attention deficit disorder (ADD) and was immediately placed on
Ritalin. Prior to administering the Ritalin, a complete blood
workup and EKG were required. The *Physicians' Desk Refer-
ence* revealed possible reactions to Ritalin including heart
problems, and the long-term side effects of prolonged usage
was not known.

When his doctor decided to increase the dosage with no
satisfactory explanation, I decided to attack the literature for
alternative treatments. The literature revealed that one of the
common denominators found in children with ADD was diet
and nutrition excesses or deficiencies.

I discovered my son was reacting to nitrate and nitrite preservatives. After six to eight weeks of eliminating processed meats and hot dogs, the Ritalin was no longer needed.

The literature also revealed the toxicity of the majority of dental materials I was using, especially mercury. After the positive experience with the nitrates, I decided to eliminate as many toxic dental materials as possible, especially mercury fillings.

**Q. How did you train for this job?**

**A.** There are no formal training programs—training is through self-motivation. All knowledge must be gained via study groups located throughout the country.

**Q. What are the most important personal and professional qualities for holistic dentists?**

**A.** The most important quality is not to dogmatically defend previous training protocols. The cliché about keeping an open mind is imperative because all holistic information and treatment is contrary to conventional medicine and dentistry. The professional organizations debunk or discredit holistic dentists, so perseverance and courage are essential personality traits.

**Q. What are some of the pros and cons of your job?**

**A.** The pros include knowing you are consciously not adding any toxic burdens to the body—there are already too many from the environment. The cons include the fact that there are very few holistic dentists, so the support groups are few and spread thinly.

**Q. What is the future employment outlook for holistic dentists?**

**A.** The timing is good because the awareness of alternative treatments is spreading, especially with the younger generation and the environmentalists. It will remain an uphill battle until the professional organizations support or at least recognize alternative treatments.

# Holistic Physicians

## OVERVIEW

*Holistic physicians* are licensed medical doctors who embrace the philosophy of treating the patient as a whole person. Their goal is to help the individual achieve maximum well-being in mind, body, and spirit. Holistic medicine emphasizes a cooperative relationship between physician and patient and focuses on educating patients in taking responsibility for their lives and their health. Holistic physicians use many approaches to diagnosis and treatment, including other alternative approaches, such as acupuncture, meditation, nutritional counseling, and lifestyle changes. They also use drugs and surgery when a less invasive treatment cannot be found. Holistic physicians are part of the rapidly growing field of alternative health care practitioners. Most work in private practice or in alternative health clinics.

## HISTORY

The modern term "holism" was first used by Jan Smuts in the 1926 book *Holism and Evolution*. Smuts championed the idea that living things are much more than just the sum of their parts. He challenged the views of modern medical science, which reduced the individual to a collection of body parts and diseases and denied the complexity of the human experience.

Dr. Evart Loomis is considered by many to be the father of modern holistic medicine. As early as 1940, Dr. Loomis believed that all aspects of an individual had to be considered in order to determine the cause of an illness. In 1958, he and his wife, Vera, founded

Meadowlark, thought to be the first holistic medical retreat center in the United States.

In the late 1950s and early 1960s, the holistic medical movement began to grow as people became increasingly aware that modern medicine did not have all the answers. Many chronic (long-term) conditions did not respond to medical treatment. Some side effects and cures even proved to be worse than the diseases. By the 1970s, *holistic* had become a common term. Currently, the use of holistic principles is increasingly incorporated into individual lifestyles and into the practice of medicine.

## THE JOB

In many ways, the primary duties of holistic physicians are much like those of allopathic physicians (conventional doctors). They care for the sick and injured and counsel patients on preventive health care. They take medical histories, examine patients, and diagnose illnesses. Holistic physicians also prescribe and perform diagnostic tests and prescribe medications. They may refer patients to specialists and other health care providers as needed. They use conventional drugs and surgery when less invasive approaches are not appropriate or effective.

An important difference between the practices of allopathic physicians and holistic physicians is the approach to the patient-doctor relationship. Holistic doctors work in partnership with their patients. To establish a partnership relationship, holistic practitioners usually spend more time with their clients than allopathic doctors do. The initial visit for an allopathic practitioner is usually 20 to 30 minutes; holistic doctors usually spend 45 minutes to an hour or more on an initial visit. For conventional physicians, most follow-up visits average seven to 10 minutes, while holistic practitioners take 30 to 45 minutes for the same visits.

During the initial history and physical, holistic physicians ask questions about all aspects of a person's life—not just the immediate symptoms of illness. If holistic practitioners are trained in homeopathy, the interview will be particularly detailed. They want to know about what their patients eat, how they sleep, what their life is like, what their stresses are, what makes them happy or sad, what their goals and beliefs are, and much more. They also ask about health history and overall health. Holistic physicians don't just want to know today's symptoms. They try to find the underlying causes of those symptoms. They listen very carefully, and they do not make personal judgments about their patients' lives. They strive to have an attitude of unconditional positive regard for and acceptance of their patients.

Holistic physicians believe that maintaining health is the best approach to eliminating illness. They discuss their patients' lifestyles and suggest ways to improve their health and life. Nutrition and exercise are often important components of a wellness program.

Holistic doctors use healing modalities that consider the whole person and support the body's natural healing capabilities. They use a variety of approaches to diagnosis and treatment. For chronic (long-term) problems, they frequently recommend natural methods of treatment that have been shown to be more effective than conventional approaches. They are usually trained in several alternative health modalities themselves, but they may refer patients to a specialist if necessary.

Like other physicians, holistic practitioners resort to using conventional drugs, laboratory tests, or surgery when necessary. They discuss the drugs, tests, or other procedures with their patients in advance. They answer questions and help patients understand their options. Holistic physicians give patients choices and involve them in decisions about their healing program.

In addition to their regular duties as health care providers, holistic physicians must complete a large amount of paperwork. Whether they work in clinics or in private practice, they keep accurate patient records. More and more insurance companies are covering alternative services that are performed by licensed physicians. Holistic practitioners must frequently submit records to insurance companies in order to be paid for their services.

Those who work in private practice must also supervise the operations of their practices. This can involve interviewing, hiring, and training. Physicians in private practice may spend a large percentage of their time on business matters.

## REQUIREMENTS

### High School

To become a holistic physician, you will have to study for 11 to 18 years after high school. Preparing for this profession is extremely demanding. Because you'll be entering a premed program in college, you'll want to take as many science classes as you can. Biology, chemistry, and physics will prepare you for college medical courses.

Holistic physicians need excellent communication abilities in order to build successful partnership relationships with their patients. Psychology, English, speech, and debate can help sharpen your communication skills. Business, mathematics, and computer courses can help you gain the skills you need to be a successful businessperson.

## Postsecondary Training

To become a holistic physician, you must first become a conventional physician. In order to do this, you must complete a bachelor's degree and medical school.

At the present time, training for competency in holistic or alternative medicine is not a part of regular medical training. At the insistence of many students, nearly a third of all conventional medical schools now include courses in alternative therapies, but they are still relatively few in number. As interest in alternative approaches grows, the number of courses available in medical schools will undoubtedly increase. Most holistic physicians train themselves in alternative modalities through special postgraduate work and continuing education. A few graduate schools now offer specialized programs in alternative health care approaches, and a very few residencies are available.

## Certification or Licensing

All 50 states, the District of Columbia, and the U.S. territories license physicians. To obtain a license, you must graduate from an accredited medical school. You must also pass a licensing exam and complete one to seven years of graduate medical education.

At this time, there is no special certification or licensing available for holistic physicians. A practitioner's decision to use the term "holistic physician" or "alternative physician" is strictly voluntary. The American Holistic Medical Association established the American Board of Integrative Holistic Medicine (ABIHM) in 1996. The ABIHM has developed a core curriculum on which it bases its board certification examination for holistic physicians. A certificate indicates that an individual has met the voluntary education and testing requirements of the organization. See the association's Web site (http://www.holisticboard.org) for more information.

## Other Requirements

To be a holistic physician, the whole-person approach to healing must be an integral part of your belief system and your life. You must have a fundamental respect for the dignity of humankind and a strong desire to help others.

Excellent listening, communication, and observational skills are essential. You also need the ability to make quick and good critical judgments and decisions in emergencies.

Practicing holistic medicine requires an open mind and a commitment to lifelong learning. Holistic physicians must be highly self-motivated and have the stamina to survive long hours and pressures of education and practice. You need to have the courage of your convictions and enjoy trail blazing. Even though alternative health care approaches have become more respected within the medical community in recent years, many physicians still do not accept them. Idealism and high ethical standards are essential. Most holistic physicians also need excellent business skills to run their own practices.

## EXPLORING

Since the study of medicine involves such a long, expensive educational process, it is a good idea to explore the field carefully in advance to decide whether a career as a holistic physician is for you. Join science clubs and design projects relating to medicine and health care.

Visit your local health food stores and explore the nutrition and homeopathic sections. Talk with the staff. You may find some very knowledgeable, helpful people. Pick up any alternative newspapers and magazines they have. Volunteer at a hospital or nursing home to see how you feel about working with people who are sick or injured.

Contact the professional associations listed at the end of this article for information. Some offer student membership. Some associations offer Web sites with chat groups; others have searchable databases. You can ask questions and receive answers from some very prominent people in the field of alternative health care.

Association Web sites also may have searchable databases of holistic physicians. Find one in your area and make an appointment for a physical exam. Experience how the practitioner works and consider whether you would like to practice medicine this way. Ask the physician about the field. Perhaps that person would be willing to hire you for a summer or part-time position or become your mentor.

## EMPLOYERS

The major employers of holistic physicians are physicians who have large practices, group practices, or alternative health clinics. An increasing number of physicians become partners or salaried employees of group practices. Working with a medical group spreads out the cost of medical equipment and other business expenses. In response to public interest and use of alternative approaches, a number of hospitals are opening alternative health care centers.

Some holistic physicians practice privately or with a partner. More holistic physicians are currently practicing on the East Coast and the West Coast in areas where alternative health care is already more accepted. However, the demand for holistic physicians is growing in all areas of the country.

## STARTING OUT

The medical school you attend will have listings for job openings for physicians. If you have established a particular rapport with a staff member, that person might be able to help you. Professional journals, daily newspapers, and the Internet also have listings.

Networking is one of the best ways to find employment. Join professional organizations, attend meetings, and get to know people in the field. Networking with others in your field gives you a better chance of getting to know physicians who share some of your philosophies about holistic health.

Working in the practice or clinic of another physician who shares your beliefs about the practice of medicine is one of the best ways to get started as a holistic physician. It is hard to learn in isolation. When you interview potential employers, learn about their approaches to medicine. Be sure the setting will help you apply the skills you have learned without compromising what you believe about good health care.

A few holistic physicians go into private practice right away. Some set up a new practice, while others purchase an established practice from a physician who is retiring or moving.

## ADVANCEMENT

Holistic physicians can advance in a variety of ways. One who starts out as a salaried employee in a large practice or clinic may eventually become a partner. Holistic practitioners also advance by building their clientele and setting up their own practices or group practices. They sometimes buy the practices of retiring practitioners to add to their own.

Another avenue for advancement is specialization. Holistic practitioners may specialize in traditional medical specialties, such as pediatrics or obstetrics and gynecology, or they may choose to specialize in an area of alternative medicine, such as acupuncture or homeopathy.

For holistic physicians, continuing education is an important part of advancement. Holistic health care requires even more continual learning than conventional medicine. You will want to keep up on developments in the alternative modalities that interest you most, such as homeopathy, herbal therapy, Oriental medicine, or nutrition. And of course, you will have to keep current on changes in conventional medicine.

Teaching, writing, and public speaking are also directions for professional improvement. A few holistic physicians become executives with state or national organizations, such as the American Holistic Health Association.

# EARNINGS

Holistic physicians generally earn about as much as allopathic physicians who work in the same settings. According to the Association of American Medical Colleges, the average first year resident received a stipend of about $44,747 a year in 2006, depending on the type of residency, the size of the hospital, and the geographic area. Fifth-year residents earned about $52,372 a year. According to Physicians Search, a physician recruitment agency, average starting salaries for family practitioners ranged from $90,000 to $150,000 in 2006. Family practitioners who had been in practice for at least three years earned salaries that ranged from $111,894 to $197,025. Internists who had been in practice for three years earned average salaries of $160,318 in 2006. Physicians who worked in specialties had the highest earnings. For example, obstetricians and gynecologists who had been in practice for at least three years had average annual salaries of approximately $248,294 in 2006.

Of course, earnings vary according to experience, skill, hours worked, geographic region, and many other factors. Some holistic practitioners may earn less because they spend more time with their patients, so they can see fewer in a day. Some make up the difference by charging more per visit.

Benefits vary according to the position of the physician. Those who work for large practices, clinics, or hospitals may receive benefit packages that include sick pay, vacation time, insurance, and other benefits. Those who are partners in a practice or are self-employed must provide their own benefits.

# WORK ENVIRONMENT

Holistic physicians work in particularly clean, quiet, comfortable surroundings. In keeping with their emphasis on whole-person relationships, many believe making their offices or clinics comfortable and pleasant is of particular importance. They may use air filtration systems and aromatherapy and choose ergonomically appropriate furniture and work stations.

Most group practices and solo practitioners have an office suite. The suite generally has a reception area. In clinics, several professionals may share this area. Most holistic physicians have a secretary or office staff. The suite also contains examining rooms and treatment rooms. In a clinic where several professionals work, there are usually separate offices for the individual professionals.

Holistic physicians who work in large practices or clinics need to work well in a group environment. They may work under supervision or in a team with other professionals. Those who work alone need a lot of self-discipline and must be highly motivated.

Most holistic physicians work four to five days a week. Some work 40 hours a week, although others put in longer hours. Larger practices and clinics may determine the hours of work, but holistic physicians in private practice can set their own. Evening and weekend hours may be scheduled to accommodate patients' needs. Physicians frequently travel between office and hospital to care for their patients.

## OUTLOOK

The *Occupational Outlook Handbook* (OOH) predicts that employment for physicians will grow faster than the average for all occupations through 2016. Demand for holistic physicians is expected to keep pace with or exceed the demand for conventional physicians due to the recent rapid growth in interest in alternative health care approaches.

Rising health care costs have caused the government to reexamine the health care system. As efforts to control health care costs increase, the general public, the government, and the insurance industry will turn more and more to physicians who provide cost-effective, quality health care services.

Employment opportunities are expected to be best for primary care physicians, including general and family practitioners, general internists, and general pediatricians. Preventive care specialists and geriatric specialists will be in demand; these are areas in which holistic physicians excel.

The OOH predicts that in the future, physicians may be more likely to work fewer hours, retire earlier, earn less, or practice in rural and lower income areas. In addition, with the rising costs of health care, physicians will be more likely to take salaried jobs in group medical practices, clinics, and integrated health care systems instead of opening their own practices.

## FOR MORE INFORMATION

*For information on integrative medicine, contact*
**American Association of Integrative Medicine**
2750 East Sunshine
Springfield, MO 65804-2047
Tel: 417-881-9995
http://www.aaimedicine.com

*For information about naturopathic medicine, contact*
  **American Association of Naturopathic Physicians**
  4435 Wisconsin Avenue, NW, Suite 403
  Washington, DC 20016-1851
  Tel: 202-237-8150
  Email: member.services@naturopathic.org
  http://www.naturopathic.org

*For information on board certification for holistic medicine, contact*
  **American Board of Holistic Medicine**
  614 Daniel Drive, NE
  East Wenachee, WA 98802-4036
  Email: holos@charter.net
  http://www.holisticboard.org

*For information on complementary, alternative, and integrative
medicine, contact*
  **American College for Advancement in Medicine**
  24411 Ridge Route, Suite 115
  Laguna Hills, CA 92653-1691
  Tel: 800-532-3688
  http://www.acamnet.org

*For articles on holistic health, self-help resources in the United States,
and a searchable database of practitioner members, contact*
  **American Holistic Health Association**
  PO Box 17400
  Anaheim, CA 92817-7400
  Tel: 714-779-6152
  Email: mail@ahha.org
  http://ahha.org

*For principals of holistic medical practice, a searchable database
of members, and to learn more about the* AHMA *Newsletter,
contact*
  **American Holistic Medical Association (AHMA)**
  23366 Commerce Park, Suite 101B
  Beechwood, OH 44122-5850
  Tel: 216-292-6644
  Email: info@holisticmedicine.org
  http://www.holisticmedicine.org

## INTERVIEW

*Jill Carnahan, M.D., ABFM, ABHM, is an integrative holistic physician in Peoria, Illinois. She discussed her career with the editors of* Careers in Focus: Complementary and Alternative Health Care.

**Q. Can you please tell us about yourself and your practice?**

**A.** I am traditionally trained in family medicine, but have always had a passion for health and healing. In addition to being board-certified in family medicine, I am also board-certified in holistic medicine. I have actively pursued additional training in diet, lifestyle and nutrition, herbal medicine, and other complementary and alternative therapies during medical school and residency. I currently practice both traditional medicine and integrative holistic medicine, although I will be soon going to an entirely holistic practice.

I seek to understand the physiology and cause of disease and correct the root problems though lifestyle modification, diet, supplementation, and teaching patients to make good healthy choices.

I am called to medicine and passionate about connecting and partnering with patients to reach their optimal health goals. For the patient, there is a big difference between just surviving and thriving, and my goal is to take each patient to a new level of health and vibrancy!

**Q. What is one thing that young people may not know about a career in holistic medicine?**

**A.** I still think a traditional medical (osteopathic or allopathic) training program is the best foundation to understand and transform modern medicine into what it could be. However, if you choose this route, you will need to supplement your education with reading and study of other disciplines in holistic healing that may not be taught in traditional medical schools.

You will not be able to master every area of holistic medicine, so pick one thing or several you are passionate about and focus on doing them with excellence. You can always refer someone to another practitioner who does something better that you are not an expert in. For example, I focus on diet, lifestyle, and nutritional counseling and refer out for acupuncture treatments or manipulative therapies (osteopathic or chiropractic adjustments).

**Q. What are the most important personal and professional qualities for holistic physicians?**

**A.** • Passion, passion, passion!—you have to be excited about and dedicated to what you do.

   • Empathy, compassion, dedication—you must be able to connect with patients and be committed to lifelong learning.

   • Love—the greatest healing on earth comes from unconditional love.

**Q. What are some of the pros and cons of your job?**

**A.** Pros: touching patients' lives and having the honor to assist them on a healing pathway to wellness.

   Cons: poor insurance reimbursement, bias from some in the traditional medical community.

**Q. What advice would you give to young people who are interested in the field?**

**A.** Go for it; the future is yours. Find an area of holistic medicine that you are excited and passionate about and go make a difference in the world. You have many options, including (but not limited to): holistic/integrative medicine (allopathic or osteopathic), chiropractic therapy, acupuncture, herbal medicine, homeopathy, traditional Chinese medicine, massage therapy, body work/energy medicine, and nutrition.

**Q. What is the future employment outlook for holistic medicine?**

**A.** Excellent. Our world is changing and patients are demanding more options for healthcare. They are willing to pay out of pocket when insurance will not cover the treatments. I think insurance companies will soon realize the value of treating chronic conditions with holistic treatment options and coverage will start to improve.

# Homeopaths

## QUICK FACTS

**School Subjects**
Biology
Chemistry
English

**Personal Skills**
Helping/teaching
Technical/scientific

**Work Environment**
Primarily indoors
Primarily one location

**Minimum Education Level**
Some postsecondary training

**Salary Range**
$30,000 to $90,000 to
$175,000

**Certification or Licensing**
Voluntary (certification)
Required by certain states
(licensing)

**Outlook**
Faster than the average

**DOT**
N/A

**GOE**
N/A

**NOC**
3232

**O*NET-SOC**
N/A

## OVERVIEW

Samuel Hahnemann, the founder of homeopathy, said, "The highest ideal of cure is the speedy, gentle, and enduring restoration of health by the most trustworthy and least harmful way." *Homeopaths* are health care professionals who practice a complete system of natural medicine called homeopathy. Homeopathic care generally costs less than conventional medical care, and homeopathic medicine is safe, effective, and natural. Homeopathy is used to maintain good health and to treat acute as well as chronic ailments. It has proven to be effective in many instances where conventional medicines have been unsuccessful. Some of its remedies are simple enough to be used by people who are not medically trained.

Homeopathy is part of the rapidly growing field of alternative/complementary health care. Unlike conventional medicine, it does not treat just the symptoms of a disease. Instead, it seeks the underlying cause of the illness. It seeks to stimulate the patient's natural defenses and the immune system so the body can heal itself. Homeopaths believe that being healthy means being balanced mentally, emotionally, and physically. In this sense, homeopathy is truly a holistic medical model.

## HISTORY

Samuel Hahnemann, a renowned German physician, founded homeopathy in 1796. Medical practices in the 1700s and 1800s often caused more harm than good. Physicians routinely used bloodletting, purging, and large doses of toxic medicines as part of their treatments. Dr. Hahnemann wanted to find a more humane approach. Through years of careful observation, experimentation, and documentation, he developed the system of medicine that he named homeopathy. Homeopathy grew because it was systematic, effective, and comparatively inexpensive. Precisely because of its benefits, the new system threatened the medical establishment. Dr. Hahnemann was persecuted and even arrested. However, he was determined and courageous, and he continued his work throughout his life. His system of medicine spread throughout the world.

Several doctors who had studied homeopathy in Europe emigrated to the United States around 1825. They introduced homeopathy to other physicians, and its popularity grew rapidly. By the mid-1800s, several medical colleges in the United States taught homeopathy. In 1844, homeopaths established the first national medical society in America, the American Institute of Homeopathy. The practice of homeopathy continued to thrive until the early 1900s. At the turn of the century, the United States had 22 homeopathic medical colleges, and one-fifth of the country's medical doctors used homeopathy.

However, like Hahnemann in Europe, the homeopaths in the United States seemed to pose a threat to the conventional medical and pharmaceutical establishments. For a variety of reasons—attacks by the medical establishment, growth in popularity of a more "mechanical" model of medicine, and discord among homeopaths themselves—the practice of homeopathy in the United States declined. By the late 1940s, there were no homeopathy courses taught in this country.

Homeopaths in other countries also experienced opposition. However, homeopathy flourished wherever people were allowed to practice it with relative freedom. Today, over 500 million people worldwide receive homeopathic treatment. Homeopathy is popular in England, France, Germany, the Netherlands, India, Pakistan, Sri Lanka, Brazil, and many other countries. Because homeopathic treatments and drugs are natural and relatively inexpensive, even countries with limited resources can take advantage of them. In this country, there has been a tremendous increase in interest in homeopathy since the 1970s. Statistics show that Americans are turning to this form of treatment in dramatic numbers. As alternative health care is growing, so is the field of homeopathy.

## THE JOB

Homeopaths help people improve their lives and get well. They look at illness differently than conventional doctors do. They view the symptoms of an illness as the body's attempts to heal itself. For example, they see a cough as the body's efforts to rid itself of something that is foreign to the system. Instead of trying to suppress the symptoms, homeopaths search for the underlying cause of the problem. They try to discover the more fundamental reason for the illness. Why was the body susceptible to a cough in the first place?

To homeopaths, people are healthy when their lives are balanced mentally, emotionally, and physically. If any aspect of the patient's life is out of balance, it could lead to illness. A symptom, such as a cough, is just the top layer of a problem, and homeopaths work to peel away all the layers and get to the root of the problem. The goal of homeopathic medicine is not just to cure the ailment, but rather to return the individual to optimum health.

To discover the reasons for an illness, homeopaths begin with a very detailed individual interview. The first interview usually takes at least an hour and may last up to two hours. Homeopathic treatment is based entirely on the individual. Homeopaths believe that every person is unique and that individuals experience the same illness differently. Although two people may complain of a cold, each of them will have unique symptoms and be affected in different ways. The homeopathic practitioner asks questions about every aspect of the individual's life—health symptoms, eating habits, sleeping patterns, reactions to heat and chill, and so on. In order to process all of this information, homeopaths must have good communication and analytical skills and be very attentive to detail. Choosing the right cure depends on understanding every aspect of the individual's situation, not just the illness.

To help guide their research, homeopaths classify people into categories called constitutional types. They determine an individual's constitutional type according to temperament, physical appearance, emotional history, previous ailments, preferences about food, reactions to the weather, and many other traits. Then they search for a constitutional medicine, one that produces symptoms that are most similar to the individual's symptoms.

Homeopathy is based upon the principle that "like cures like," also called the Law of Similars. Dr. Hahnemann observed that a substance that produces the symptoms of an illness when given in a large dose could cure the illness if it were given in a minute dose. The theory is that the small dose stimulates the body's natural healing power to fight off the illness. Hippocrates first recognized this principle in 4 B.C. The Law of Similars is also the theory behind some conventional medicines, such as vaccinations and allergy shots.

After determining the individual's constitutional type, homeopaths seek out the substance that is capable of producing the same symptoms that the individual is experiencing. They can spend much of their day at the office studying their notes and researching. They search through books called repertories or use computers to find the right constitutional medicine.

Homeopaths use very small doses of natural medicines to stimulate the body to heal itself. The Law of the Infinitesimal Dose is another important principle of homeopathic medicine. It states that the more dilute a remedy is, the more powerful it is. Although this seems paradoxical, years of clinical study have shown the small doses to be effective.

Homeopathic medicines are natural, safe, and effective. They are specially prepared from plant, animal, or mineral extracts. The raw material is dissolved in a mixture of alcohol and water. Then it is diluted several times and shaken vigorously. The Food and Drug Administration (FDA) recognizes homeopathic remedies as official drugs. It regulates their production, labeling, and distribution just as it does conventional medicines. Homeopathic remedies are collected in an official compendium, the *Homeopathic Pharmacopoeia of the United States,* which was first published in 1894.

After homeopaths choose a remedy, they instruct the individual in its use. This may happen at the end of the initial interview if the person's symptoms point to an obvious cure. Many times, however, homeopaths must spend a long time searching for the remedy that matches the essence of the person's symptoms. When that is the case, they may not give the individual a remedy at the first session. Finding the exact constitutional medicine requires patience, experience, problem-solving ability, and intuition.

The course of treatment depends on the individual's circumstances, symptoms, and prognosis. After a prescribed period of time, the individual generally returns for a follow-up visit. This visit typically lasts from 15 to 45 minutes. During this time, homeopaths look for signs of improvement and sometimes choose a different remedy if the desired result has not been obtained. Usually only one remedy is given at a time because the goal is to stimulate the body's natural defenses with a minimal amount of medicine. Homeopaths tend to discourage frequent visits unless they are medically necessary. The time between visits is usually from one to six months.

Most homeopaths work in private practice, so they must know how to handle paperwork and run a business. Many are health care professionals who are licensed in other medical fields, such as acupuncturists, chiropractors, physicians, naturopaths, nurse practitioners, and osteopaths. Licensed professionals must understand and manage their own malpractice insurance and their patients' insurance claims. More and more insurance policies cover visits to homeopaths who are also licensed health practitioners. If homeopaths are not licensed, insurance will probably not cover their treatments. The use of the computer is becoming increasingly important to homeopaths. The collected wisdom of centuries of homeopathy is rapidly being made available in computerized databases, and this is an invaluable aid to the arduous research of the homeopath.

Homeopathic practitioners are usually highly dedicated individuals. As Sharon Stevenson, former executive director of the National Center for Homeopathy, put it, "Once they catch the 'fever' they just can't help themselves. They get satisfaction from working with a kind of medicine that really cures and doesn't just cover up illness. And the medicines aren't going to make the patients sick."

Homeopaths believe strongly in the benefits homeopathic care can bring to their patients and to the world. They have the great reward of helping people and seeing them get well. In addition to their practices, many homeopaths are involved in the effort to expand the understanding and acceptance of homeopathy throughout the country. They participate in research and give lectures. Some are involved in politics, fighting for legislation to benefit homeopathy.

## REQUIREMENTS

People from many different backgrounds practice homeopathy. Most homeopaths in the United States are licensed health professionals. Among them, medical doctors are the majority. Many other licensed professionals, such as acupuncturists, chiropractors, naturopaths, medical assistants, nurse practitioners, and nurses, also specialize in homeopathy. In addition, there is a small group of practitioners of homeopathy who do not have licenses in a health care field. The basic skills, interests, and talents required to be a good homeopath are common to all of these professionals, but educational requirements differ according to the individual health field.

### High School

Because of its medical nature, homeopathy requires a solid background in the sciences. Biology and chemistry will help you prepare for a career in homeopathy. The emphasis on careful interviews and detailed documentation make English, journalism, speech, debate, psychology, and sociology classes very valuable. Since most homeopaths are solo practitioners, business and computer courses are also recommended. The basics you learn in high school will help you become familiar with standard medical knowledge and be able to use this information as a foundation for in-depth study of homeopathy.

## Postsecondary Training

If a career in homeopathy interests you, there are many paths from which to choose. Most future homeopaths study health-related fields in college, for example, nutrition, biology, premed, or nursing. Careers such as nutritionist, medical assistant, and nurse require fewer years of training to become licensed. Others, like chiropractor, naturopathic physician, or physician, require considerably more years of study. The specific courses you need will depend upon your choice of health field. Particularly beneficial areas of study include anatomy, physiology, and pathology. In many cases, individuals complete their studies for their licenses and then take courses in homeopathy that are offered at several institutions around the country.

After college, some future homeopaths go to medical school. There is a growing interest in homeopathy among physicians, and homeopaths are working toward integrating homeopathy into the curricula of conventional medical schools.

Another path toward a career in homeopathy is to earn a doctorate in naturopathic medicine. Naturopathic medicine is an approach to natural healing that incorporates an array of healing modalities, including homeopathy. There are only six accredited naturopathic medical schools in North America. They offer four-year programs with homeopathy as a specialty. These schools require at least two years of chemistry, a year of biology, and some other premedical course work prior to admission.

It is easier to practice homeopathy if you are also licensed to practice conventional or naturopathic medicine. However, there are some programs for those who are not medically trained. Training in homeopathy can demand as much time and effort as medical studies. Programs are available on a part-time basis for those who need flexible class hours. There are also a few respected correspondence courses. If you are interested in studying abroad, England, India, and France have schools for classical homeopathy.

There are no federally funded programs for student aid for homeopathy. Some of the professional societies do offer scholarships or other assistance. If you are seriously considering a career in homeopathy, contact the national homeopathic associations listed at the end of this article for information about programs, requirements, and scholarship funds.

## Certification or Licensing

Certification indicates that a homeopath has met the standards of education and knowledge set by a particular professional association. The Council for Homeopathic Certification offers the certified in classical homeopathy credential to those who pass written and oral examinations. The North American Society of Homeopaths also offers certification. Contact these organizations for more information about certification.

An individual can be a certified homeopath but still not be licensed to practice medicine. Licensing is a requirement established by government. Homeopaths who are licensed health care practitioners in other fields, such as chiropractors, physicians, naturopathic physicians, nurses, and nurse practitioners, must maintain the appropriate licenses for their specific fields.

Both certification and licensing requirements for homeopaths vary according to state. Some states do not consider homeopathy to be the practice of medicine, so they do not regulate its practice. Other states require homeopaths to be licensed in some other form of health care. Arizona, Connecticut, and Nevada offer homeopathic medical licenses. Check with the office of the attorney general in your state to be sure you know its certification and licensing requirements. Although some homeopaths currently practice without a medical license, professionals in the field agree that the trend is toward certification and licensing. If you are interested in a career in homeopathy, it is recommended that you acquire a license in some related field of medicine.

### Other Requirements

To be a successful homeopath, you need to enjoy helping and working with people. On the other hand, you must also be self-motivated and enjoy researching and working alone. You need to be inquisitive, detail oriented, independent, and self-reliant. It helps to enjoy solving mysteries and puzzles.

In addition, you must know your own mind and have the courage of your convictions. Because homeopathy is re-emerging as an important form of alternative health care in this country, homeopaths need to have strong convictions and be able to take criticism. They may have to defend their work or try to educate others who know little about homeopathy. It helps for a homeopath to be a bit of a crusader.

## EXPLORING

There are many ways for you to learn about homeopathy right now. Ask your librarian for homeopathic journals, newsletters (such as *Homeopathy Today,* http://homeopathytoday.org), and books. Visit your local health food stores and explore the homeopathic section. Talk with the staff. You may find some very knowledgeable, helpful people. Pick up any alternative newspapers and magazines they have. Ask if there are homeopathic practitioners or pharmacists in the area.

If there are, visit them and talk to them about their work. There are still relatively few homeopaths in this country, but they are generally enthusiastic supporters of others who are interested in the career. Surf the Internet. There is a wealth of information online, and there are alternative medicine/holistic health forums where you can discuss homeopathic medicine with people in the field. If possible, make an appointment with a homeopath so you can experience this approach to health care for yourself.

The National Center for Homeopathy has information on training sessions and seminars located throughout the country where beginners can study. Students can study a variety of topics and live and learn with others interested in the field, from beginners to experts. Sharon Stevenson says the programs "are a wonderful, intensive experience where you get to rub elbows with homeopaths from all over the country. You live in a dorm, study, eat, and relax together. Bonds are formed that last a lifetime."

## EMPLOYERS

Most homeopaths practice on their own or with a partner. Working with a partner makes practicing easier because the costs of running an office are shared. Other tasks, such as bookkeeping and record keeping, can also be shared. Alternative health clinics and some other health care professionals may hire homeopaths. Hospitals and other health care agencies generally do not hire homeopaths, but they may as the alternative health care movement grows.

It is easier to practice homeopathy in some areas of the United States, such as on the West Coast and in larger cities, but there are practicing homeopaths throughout the country.

## STARTING OUT

Since homeopaths come from so many different backgrounds, ways to get started vary, too. Licensed professionals generally begin practicing the discipline in which they are licensed. Some build their homeopathic practice along with the other practice. Others just begin a homeopathic practice. Unlicensed homeopaths may work with licensed individuals. In these cases, the licensed professional is generally legally responsible for the work of the unlicensed homeopath. Some unlicensed individuals have been known to offer their services for free at the beginning, just to gain experience.

Homeopathy is a growing field, but it is still a relatively small community of professionals. Once you get to know others in the field, you may be able to find a mentor who will help you learn how to get started. Networking with others in the field can be an extremely valuable way to learn and grow.

## ADVANCEMENT

Advancement comes with building a solid reputation. Homeopaths whose practices grow may eventually need to look for partners in order to take care of more patients. Many homeopaths are active promoters of the discipline. They write articles for journals or magazines or present information on homeopathy in public forums, such as on radio and television.

Others pursue research into homeopathic treatments and present their findings to colleagues at conventions or publish their work in the homeopathic journals. A few may work with the homeopathic pharmaceutical companies.

## EARNINGS

Since many homeopaths are in solo practice, incomes vary widely according to the number of hours worked and the rates charged. Statistics on earnings in the field are not yet available, but professionals tend to agree that homeopathic physicians charge between $100 and $300 for an initial visit of 60 to 90 minutes and $50 to $100 for a follow-up visit of 15 to 45 minutes. Unlicensed homeopaths charge between $50 and $250 for the same initial visit and $30 to $80 for a follow-up. They may take several years to build a practice, and their rates will usually remain on the lower end of the scale. Fees tend to increase the longer the individual has been practicing.

According to Dana Ullman, nationally known expert on homeopathy, licensed professionals earn about the average for their professions or a little less. For example, homeopathic physicians earn $90,000 to $175,000 a year. They have good incomes, but generally not as high as the average medical doctor. (Mean earnings of general practitioners in 2007 were $153,640, according to the U.S. Department of Labor.) Other licensed professionals, such as homeopathic nurses, might earn $60,000 to $100,000. Unlicensed homeopaths usually earn less, perhaps beginning around $30,000. As with all self-employed individuals, income is directly related to number of hours worked and fees charged.

Since most homeopaths are solo practitioners, they must supply their own benefits, such as vacations, insurance, and retirement funds. In addition, licensed professionals must maintain their licenses and pay for their own malpractice insurance.

## WORK ENVIRONMENT

Homeopaths work indoors, usually in their own offices, and sometimes even in their homes. As a result, they have the surroundings of their choice. Since they meet with patients and also spend time in research, they frequently have quiet, pleasant offices. Most work on their own with little, if any, supervision, so it is important to be self-motivated. Many homeopaths also have the ability to determine the number of hours and days they work per week. They may set schedules that make it easy for their patients to make appointments.

## OUTLOOK

The field of homeopathy is growing rapidly along with the national interest in alternative health care. Sharon Stevenson states that there has been a shortage of trained homeopaths; many established homeopathic practitioners have waiting lists ranging from two months to one year.

Homeopathy can be combined with a variety of health care professions. Many practitioners include it among other healing approaches they use. However, many homeopaths believe that it is best to specialize in homeopathy. The amount of experience and the complexity of the knowledge required to become a good practitioner make homeopathy a lifelong education.

The World Health Organization (WHO), the medical branch of the United Nations, cited homeopathy as one of the systems of traditional medicine that should be integrated worldwide with conventional medicine in order to provide adequate global health care in the next century. The field of homeopathy is growing much faster than the average. According to Dana Ullman, "Homeopathy is not mainstream medicine. It is on the cutting edge of medicine and healing. If you are good at homeopathy, you will always have plenty of patients, and you will be in demand anywhere in the world."

## FOR MORE INFORMATION

*This national organization certifies practitioners of classical homeopathy.*

**Council for Homeopathic Certification**
PMB 187
16915 SE 272nd Street, Suite 100
Covington, WA 98042-7347
Tel: 866-242-3399
Email: chcinfo@homeopathicdirectory.com
http://www.homeopathicdirectory.com

*This professional association provides education and training for homeopathic professionals and for interested consumers who want to learn homeopathy for their own use.*
   **National Center for Homeopathy**
   801 North Fairfax Street, Suite 306
   Alexandria, VA 22314-1775
   Tel: 703-548-7790
   Email: info@homeopathic.org
   http://homeopathic.org

*For information on education, certification, and homeopathic research, contact*
   **North American Society of Homeopaths**
   PO Box 450039
   Sunrise, FL 33345-0039
   Tel: 206-720-7000
   Email: NashInfo@homeopathy.org
   http://www.homeopathy.org

*For comprehensive Internet information on alternative health care in general and homeopathy in particular as well as extensive links, visit*
   **HealthWorld Online**
   http://www.healthy.net

   **Homeopathic Educational Services**
   http://www.homeopathic.com

   **Homeopathy Home**
   http://www.homeopathyhome.com

## ━━━━━━━ INTERVIEW ━━━━━━━

*Dr. Kimberly Lane is the owner of Wellness Lane, LLC, a classical homeopathy and health consultation practice in Minnesota. (Visit http://www.wellnesslane.org to learn more about her practice.) Dr. Lane discussed her career with the editors of* Careers in Focus: Complementary and Alternative Health Care.

**Q. How long have you worked as a homeopath?**
**A.** I graduated in 2005 and had been using homeopathy in my previous practice, but I opened up a classical homeopathy practice in October 2007.

**Q. Why did you decide to become a homeopath?**
**A.** I have been intrigued with the way homeopathy works—more gentle and deep healing. I also have found allopathic medicine

cannot deal with everything and in some chronic diseases has nothing more to offer. Some of the allopathic prescriptions bring significant unwanted side effects in trying to get the hoped-for effects. Homeopathic remedies use the energy of the substance from which they are made—they will work to stimulate each person's vital force to heal from within. Homeopathy is quite amazing as one witnesses the remedy working.

**Q. What type of educational path did you pursue to become a homeopath?**

**A.** There are several homeopathy schools in the United States and in the world. They can be full or part time and run from one to four years. I attended the Northwestern Academy of Homeopathy in Minneapolis, Minnesota. It is a four+ year program that meets four eight-hour days a month. It is the only school in the U.S. that has a clinical component for the last two years.

**Q. What are the most important professional qualities for homeopaths?**

**A.** One needs integrity, curiosity, and the ability and desire to see the inter-relatedness or patterns for evaluation and understanding the patient and the remedies. I think the ability to forego judgment and instead seek understanding (from the patient's point of view) of why one does what one does is also very important.

**Q. What do you like most and least about your job?**

**A.** I like most the fun of seeing patients get better, returning to health. The part I least like is being unable to assist a person's return to better health; it may be the person is unable to change some habits or continue coming to follow up appointments or the remedy is not working as fast as they (or I) would like.

**Q. What is the future employment outlook in the field?**

**A.** Very good for me with my background. I am an M.D., board certified in holistic medicine and family practice who has a degree in homeopathy. I also think the field of homeopathy is in resurgence as people seek a different alternative to health care as our country knows it. FYI: The University of Minnesota Medical School used to be the School of Homeopathy, Medicine, and Surgery until 1914. Homeopathy was quite prevalent in the 1800s and even into the mid-1900s. It is very prevalent in the rest of the world—Canada, England, Europe, India, and the "down-under" countries.

# Horticultural Therapists

## QUICK FACTS

**School Subjects**
Agriculture
Biology
Psychology

**Personal Skills**
Helping/teaching
Mechanical/manipulative

**Work Environment**
Indoors and outdoors
Primarily one location

**Minimum Education Level**
Bachelor's degree

**Salary Range**
$21,770 to $36,295 to
$58,030+

**Certification or Licensing**
Voluntary

**Outlook**
About as fast as the average

**DOT**
N/A

**GOE**
N/A

**NOC**
N/A

**O*NET-SOC**
29-1125.00

## OVERVIEW

*Horticultural therapists* combine their love of plants and nature with their desire to help people improve their lives. They use gardening, plant care, and other nature activities as therapy tools for helping their clients. These activities help clients feel better by focusing on a project, improving social skills, and being physically active. In addition to these benefits, clients experience emotional benefits, such as feeling secure, responsible, and needed. Horticultural therapists' clients can include nursing home residents, psychiatric patients, prison inmates, "at risk" youth, and the mentally disabled. Frequently horticultural therapists work as part of a health care team, which may include doctors, physical therapists, nurses, social workers, and others.

## HISTORY

Gardens have been grown for thousands of years, both for their beauty as well as their products. In the Middle Ages, for example, gardening took place mainly within the walls of monasteries; gardens included herbs for medicinal purposes, flowers for the church, and fruits and vegetables for the monks to eat. In the United States, people also gardened for pleasure as well as practicality. With the opening of the Friends Asylum for the Insane in Pennsylvania in 1817, however, gardening and nature activities took on an additional function. The Friends Asylum, a hospital for the mentally ill, was built on a farm and had walkways, gardens, and tree-filled areas. As part of their treatment, patients were expected to participate in the upkeep of the grounds. In 1879, the Friends Asylum built a greenhouse for patient use and today is recognized as the first U.S. hospital to treat patients with what is now known as horticultural therapy.

The use of horticultural therapy did not become popular, however, until after World War II. Garden club groups, wanting to help wounded servicemen at veterans' hospitals, began volunteering and sharing their gardening know-how. By 1955, Michigan State University was the first university to award an undergraduate degree in horticultural therapy. Today horticultural therapists undergo special training, and a number of colleges and universities offer degrees or programs in horticultural therapy.

## THE JOB

During an average workday, horticultural therapists usually spend much of their time working directly with clients. In addition to working with clients, horticultural therapists who hold management positions need to spend time managing staff, arranging schedules, and perhaps overseeing the work of volunteers. One of horticultural therapists' most important responsibilities is to assign the right task to each client so that their skills are enhanced and their confidence is boosted. After all, clients who are already depressed, for example, won't feel much better when the hard-to-grow plants that they were assigned to watch over suddenly die. In order to determine what projects will suit their clients, horticultural therapists begin by assessing each client's mental and physical state. This assessment may involve talking to the clients, reviewing medical records, and consulting with a physician or other health care professional about a treatment plan.

With the results from the assessment, therapists determine what kind of work will benefit the client. Therapists then assign the client a job. Therapists and clients may work in greenhouses, in outdoor garden areas on hospital grounds, in classroom-type settings to which the therapists have brought all the necessary supplies, or at community botanical gardens, to name a few locations. Depending on the work area, a client may be asked to put soil in cups to plant seeds, water a garden, or be part of a group activity in which something will be made from the garden's products, such as tea or dried flower arrangements. In some cases, the gardens' produce and plants are sold to help pay for expenses, such as the purchasing of new seeds and plants. In this way, clients may be involved in business goals and continue to develop their sense of accomplishment.

Establishing a place where clients can feel safe and useful is an important part of horticultural therapists' work. This may mean allowing clients to work at their own pace to complete a task, giving praise for accomplishments (no matter how small), encouraging clients to talk to each other to decrease feelings of loneliness, and ensuring that the atmosphere of the therapy session stays positive. Horticultural therapist Lorraine Hanson explains, "One of the benefits of this treatment is that patients get a chance to socialize with each other while they work. They look forward to that, and it helps them prepare to reenter their communities."

In addition to working with clients, horticultural therapists who are part of a health care team will likely need to spend some of their time attending meetings with other team members to report on a client's progress and discuss a continuing treatment plan. Horticultural therapists must also do some paperwork, keeping their own records about clients, projects that have been completed, and even expenses. A successful horticultural therapist must be creative in order to think of new projects for clients to work on as well as figure out how to tailor projects and tasks to meet the needs of each client.

Because horticultural therapists often work with clients who have profound or complex problems, such as people with Alzheimer's disease, they may face situations in which the client doesn't improve or doesn't feel the therapy has been helpful. This can be frustrating and even discouraging for the therapist, but it is also an aspect of the job that each therapist needs to deal with.

Some horticultural therapists also provide consulting services, usually to architects, designers, and administrators of health care or human services facilities. For example, they may offer their professional advice during the building or redesigning of hospitals, schools, and assisted-living communities. They may help with landscaping, selecting plants that are suitable for the region and offer a variety of colors, shapes, and smells. They may advise on the creation of "barrier free" gardens that are accessible to those with disabilities. And, they may design interior spaces, such as greenhouses and solariums.

## REQUIREMENTS

### High School
You can begin to prepare for this career while you are still in high school. Science classes, including biology, chemistry, and earth science, will give you a basic understanding of growth processes. Be sure to take agriculture classes if your school offers them, particularly classes dealing with plants. To learn about different groups of people and how to relate to them, take sociology and psychology classes. English classes will help you develop your communication skills, which are vital in this profession. Other important classes to take to prepare you for college and work include mathematics, economics, and computer science.

## Postsecondary Training

Horticultural therapy has only fairly recently been recognized as a profession in the United States (as you recall, the first undergraduate degree in the field was given in 1955), and routes to enter this field have not yet become firmly established. To become registered by the American Horticultural Therapy Association (AHTA), however, you will need at least some related educational experience. Those in the field recommend that anyone wanting to work as a horticultural therapist should have, at a minimum, a bachelor's degree. A number of colleges offer degrees in horticultural therapy or horticulture degrees with a concentration in horticultural therapy, including Kansas State University, Rutgers University, and the University of Maine-Orono. The AHTA provides a listing of schools offering these programs on its Web site, http://www.ahta.org. Course work generally includes studies in botany, plant pathology, soil science, psychology, group dynamics, counseling, communications, business management, and economics, to name a few areas. In addition, an internship involving direct work with clients is usually required. Other facilities, such as botanic gardens, may offer certificate programs, but, naturally, these programs are much smaller in scope than horticulture degree programs.

## Certification or Licensing

The AHTA offers voluntary certification in the form of the horticultural therapist registered (HTR) designation. Applicants for the HTR credential must have a four-year college degree (with required course content in horticulture, human services, and horticultural therapy) and complete a 480-hour internship (field work) under the supervision of an AHTA-registered horticultural therapist. Currently no licensing exists for horticultural therapists.

## Other Requirements

Horticultural therapists must have a strong desire to help people, enjoy working with diverse populations, and be able to see each client as an individual. Just as important, of course, horticultural therapists must have an interest in science, a love of nature, and a "green thumb." These therapists need to be creative, perceptive, and able to manage groups. They must be able to interact with a variety of professionals, such as doctors, social workers, administrators, and architects, and work well as part of a team. As therapists, they may develop close emotional relationships with their clients, but they also must stop themselves from becoming emotionally over involved and realize the limits of their responsibilities. This work can often be quite physical, involving lifting and carrying, outdoor work, and work with the hands, so horticultural therapists should be in good physical shape.

## EXPLORING

There are a number of ways you can explore your interest in this field. No matter where you live, become involved in gardening. This may mean gardening in your own backyard, creating a window box garden, or working at a community garden. To increase your gardening knowledge, join gardening groups and read about gardening on Web sites such as those by the National Gardening Association and the Garden Club of America (see the end of this article for contact information). Such sites usually provide tips for gardeners as well as information on gardening events. Volunteer at a local public facility, such as a museum with a garden, a botanic garden, or a nature trail, to meet others interested in and knowledgeable about gardening. Keep up-to-date by reading gardening magazines and talking to professionals, such as greenhouse managers. You can also get a part-time or summer job at a gardening supply store, greenhouse, or even the floral section of a grocery store.

Of course, it is just as important to explore your interest in working with people who need some type of assistance. Therefore, try to find paid part-time or summer work at a nursing home, hospital, assisted-care facility, or even a daycare center. If you are unable to find paid work, get experience by volunteering at one of these places.

## EMPLOYERS

Hospitals, rehabilitation centers, botanical centers, government social service agencies, and prisons are among the institutions that may employ horticultural therapists. In addition, horticultural therapists may work independently as consultants.

## STARTING OUT

An internship completed during your college years provides an excellent way to make contacts with professionals in the field. These contacts may be able to help you find a job once you graduate. Also, by joining the AHTA, you will be able to network with other professionals and find out about job openings. Your school's career center may be able to provide you with information about employers looking to hire horticultural therapists. You can also apply directly to facilities such as hospitals, nursing homes, and botanical centers.

## ADVANCEMENT

Advancement in this profession typically comes with increased education and experience. Horticultural therapists who pursue advanced training may move into management positions and oversee the work of other therapists on staff. Some may advance by adding consulting to their current responsibilities. Others may consider it an advancement to move into consulting full time. Still others may move into teaching at schools offering horticultural therapy programs.

## EARNINGS

The U.S. Department of Labor reports that the median annual earnings of recreational therapists were $36,940 in 2007. Salaries ranged from less than $21,770 to more than $58,030 a year. Rehabilitation counselors had median annual earnings of $29,630, and mental health counselors had median earnings of $36,000. According to the most recent AHTA survey available, beginning horticultural therapists make approximately $25,315. Those with five to 10 years of experience have annual earnings of approximately $31,750, and those with more than 10 years of experience earn approximately $36,295.

Benefits will depend on the employer but generally include standard ones, such as paid vacation and sick days and health insurance. Those who work as independent consultants will need to provide for their own health insurance and other benefits.

## WORK ENVIRONMENT

Horticultural therapists work in many different environments. Big city community gardens, classrooms, greenhouses, and hospital psychiatric wards are just a few of the settings. Work environments, therefore, can include being outdoors in the sun all day; being in a locked facility, such as for psychiatric patients or prisoners; being in warm, stuffy greenhouses; and being in an air-conditioned school. No matter where horticultural therapists work, though, they are in the business of helping people, and they spend most of their day interacting with others, such as clients, doctors, and volunteers. Because the therapists try to create calm, safe environments for their clients, the environments the therapists spend much of their time working in will be calm as well. Horticultural therapists shouldn't mind getting a bit dirty during the course of the day; after all, they may need to demonstrate activities such as planting a row of seeds in wet soil.

## OUTLOOK

The outlook for horticultural therapists is good. The U.S. Department of Labor reports that counselors will have much-faster-than-average employment growth, while recreational therapists will have slower-than-average employment growth. As horticultural therapy gains recognition both from professionals and the public, the demand for it is likely to increase.

One factor that may affect the availability of full-time jobs in hospitals is the cost-cutting measures implemented by managed care and other insurance companies to severely limit patients' hospital stays. However, this may create more opportunities for those working at outpatient centers and other facilities.

## FOR MORE INFORMATION

*For more information on the career, schools with horticultural therapy programs, registration, and publications, contact*
**American Horticultural Therapy Association**
201 East Main Street, Suite 1405
Lexington, KY 40507-2004
Tel: 800-634-1603
Email: info@ahta.org
http://www.ahta.org

*To learn more about gardening, contact the following associations:*
**American Community Gardening Association**
1777 East Broad Street
Columbus, OH 43203-2040
Tel: 877-ASK-ACGA
Email: info@communitygarden.org
http://www.communitygarden.org

**Garden Club of America**
14 East 60th Street, 3rd Floor
New York, NY 10022-7147
Tel: 212-753-8287
Email: info@gcamerica.org
http://www.gcamerica.org

**National Gardening Association**
1100 Dorset Street
South Burlington, VT 05403-8000
Tel: 802-863-5251
http://www.garden.org

# Hypnotherapists

## OVERVIEW

Hypnosis is a sleep-like state brought on by another person's suggestions. People under hypnosis may be suggested to relax, change their way of thinking, or even move under direction. *Hypnotherapists* help people use the powers of their minds to increase motivation, change behavior, and promote healing.

## HISTORY

Hypnosis has been a phenomenon for thousands of years; shamans, healers, and medicine men and women of ancient tribes used trance and other states of consciousness to heal sickness and appease their gods. Some of today's professional hypnotherapists suggest that hypnotherapy began with these ancient healers.

The first recorded instance of hypnosis in modern times occurred in the 1700s, when Austrian physician Franz Mesmer touted the healing potential of the trance state in his patients. Mesmer had a very flamboyant hypnotic style, and he claimed considerable success in helping his patients to heal. This trance state became know as "mesmerism," in honor of this early practitioner.

Mesmerism continued to be used in Europe in the mid-1800s, albeit sparingly and with little encouragement from the established medical community. Records indicate that Scottish surgeon James Esdaile used mesmerism as the sole anesthetic during surgery, and John Elliotson, a British surgeon, had similar success in pain management. English physician James Braid coined the word "hypnosis" in the late 1800s, using the Greek word for sleep, *hypnos*.

In the years that followed, a number of French physicians began to investigate hypnosis more earnestly. Jean Martin Charcot determined

**QUICK FACTS**

**School Subjects**
Biology
Health
Psychology

**Personal Skills**
Communication/ideas
Helping/teaching

**Work Environment**
Primarily indoors
Primarily one location

**Minimum Education Level**
Some postsecondary training

**Salary Range**
$20,000 to $45,000 to
$100,000+

**Certification or Licensing**
Recommended (certification)
Required by certain states
(licensing)

**Outlook**
About as fast as the average

**DOT**
079

**GOE**
N/A

**NOC**
N/A

**O*NET-SOC**
N/A

that hypnosis was an abnormal, unsafe state. However, French physicians August Ambrose Liébeault and Hippolyte Bernheim actually considered hypnosis to be a very normal state of mind that was largely untapped. They did more research into the idea of suggestibility during the hypnotic state. Gradually, hypnosis became more accepted in wider circles.

In the early 1900s, Sigmund Freud also began to investigate hypnosis to explore his patients' psyches, but he eventually rejected it in favor of dream analysis and psychoanalysis. Freud's early rejection of hypnotherapy caused many in the medical establishment to lose interest in the field until the 1950s, when hypnosis regained popularity. The establishment of the National Guild of Hypnotists in 1951 helped bring solidarity and credibility to the profession.

In the 1960s and 1970s, hypnotherapy became a popular alternative therapy in the United States and the United Kingdom. Today, hypnotherapy is gaining more acceptance in the mainstream, although it may never reach the level of acceptance of more traditional therapies.

## THE JOB

"You are getting very sleepy. When I snap my fingers, you will begin yodeling. After you awaken, you will cluck like a chicken every time the phone rings." Is this hypnotism? Perhaps, but the hypnotist acts of magic shows and clubs have little in common with certified hypnotherapy.

Hypnotherapists induce a hypnotic state in others in order to bring about a desired effect, such as increasing motivation or changing a behavior. They may also train people in self-hypnosis techniques. Hypnotherapists don't cast a spell, gain control of a person's mind, or do anything else that's magical or strange. Instead, they use hypnosis to help people tap the power of their own minds to help themselves.

Hypnosis has been proven to work in hundreds of ways, from helping people stop smoking to easing the pain of childbirth. Although hypnosis has been studied for centuries, exactly what makes hypnosis work is still being explored.

A hypnotic state is a sleep-like condition in which the brain waves have slowed and the client is much more relaxed than normal. He or she is not asleep, but aware of and sensitive to the surroundings. But where a fully alert mind might normally break in and stop the acceptance of a suggestion, the brain appears to accept ideas more readily under hypnosis.

Clients are always in control in the hypnotic state—they won't do or say anything that they wouldn't normally do or say. "It's a myth that you can get someone to do something against their morals or ethics," stresses Dr. Dwight F. Damon, president of the National Guild of Hypnotists (NGH).

Founded in 1951, the NGH is one of the oldest and largest organizations for hypnotherapists worldwide, with chapters in cities across the United States and Canada. Damon adds, "I could tell you, 'Go stand on your head in the corner,' and if you wouldn't do it normally if I suggested it, you wouldn't do it under hypnosis."

A typical session with a hypnotherapist takes place in an office or quiet room. The hypnotherapist begins by discussing with the clients what goals and expectations they may have. Does she want to quit biting her nails so she looks good for her wedding? Does he hope to overcome a fear of flying so he can visit his elderly grandfather in Europe? Does the couple want to stop smoking and eat a more healthy diet so they can set a good example for their children? Whatever the reason, hypnotherapists need to know why the client wants to accomplish his or her goal.

Most hypnotherapists also try to find out about the health, background, and lifestyle of their clients. "Then we explain to the patient what hypnosis is—or really, what hypnosis is not, because people have a lot of misconceptions about it," says Damon. "They think it's sleep, or that they're going to reveal some deep dark secret, or that someone's going to get control over their mind. But none of this is true."

Next, the hypnotherapist does conditioning or susceptibility tests, which check to see how open to suggestion the client is and which hypnosis techniques are likely to work best. For example, the hypnotherapist could have a client look steadily at an object while he or she talks in a monotone. Sounds like ocean waves, a ticking clock, or an air conditioner may help a client relax and focus. "I might have you look at a spot on the wall and say to you, 'Your eyelids are getting heavy, drowsy, tired. . . . But do not close your eyes yet; look at the spot on the wall. . . . Your eyelids are getting heavy, drowsy, tired. . . . But do not close your eyes yet; look at the spot on the wall,'" Damon says. Guided by these suggestions, the client becomes more and more relaxed, drifting into a hypnotic state.

Under hypnosis, the client's attention is very concentrated on the hypnotherapist's voice. If a suggestion is made that the client accepts, such as, "You want to quit smoking," his or her mind will be highly responsive to the suggestion and accept it. "How long the process takes depends on what you're doing, but you usually don't need a lot of time," says Damon. One of the phenomena of hypnosis is that subjects often think they've been "under" for a shorter time than they actually have. "People may think they've been hypnotized for a few minutes, when actually it was 20 minutes," he says.

Sometimes it takes a few sessions before hypnosis works, that is, before the hypnotherapist is able to help clients enter a hypnotic state.

Hypnosis is also used in medical or clinical settings, and even in emergency situations. "Many of our people are training EMTs [emergency medical technicians] and paramedics in hypnosis," adds Damon. These workers may use hypnosis to help people under their care slow down the flow of blood, control breathing, and reduce pain and anxiety through positive suggestions.

Hypnosis is also helpful to mental health professionals. In the hypnotic state, a person may be more open to remembering past events that have affected them traumatically. Once these are remembered, a psychologist or other mental health professional can help the patient deal with them through therapy. Hypnotherapy can also help people replace negative thoughts with positive ones or deal with their fears.

Hypnosis has been used in the treatment of depression, schizophrenia, sleep disorders, anorexia, panic attacks, neuroses, attention deficit disorder, asthma, allergies, heart disease, headaches, arthritis, colon and bowel problems, and more. Experimental research is testing its use with cancer. Young children, for example, have been taught to picture good white blood cells eating cancer cells like the Pac-Man video game.

## REQUIREMENTS

### High School

If you're planning to make hypnotherapy your career, take a college-preparatory course of study in high school. Courses in health, biology, anatomy, and chemistry will give you a better understanding of the mind-body connection that is key to hypnotherapy. You may wish to study speech, communications, psychology, and sociology as well to help you learn to deal with clients and approach their treatments in the most effective manner.

You may prefer to use hypnosis as part of another career. If this is the case, you should do course work pertaining to your future field, for example, if you plan to use hypnotherapy in a dental practice. Advanced science and math classes in high school will prepare you for college, medical school, and beyond.

### Postsecondary Training

If you wish to work only as a hypnotherapist (not combining hypnotherapy with the practices of another profession), you do not need a four-year college degree. You will, however, need some postsecondary training. Many schools across the country offer training in hypnosis, but it will be a key factor in your future success to attend a respected and accredited program. Look for a school or program that has been accredited by a professional organization, such as the American Council of Hypnotist Examiners (ACHE) or the NGH, as well as approved by the state's department of education. If you attend a program without these credentials, you will have difficulty getting certification or licensing later on.

Course work tends to vary from school to school. NGH-certified instructors, however, teach a standard curriculum. Dr. Dwight Damon explains that this way, the association knows its students are getting the same basic education no matter where they're located in the world. "The core curricula is a work in progress; we keep adding to it," says Damon. It is built on what he describes as a "basic, classic approach to hypnosis," including study of and practice in hypnosis techniques, such as progressive relaxation, introduction to psychology, introduction to ethics, and practical information about running your own business. You are not taught how to be a psychologist, psychiatrist, or counselor, Damon emphasizes, but you must be able to refer people to these professionals for serious problems.

If you want to use hypnosis with a medical, dental, psychological, social work, religious, or other profession, you will first need to earn your college and, in some cases, advanced degree in the particular field that interests you and then pursue training in hypnosis. Some medical and dental schools now offer courses in clinical hypnosis, although, again, this is still relatively rare. The major professional associations also provide certification in clinical hypnosis.

### Certification or Licensing

A number of associations offer certification, but the two best-known certifying groups are the ACHE and the NGH. The ACHE offers two levels of certification: certified hypnotherapist and certified clinical hypnotherapist. To attain the certified hypnotherapist designation, you must complete at least 200 hours of instruction from an approved school and pass a written and practical skills exam. To attain the certified clinical hypnotherapist designation, you must complete at least 300 hours of instruction from an approved school and pass an examination. The NGH also offers a certification for instructors. Certification is highly recommended because it demonstrates both to your peers and your clients that you have received thorough training and are keeping up with developments in the field.

While most states do not license hypnotherapists, legislation for licensure is being considered in many states. You will need to check with your state's licensing board for specific requirements in your area. In addition, hypnotherapists who run their own businesses will need a business license.

## Other Requirements

In order to succeed as a hypnotherapist, you should be able to inspire trust in others. Because you will be asking clients to let their guard down and become open to a higher level of suggestibility, they will need to feel very comfortable with you. A calm, soothing personality, and a voice to match, will help you ease clients into a hypnotic state. You will also need to be able to interact well with a variety of people and have a true interest in helping them. Because hypnotherapy works differently for each person, you should be creative and patient in your approach to your clients and their needs.

Finally, hypnotherapists need high moral and ethical standards. People who seek out hypnotherapy to help overcome a particular obstacle are often very vulnerable, either professionally or personally. A high-profile government leader, for instance, may look to hypnotherapy to help him overcome an addiction to prescription painkillers. Practitioners of hypnotherapy must be sensitive to their clients' needs and wishes and take privacy issues very seriously.

## EXPLORING

If you are interested in doing hypnotherapy work, you should contact a professional hypnotherapist organization for guidance. You may qualify for a student membership. Also, many associations hold workshops or have conferences in all areas of the country (and world) throughout the year. Find out how you can attend such a session.

Check out books on hypnotherapy and self-hypnotism from your local library. These guides can teach you the theoretical basis of hypnotism as well as help you learn techniques to apply hypnotism to yourself and your own needs.

Volunteer at a local hospital, hospice, or other extended care facility that employs hypnotherapists as part of their treatment programs. You may be allowed to sit in on a hypnotherapy session or talk to patients to see what progress they make with hypnotism.

Make an appointment to see a hypnotherapist yourself to get a feel for the field. Your hypnotherapist may help you learn more about how you respond to hypnotic suggestion and how you can help others through hypnotherapy.

## EMPLOYERS

Because many professionals use hypnosis as part of another career, it's difficult to list all possible places a hypnotherapist may work. The health fields, of course, are the main arenas for hypnotherapists.

A dentist may use hypnosis to help a patient deal with the pain of a root canal, or a psychologist may prescribe hypnotherapy to a client who is having an extended bout of insomnia. Hospitals may have hypnotherapists on call to assist with an emergency room patient, or emergency medical technicians may use hypnosis techniques to help injured people on the scene. A nurse-midwife may use hypnosis to help pregnant women ease the pain of childbirth, or a sports physician may help a football player ease the pain of an injury.

Hypnotherapists work in all fields of medicine: medicine for the body and medicine for the mind. Hypnotherapists work in hospitals, clinics, medical practices, and social and religious organizations. They work as counselors or advisers. A hypnotherapist may work as a teacher of hypnosis or as a consultant.

## STARTING OUT

Most people who practice hypnotherapy as their primary occupation set up and run their own businesses. After becoming certified and getting a business license, they rent office space or work out of their homes and start advertising for business. They may network with doctors, dentists, and psychologists to develop a client base. New hypnotherapists may arrange to speak to community, church, or professional groups to educate the public and attract clients. They may also advertise in local newspapers, distribute brochures, or set up a Web site to announce their services. Some hypnotherapists rent space in a medical office suite and build a clientele with the office's patients.

Few professionals rely on hypnotherapy alone; the vast majority of practitioners use hypnotherapy as part of another health-related profession. Therefore, most certified hypnotherapists begin practicing in their primary field first, and then incorporate hypnotherapy into treatments. They may begin by identifying a patient who may be particularly responsive to hypnosis. After suggesting hypnotherapy as a treatment option, the hypnotherapist and the patient work together to deal with the patient's needs through hypnosis. As practitioners become more accomplished using hypnotherapy as part of their practices, they may branch out into using hypnosis for more of their patients, or they may even move toward hypnotherapy as a primary career.

## ADVANCEMENT

Hypnotherapists with their own businesses can build on their knowledge and skills. Research in the field continues, and hypnotherapists need to make sure they know all the latest techniques. They can learn and become certified in more counseling or healing arts practices. They can also market their services more aggressively to build a larger client base.

Those in medical or other fields also need to keep their skills up to date. They can study hypnosis techniques at the doctoral or postdoctoral level. Practitioners with advanced study and more credentials can usually command higher salaries. Some professional associations now award advanced credentials and recognition to exceptional hypnotherapists. This may include awards for outstanding contributions to the field.

Accomplished hypnotherapists may also move away from client interaction and more toward the administration of hypnotherapy programs. They may focus their time on research in the field, writing books, or publishing papers in professional hypnotherapy or medical research journals. Hypnotherapists may become instructors of hypnosis, or they may use their training and experience to help them pursue an advanced degree in another medical field that may be enriched by hypnotherapy techniques.

## EARNINGS

Salaries for people who do hypnosis for a living vary widely. A hypnotherapist in a large urban area may charge from $50 per hour to $150 per hour, depending on his or her experience and ability.

Many people practice hypnotherapy part time, while others combine it with another job. According to the Hypnotherapy Academy of America, an ACHE-approved school, a certified hypnotherapist can earn $45,000 or more per year. Average salaries for medical professionals like doctors or dentists may be well over $100,000 per year.

According to the National Board for Professional and Ethical Standards, Hypnosis Education and Certification, a qualified hypnotherapist can earn between $75 and $175 an hour. Many practitioners working part time with four or five clients can earn $400 to $600 a week. Full-time professionals can earn $75,000 or more a year.

Hypnotherapists who work for an established hospital, school, or other company generally enjoy a full complement of benefits, including paid vacation time, sick days, and medical and dental care. Self-employed practitioners must take care of their own benefits.

## WORK ENVIRONMENT

People who use hypnotherapy as part of a medical practice generally work in clean, comfortable, soothing surroundings. Because hypnotherapists work to put their patients into a calm, relaxed state for treatment, most offices will be free of extra noise, light, and other distractions. Hypnotherapists often have a monotonous noise-maker—such as a metronome or loud clock—for patients to focus on while they are being hypnotized. The patient may be seated in a comfortable chair or lying down on a sofa.

Practitioners who use hypnotherapy as part of an emergency medical team, such as EMTs, will have a much more frenzied environment. They use hypnotherapy techniques in emergency (and often dangerous) situations, and they need to be prepared for any eventuality.

## OUTLOOK

There has been a growing acceptance of hypnotherapy by the conventional medical establishment and the general public over the past decade. According to the *Occupational Outlook Handbook,* the best opportunities in hypnotherapy are for those who add hypnosis skills to other medical or therapeutic skills, such as dentistry or psychology. People trained only in hypnotherapy generally have a more difficult path. Working for themselves, they need to advertise their services and develop a client base. It can take time to build up a business to the point where it can support you. Competition may also be tough, especially in areas where hypnotism is popular, such as California. Hypnotherapists with limited training often drop out of the field.

In some states, legislation may have an impact on the extent to which hypnotherapy can be practiced and who can practice it.

## FOR MORE INFORMATION

*Visit this professional organization's Web site to read articles about hypnotherapy.*
American Association of Professional Hypnotherapists
16055 SW Walker Road, #406
Beaverton, OR 97006-4942
Tel: 503-533-7106
http://www.aaph.org

*For information on certification and approved programs, contact*
American Council of Hypnotist Examiners
700 South Central Avenue
Glendale, CA 91204-2011
Tel: 818-242-1159
Email: hypnotismla@earthlink.net
http://www.hypnotistexaminers.org

*For certification and degree programs in hypnotherapy, contact*
**American Pacific University**
615 Piikoi Street, Suite 501
Honolulu, HI 96814-3140
Tel: 877-AMPAC-41
Email: info@ampac.edu
http://www.ampac.edu

*The NGH is one of the oldest hypnotherapy organizations in the United States. For information on certification and hypnotherapy, contact*
**National Guild of Hypnotists (NGH)**
PO Box 308
Merrimack, NH 03054-0308
Tel: 603-429-9438
Email: ngh@ngh.net
http://www.ngh.net

# Kinesiologists

## OVERVIEW

*Kinesiologists* (also known as *kinesiotherapists*) are health care workers who plan and conduct exercise programs to help their clients develop or maintain endurance, strength, mobility, and coordination. Many of their clients are people who have disabilities. They also work with people who are recovering from injuries or illnesses and need help to keep their muscle tone during long periods of inactivity.

Kinesiology is based on the belief that each muscle in the body relates to a specific meridian—or energy pathway—in the body. These meridians also relate to organs, allowing the muscles to give us information about organ function and energy. The profession builds on basic principles from Chinese medicine, acupressure, and massage therapy to bring the body into balance. The goal is to release physical and mental pain, and alleviate tension in the mind and body. Relieving stress—be it physical, mental, emotional, chemical, environmental, or behavioral—is a main element of kinesiology. Various techniques are combined with visualization, massage, and movement exercises to help patients heal.

## HISTORY

Kinesiology studies how the principles of mechanics and anatomy affect human movement. The word *kinesio* is derived from the Greek work kinesis, meaning motion. Kinesiology literally means the study of motion, or motion therapy. Kinesiology is based on the idea that physical education is a science.

Scientists throughout the centuries have studied how the body works: how muscles are connected, how bones grow, how blood flows.

Kinesiology builds on all that knowledge. The practice of kinesiology developed during World War II, when physicians in military hospitals saw that appropriate exercise could help wounded patients heal faster and with better results than they had before. This exercise therapy proved particularly useful for injuries to the arms and legs.

By 1946, Veterans Administration hospitals were using prescribed exercise programs in rehabilitation treatment. Before long, other hospitals and clinics recognized the benefits of kinesiology and instituted similar programs. Within a few years the new therapy was an important part of many treatment programs, including programs for chronically disabled patients.

In the 1950s, a number of studies indicated that European children were more physically fit than American children were. To decrease the gap in fitness levels, the United States government instituted physical fitness programs in schools. This practical application of kinesiology to otherwise healthy children boosted the field dramatically.

Today, the study of physical fitness and the movement of the body are illustrated in countless fields. Although kinesiologists have historically worked with injured or disabled patients, kinesiologists and other health care professionals will be in higher demand to help people of all abilities maintain good health and fitness as humans move towards a more computerized, less active lifestyle.

## THE JOB

Kinesiology is a broad field covering the study of how muscles act and coordinate to move the body. Many diverse career opportunities are open to those who have studied kinesiology; for example, jobs in this area include physical education or dance teachers, coaches of sports teams, health and fitness consultants, athletic or personal trainers, and researchers in biomechanics. Kinesiologists are usually identified by their specialty, such as athletic trainer, but for the purposes of this article we will examine the broader, interchangeable titles of kinesiologist and kinesiotherapist. All kinesiologists use muscle testing and physical therapy to evaluate and correct the state of various bodily functions in their patients. Kinesiologists take all body systems into account when treating a patient. Thus, the aim of kinesiology is to treat the whole patient, not to correct a disorder. Kinesiologists allow patients to work through a disability or disorder.

Kinesiologists work with a wide range of people, both individually and in groups. Their patients may be disabled children or adults, geriatric patients, psychiatric patients, the developmentally disabled, or amputees. Some may have had heart attacks, strokes, or spinal injuries. Others may be affected by such conditions as arthritis, impaired circulation, or cerebral palsy. Kinesiologists also work with people who were involved in automobile accidents, have congenital birth defects, or have sustained sports injuries.

These professionals work to help their clients be more self-reliant, enjoy leisure activities, and even adapt to new ways of living, working, and thriving. Although kinesiologists work with their patients physically, giving them constant encouragement and emotional support is also an important part of their work.

Kinesiologists' responsibilities may include teaching patients to use artificial limbs or walk with canes, crutches, or braces. They may help visually impaired people learn how to move around without help or teach patients who cannot walk how to drive cars with hand controls. For mentally ill people, kinesiologists may develop therapeutic activities that help patients release tension or learn how to cooperate with others.

The work is often physically demanding. Kinesiologists work with such equipment as weights, pulleys, bikes, and rowing machines. They demonstrate exercises so their patients can learn to do them and also may teach members of their patients' families to help the patients exercise. They may work with their patients in swimming pools, whirlpools, saunas, or other therapeutic settings. When patients are very weak or have limited mobility, therapists may help them exercise by lifting them or moving their limbs.

Kinesiologists work as members of medical teams. Physicians describe the kind of exercise their patients should have, and then the therapists develop programs to meet the specific needs of the patients. Other members of the medical team may include nurses, psychologists, psychiatrists, social workers, massage therapists, physical therapists, acupuncturists, and vocational counselors.

Kinesiologists write reports on the clients' progress to provide necessary information for other members of the medical team. These reports, which describe the treatments and their results, may also provide useful information for researchers and other members of the health care team.

These therapists do not do the same work as physical therapists, orthotists, or prosthetists. *Physical therapists* test and measure the functions of the musculoskeletal, neurological, pulmonary, and cardiovascular systems and treat the problems that occur in these systems. *Orthotists* are concerned with supporting and bracing weak or ineffective joints and muscles, and *prosthetists* are concerned with replacing missing body parts with artificial devices. Kinesiologists focus instead on the interconnection of all these systems. In certain cases, they may refer a patient to another specialist for additional treatment.

# REQUIREMENTS

## High School

If you are interested in this field, you should prepare for your college studies by taking a strong college-preparatory course load. Classes in anatomy, chemistry, biology, mathematics, and physics will give you the basic science background you will need to study kinesiology in college. Health, psychology, and social science will also be very helpful. Be sure to take physical education classes in order to gain a better appreciation for the nature of movement and muscles. Participating in a sport will also help you understand kinesiology from the patient's perspective.

## Postsecondary Training

In order to practice kinesiology, you will need to earn a bachelor's degree from a four-year program at an accredited school. Curriculum standards have been established by the Committee on Accreditation of Education Programs for Kinesiotherapy, which also reviews programs and makes recommendations for accreditation to the Commission on Accreditation of Allied Health Education Programs (CAAHEP). To find out more about accredited programs, visit the CAAHEP's Web site, http://www.caahep.org. Some kinesiologists major in physical education, exercise science, or health science and have kinesiology as a specialty, but a growing number of institutions in the United States are starting to offer undergraduate degrees in kinesiology. Approved programs include classes in education, clinical practice, biological sciences, and behavioral sciences. Specific courses may have titles such as Movement Coordination, Control, and Skill; Performance and Physical Activity; Biomechanics; Developmental Games; Personal and Community Health; and Motor Learning. Master's degrees in kinesiology and related programs are currently offered at more than 100 institutions; doctorates in the field are offered at approximately 55 universities.

Clinical internships are also required. These internships generally consist of at least 1,000 hours of training at an approved health facility under the supervision of certified kinesiologists. You may also seek out an assistantship with a practicing kinesiologist.

## Certification or Licensing

Although certification is not mandatory for every job, it is highly recommended as a way of showing professional achievement. Certification is offered in the form of registration by the Council on Professional Standards for Kinesiotherapy (COPS-KT) through the American Kinesiotherapy Association. To receive registration from COPS-KT, applicants must have at least a bachelor's degree in kinesiotherapy, exercise science, or a related field, complete core course requirements as specified by COPS-KT, have at least 1,000 hours of clinical experience under the supervision of a registered kinesiotherapist, and pass an examination. Those who meet these requirements receive the designation registered kinesiotherapist. To keep this designation, kinesiotherapists must complete continuing education credits each year.

If a kinesiotherapist has earned an undergraduate degree in physical education, he or she also may become a state-certified physical education teacher after meeting the certification requirements for his or her state.

Other certifications are available based on the kinesiologist's specialty. For example, the American College of Sports Medicine offers certifications for health and fitness instructors, specialists, and physiologists. Athletic trainers are certified by the Board of Certification for the National Athletic Trainers' Association. Such certifications typically require having completed an accredited education program as well as passing an exam.

### Other Requirements
To work as a kinesiologist, you must be mature and objective and able to work well with patients and other staff members. You must have

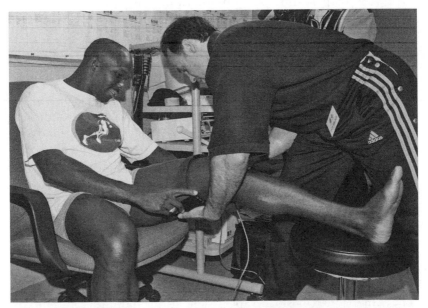

A kinesiologist *(right)* hooks up an athlete to a Bioflex low-level laser that treats damaged muscles. *(Aaron Harris, AP Photo)*

excellent communication skills to explain the exercises so patients can understand your instructions and perform the exercises properly.

You will also need stamina to demonstrate the exercises and help patients with them. You should be patient since many exercise programs are repetitive and are carried out over long periods. A good sense of humor also helps to keep up patient morale. As a kinesiologist, you also must know how to plan and carry out a program, and stay current on new developments in the field. Certification usually requires continuing education courses.

## EXPLORING

If you are a high school student interested in this type of work, you can get experience in several ways. Basic physical education courses as well as team sports, like volleyball or track, will help you gain an appreciation for the possibilities and limitations of the body. Plan and carry out exercise programs, or instruct others in proper exercise techniques. Many exercise classes are often offered in scouting and by organizations such as the YMCA and YWCA.

Opportunities for volunteer, part-time, or summer work may be available at facilities that have kinesiology or kinesiotherapy programs, such as hospitals, clinics, nursing homes, and summer camps for disabled children. Health and exercise clubs also may have summer work or part-time jobs. In addition, you may be able to visit kinesiology departments at health care centers to talk with staff members and see how they work.

## EMPLOYERS

Kinesiologists work in many types of organizations. They work for the government in the Department of Veterans Affairs, public and private hospitals, sports medicine facilities, and rehabilitation facilities. Learning disability centers, grammar schools and high schools, colleges and universities, and health clubs also employ kinesiologists. Other kinesiologists work in private practice or as exercise consultants. Kinesiologists can also find employment with sports teams, or they may write for or edit sports, rehabilitative, and other medical journals. Many kinesiologists also teach in the field or do research.

## STARTING OUT

The American Kinesiotherapy Association maintains an employment service for certified kinesiologists and kinesiotherapists. Plus, most colleges and universities offer job placement assistance for their alumni. Therapists also may apply at health facilities that have kinesiotherapy programs, including private and state hospitals, Department of Veterans Affairs hospitals, clinics, health clubs, chiropractic clinics, and rehabilitation centers. Many kinesiologists find employment by networking with other professionals in the field. Most professional organizations and associations maintain listings of positions open in various locations.

Beginning kinesiologists may gain paid employment with a facility if they start out doing volunteer work. Some organizations prefer to hire therapists with some work experience, and volunteer work gives the new kinesiotherapist a great opportunity to learn more about the field and a particular organization.

## ADVANCEMENT

Kinesiologists usually start as staff therapists at hospitals, clinics, or other health care facilities. After several years, they may become supervisors or department heads. Some move on to do consultant work for health care facilities. Some kinesiologists use their practical experience to do more research in the field, or they may teach at a kinesiology program. They may write for field newsletters or journals, reporting on their progress in rehabilitating a particular patient or in treating a specific disability. With advanced training, experienced kinesiologists may go on to more senior positions at health care centers, clinics, colleges, and related facilities.

## EARNINGS

According to the American Kinesiotherapy Association, the average starting salary for kinesiologists is between $34,000 and $37,000. This, of course, depends on the experience of the kinesiologist and the location of the job. Since kinesiology is a relatively new field, few reliable salary sources exist, but salaries are probably comparable to related health professions.

According to 2007 information from the U.S. Department of Labor, the median salary for occupational therapy assistants was $45,050, while the median for occupational therapists was $63,790. Kinesiologist salaries are likely to be somewhere in those ranges. Those working in hospitals tend to earn less than those in private practice.

Depending on their employers, most kinesiologists enjoy a full complement of benefits, including vacation and sick time as well as holidays and medical and dental insurance. Kinesiologists who work in a health care facility usually get free use of the exercise equipment.

## WORK ENVIRONMENT

Kinesiologists who are employed in hospitals and clinics usually work a typical 40-hour workweek, with hours somewhere between 8:00 A.M. and 6:00 P.M., Monday through Friday. Some may work evenings and weekends instead in order to accommodate their clients' schedules. Because of the long-range, rehabilitative nature of the work, most kinesiologists work a set schedule and generally don't have to be available for emergency situations.

The number of patients the therapist works with usually depends on the size and function of the facility. When leading a rehabilitation group, the kinesiologist may work with three to five patients at a time, helping them work on their own and as part of a team. Therapists may see their patients in hospitals and other health centers, or they may visit patients in their homes, or arrange for rehabilitative outings. Their clients may be confined to beds, chairs, or wheelchairs. Exercises are often performed in pools or on ramps, stairways, or exercise tables.

## OUTLOOK

Employment for kinesiologists is expected to grow about as fast as the average for all occupations for the next few years. The demand for their services may grow somewhat because of the increasing emphasis on services for disabled people, patients with specific disorders, and the growing number of older adults. Some medical workers also handle patients with chronic pain by using the physical rehabilitation and retraining at the base of kinesiology. Plus, kinesiology is certain to grow as a profession as more is learned about the field.

As health costs rise, the importance of outpatient care is expected to increase as well. Many insurance companies prefer to pay for home health care or outpatient care instead of lengthy, expensive—and often unnecessary—hospital stays. Part-time workers in the field will also see increased opportunities. In addition, openings will occur as many of the early kinesiotherapists reach retirement age and others change jobs or leave for other reasons.

## FOR MORE INFORMATION

*For career information, contact*
**American Academy of Kinesiology and Physical Education**
c/o Human Kinetics
PO Box 5076

Champaign, IL 61820-2200
Tel: 800-747-4457
Email: kims@aakpe.org
http://www.aakpe.org

*The AAHPERD is an umbrella organization for a number of groups
dedicated to health and fitness. For more detailed information on
kinesiology and related fields, contact*
**American Alliance for Health, Physical Education, Recreation
   and Dance (AAHPERD)**
1900 Association Drive
Reston, VA 20191-1598
Tel: 800-213-7193
Email: info@aahperd.org
http://www.aahperd.org

*For more information about education and certification, contact*
**American Kinesiotherapy Association**
118 College Drive, #5142
Hattiesburg, MS 39406-0001
Tel: 800-296-2582
Email: info@akta.org
http://www.akta.org

*For information on accredited programs, contact*
**Commission on Accreditation of Allied Health Education
   Programs**
1361 Park Street
Clearwater, FL 33756-6039
Tel: 727-210-2350
Email: mail@caahep.org
http://www.caahep.org

*To learn more about biomechanics, visit the society's Web site.*
**American Society of Biomechanics**
http://www.asbweb.org

*For information on kinesiology, contact*
**International College of Applied Kinesiology**
http://www.icak.com

# Massage Therapists

## QUICK FACTS

**School Subjects**
Health
Physical education

**Personal Skills**
Helping/teaching
Mechanical/manipulative

**Work Environment**
Primarily indoors
Primarily one location

**Minimum Education Level**
Some postsecondary training

**Salary Range**
$13,624 to $34,870 to
$70,840+

**Certification or Licensing**
Recommended (certification)
Required by certain states
(licensing)

**Outlook**
Faster than the average

**DOT**
334

**GOE**
14.06.01

**NOC**
3235

**O*NET-SOC**
31-9011.00

## OVERVIEW

Massage therapy is a broad term referring to a number of health-related practices, including Swedish massage, sports massage, Rolfing, Shiatsu and acupressure, trigger point therapy, and reflexology. Although the techniques vary, most *massage therapists* (or *massotherapists*) press and rub the skin and muscles. Relaxed muscles, improved blood circulation and joint mobility, reduced stress and anxiety, and decreased recovery time from sprains and injured muscles are just a few of the potential benefits of massage therapy. Massage therapists are sometimes called *bodyworkers*. The titles *masseur* and *masseuse,* once common, are now rare among those who use massage for therapy and rehabilitation. There are approximately 118,000 massage therapists employed in the United States.

## HISTORY

Getting a massage used to be considered a luxury reserved only for the very wealthy, or an occasional splurge for the less affluent. Some people thought massage to be a cover for illicit activities such as prostitution. With increased regulation of certification and a trend toward ergonomics in the home and workplace, however, massage therapy is recognized as an important tool in both alternative and preventative health care. Regular massage can help alleviate physical ailments faced by people today: physical stress brought on by an increase in sedentary lifestyle, aches and pains from hours spent in front of the computer, as well as injuries of the weekend warrior trying to make up for five days of inactivity.

# THE JOB

Massage therapists work to produce physical, mental, and emotional benefits through the manipulation of the body's soft tissue. Auxiliary methods, such as the movement of joints and the application of dry and steam heat, are also used. Among the potential physical benefits are the release of muscle tension and stiffness, reduced blood pressure, better blood circulation, a shorter healing time for sprains and pulled muscles, increased flexibility and greater range of motion in the joints, and reduced swelling from edema (excess fluid buildup in body tissue). Massage may also improve posture, strengthen the immune system, and reduce the formation of scar tissue.

Mental and emotional benefits include a relaxed state of mind, reduced stress and anxiety, clearer thinking, and a general sense of well-being. Physical, mental, and emotional health are all interconnected: Being physically fit and healthy can improve emotional health, just as a positive mental attitude can bolster the immune system to help the body fight off infection. A release of muscle tension also leads to reduced stress and anxiety, and physical manipulation of sore muscles can help speed the healing process.

There are many different approaches a massage therapist may take. Among the most popular are Swedish massage, sports massage, Rolfing, Shiatsu and acupressure, and trigger point therapy.

In Swedish massage the traditional techniques are effleurage, petrissage, friction, and tapotement. Effleurage (stroking) uses light and hard rhythmic strokes to relax muscles and improve blood circulation. It is often performed at the beginning and end of a massage session. Petrissage (kneading) is the rhythmic squeezing, pressing, and lifting of a muscle. For friction, the fingers, thumb, or palm or heel of the hand are pressed into the skin with a small circular movement. The massage therapist's fingers are sometimes pressed deeply into a joint. Tapotement (tapping), in which the hands strike the skin in rapid succession, is used to improve blood circulation.

During the session the client, covered with sheets, lies undressed on a padded table. Oil or lotion is used to smooth the skin. Some massage therapists use aromatherapy, adding fragrant essences to the oil to relax the client and stimulate circulation. Swedish massage may employ a number of auxiliary techniques, including the use of rollers, belts, and vibrators; steam and dry heat; ultraviolet and infrared light; and saunas, whirlpools, steam baths, and packs of hot water or ice.

Sports massage is essentially Swedish massage used in the context of athletics. A light massage generally is given before an event or game to loosen and warm the muscles. This reduces the chance of injury and may improve performance. After the event the athlete is massaged more deeply to alleviate pain, reduce stiffness, and promote healing.

Rolfing, developed by American Ida Rolf, involves deep, sometimes painful massage. Intense pressure is applied to various parts of the body. Rolfing practitioners believe that emotional disturbances, physical pain, and other problems can occur when the body is out of alignment—for example, as a result of poor posture. This method takes 10 sessions to complete.

Like the ancient Oriental science of acupuncture, Shiatsu and acupressure are based on the concept of meridians, or invisible channels of flowing energy in the body. The massage therapist presses down on particular points along these channels to release blocked energy and untie knots of muscle tension. For this approach the patient wears loosely fitted clothes, lies on the floor or on a futon, and is not given oil or lotion for the skin.

Trigger point therapy, a neuromuscular technique, focuses in on a painful area, or trigger point, in a muscle. A trigger point might be associated with a problem in another part of the body. Using the fingers or an instrument, such as a rounded piece of wood, concentrated pressure is placed on the irritated area in order to "deactivate" the trigger point.

All of these methods of massage can be altered and intermingled depending on the client's needs. Massage therapists can be proficient in one or many of the methods, and usually tailor a session to the individual.

## REQUIREMENTS

### High School

Since massage therapists need to know more than just technical skills, many practitioners use the basic knowledge learned in high school as a foundation to build a solid career in the field. During your high school years, you should take fundamental science courses, such as chemistry, anatomy, and biology. These classes will give you a basic understanding of the human body and prepare you for the health and anatomy classes you will take while completing your postsecondary education. English, psychology, and other classes relating to communications and human development will also be useful as the successful massage therapist is able to express his or her ideas with clients as well as understand the clients' reactions to the therapy. If you think you might wish to run your own massage therapy business someday, computer and business courses are essential. Finally, do not neglect your own physical well-being.

Take physical education and health courses to strengthen your body and your understanding of your own conditioning.

## Postsecondary Training

The best way to become a successful massage therapist is to attend an accredited massage therapy school after you have finished high school. There are more than 300 state-accredited massage schools located throughout the United States. More than 85 of these schools are accredited or approved by the Commission on Massage Therapy Accreditation (COMTA), a major accrediting agency for massage therapy programs and an affiliate of the American Massage Therapy Association (AMTA). COMTA-accredited and -approved schools must provide at least 500 hours of classroom instruction. (The average massage therapist has 688 hours of initial training, according to the AMTA.) Studies should include such courses as anatomy, physiology, theory and practice of massage therapy, and ethics. In addition, students should receive supervised hands-on experience. Most programs offer students the opportunity to participate at clinics, such as those providing massage services at hospices, hospitals, and shelters, or at school clinics that are open to the general public.

Massage therapy training programs typically take about a year to complete. Students can specialize in particular disciplines, such as infant massage or rehabilitative massage. Basic first aid and cardiopulmonary resuscitation (CPR) must also be learned. When choosing a school, you should pay close attention to the philosophy and curricula of the program, since a wide range of program options exists. Also, keep in mind that licensure requirements for massage therapists vary by state. For example, some state medical boards require students to have completed more than 500 hours of instruction before they can be recognized as massage therapists. Part of your process for choosing a school, therefore, should include making sure that the school's curriculum will allow you to meet your state's requirements.

## Certification or Licensing

Currently, 38 states and the District of Columbia regulate the practice of massage therapy, requiring licensure, certification, or registration. Because requirements for licensing, certification, registration, and even local ordinances vary, however, you will need to check with your state's department of regulatory agencies to get specifics for your area. Typically, requirements include completing an accredited program and passing a written test and a demonstration of massage therapy techniques.

The National Certification Board for Therapeutic Massage and Bodywork offers two national certification examinations for massage therapists: the National Certification Examination for Therapeutic Massage and Bodywork and the National Certification Examination for Therapeutic Massage. To learn more about each exam, visit http://www.ncbtmb.com. Certification is highly recommended, since it demonstrates a therapist's high-level of education and achievement. Certification may also make a therapist a more desirable candidate for job openings.

### Other Requirements

Physical requirements of massage therapists generally include the ability to use their hands and other tools to rub or press on the client's body. Manual dexterity is usually required to administer the treatments, as is the ability to stand for at least an hour at a time. Special modifications or accommodations can often be made for people with different abilities.

If you are interested in becoming a massage therapist, you should be, above all, nurturing and caring. Constance Bickford, a certified massage therapist in Chicago, thinks that it is necessary to be both flexible and creative: easily adaptable to the needs of the client, as well as able to use different techniques to help the client feel better. Listening well and responding to the client is vital, as is focusing all attention on the task at hand. Massage therapists need to tune in to their client rather than zone out, thinking about the grocery list or what to cook for supper. An effective massage is a mindful one, where massage therapist and client work together toward improved health.

To be a successful massage therapist, you should also be trustworthy and sensitive. Someone receiving a massage may feel awkward lying naked in an office covered by a sheet, listening to music while a stranger kneads his or her muscles. A good massage therapist will make the client feel comfortable in what could potentially be perceived as a vulnerable situation.

Therapists considering opening up their own business should be prepared for busy and slow times. In order to both serve their clients well and stay in business, they should be adequately staffed during rush seasons, and must be financially able to withstand dry spells.

## EXPLORING

The best way to become familiar with massage therapy is to get a massage. Look for a certified therapist in your area and make an appointment for a session. If you can afford it, consider going to

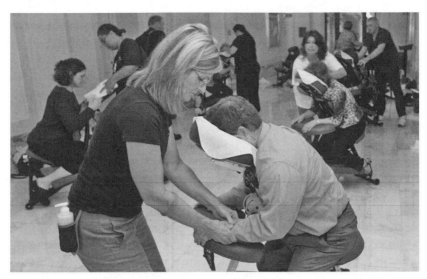

A certified massage therapist gives a chair massage to a client. *(AP Photo)*

several different therapists who offer different types of massage. Also, ask if you can set up an information interview with one of the therapists. Explain that you are interested in pursuing this career and come to the interview prepared to ask questions. What is this massage therapist's educational background? Why was he or she drawn to the job? What is the best part of this work? By talking to a massage therapist, you may also have the chance to develop a mentoring relationship with him or her.

A less costly approach is to find a book on massage instruction at a local public library or bookstore. Massage techniques can then be practiced at home. Books on self-massage are available. Many books discuss in detail the theoretical basis for the techniques. Videos that demonstrate massage techniques are available as well.

Consider volunteering at a hospice, nursing home, or shelter. This work will give you experience in caring for others and help you develop good listening skills. It is important for massage therapists to listen well and respond appropriately to their clients' needs. The massage therapist must make clients feel comfortable, and volunteer work can help foster the skills necessary to achieve this.

## EMPLOYERS

Approximately 118,000 massage therapists are employed in the United States. After graduating from an accredited school of massage therapy, there are a number of possibilities for employment. Doctors' offices, hospitals, clinics, health clubs, resorts, country clubs, cruise ships, community service organizations, and nursing homes, for example, all employ massage therapists. Some chiropractors have a massage therapist on staff to whom they can refer patients. A number of massage therapists run their own businesses. Most opportunities for work will be in larger, urban areas with population growth, although massage therapy is slowly spreading to more rural areas as well.

## STARTING OUT

There are a number of resources you can use to locate a job in massage therapy. The AMTA offers job placement information to certified massage therapists who belong to the organization. Massage therapy schools have career services offices. Newspapers often list jobs. Some graduates are able to enter the field as self-employed massage therapists, scheduling their own appointments and managing their own offices.

Networking is a valuable tool in maintaining a successful massage therapy enterprise. Many massage therapists get clients through referrals and often rely on word of mouth to build a solid customer base. Beginning massage therapists might wish to consult businesses about arranging on-site massage sessions for their employees.

Health fairs are also good places to distribute information about massage therapy practices and learn about other services in the industry. Often, organizers of large sporting events will employ massage therapists to give massages to athletes at the finish line. These events may include marathons and runs or bike rides held to raise money for charitable organizations.

## ADVANCEMENT

For self-employed massage therapists, advancement is measured by reputation, the ability to attract clients, and the fees charged for services. Health clubs, country clubs, and other institutions have supervisory positions for massage therapists. In a community service organization, massage therapists may be promoted to the position of health service director. Licensed massage therapists often become instructors or advisers at schools for massage therapy. They may also make themselves available to advise individuals or companies on the short- and long-term benefits of massage therapy, and how massage therapy can be introduced into professional work environments.

## EARNINGS

The earnings of massage therapists vary greatly with the level of experience and location of practice. Therapists in New York and

California, for example, typically charge higher rates than those in other parts of the country. Some entry-level massage therapists earn as little as minimum wage (ending up with a yearly income of around $13,624), but with experience, a massage therapist can charge from $45 to $70 for a one-hour session.

The U.S. Department of Labor reports that massage therapists earned a median salary of $34,870 a year in 2007. The lowest 10 percent earned $16,000 or less, while the highest 10 percent earned $70,840 or more. The American Massage Therapy Association reports that massage therapists charge an average of $60 for a one-hour massage. Those with earnings at the high end typically worked in higher paying geographic areas (such as large cities), had years of experience, and had built up a large clientele.

Approximately 64 percent of all massage therapists are self-employed, and self-employed therapists are not paid for the time spent on bookkeeping, maintaining their offices, waiting for customers to arrive, and looking for new clients. In addition, they must pay a self-employment tax and provide their own benefits. With membership in some national organizations, self-employed massage therapists may be eligible for group life, health, liability, and renter's insurance through the organization's insurance agency.

Massage therapists employed by a health club usually get free or discounted memberships to the club. Those who work for resorts or on cruise ships can get free or discounted travel and accommodations, in addition to full access to facilities when not on duty. Massage therapists employed by a sports team often get to attend the team's sporting events.

## WORK ENVIRONMENT

Massage therapists work in clean, comfortable settings. Because a relaxed environment is essential, the massage room may be dim, and soft music, scents, and oils are often used. Since massage therapists may see a number of people per day, it is important to maintain a hygienic working area. This involves changing sheets on the massage table after each client, cleaning and sterilizing any implements used, and washing hands frequently.

Massage therapists employed by businesses may use a portable massage chair—that is, a padded chair that leaves the client in a forward-leaning position ideal for massage of the back and neck. Some massage therapists work out of their homes or travel to the homes of their clients.

The workweek of a massage therapist is typically 35 to 40 hours, which may include evenings and weekends. On average, 19 hours per week are spent with clients, and the other hours are spent making appointments and taking care of other business-related details.

Since the physical work is sometimes demanding, massage therapists need to take measures to prevent repetitive stress disorders, such as carpal tunnel syndrome. Also, for their own personal safety, massage therapists who work out of their homes or have odd office hours need to be particularly careful about scheduling appointments with unknown clients.

## OUTLOOK

The industry predicts a strong employment outlook for massage therapists through the next several years. The growing acceptance of massage therapy as an important health care discipline has led to the creation of additional jobs for massage therapists in many sectors. Opportunities should be strongest for women, as clients—both male and female—report that they are more comfortable receiving a massage from a female therapist. Approximately 84 percent of massage therapists are women.

One certified massage therapist points to sports massage as one of the fastest growing specialties in the field. The increasing popularity of professional sports has given massage therapists new opportunities to work as key members of a team's staff. Their growing presence in sports has made massage therapy more visible to the public, spreading the awareness of the physical benefits of massage.

Massages aren't just for athletes. According to a survey by the American Massage Therapy Association, 24 percent of Americans surveyed in June 2007 had a massage in the past 12 months. The survey found that people are getting massages not just for medical reasons, but to relax and reduce stress.

There is a growing opportunity for massage therapists in the corporate world. Many employers eager to hold on to good employees offer perks, such as workplace massages. As a result, many massage therapists are working as mobile business consultants.

## FOR MORE INFORMATION

*For information on careers and education programs, contact*
**American Massage Therapy Association**
500 Davis Street
Evanston, IL 60201-4695
Tel: 877-905-2700
Email: info@amtamassage.org
http://www.amtamassage.org

*For information on careers in the field (including the brochure,* Your Massage & Bodywork Career*), state board requirements, and training programs, contact*
> **Associated Bodywork and Massage Professionals**
> 25188 Genesee Trail Road
> Golden, CO 80401-5702
> Tel: 800-458-2267
> Email: expectmore@abmp.com
> http://www.abmp.com
> http://www.massagetherapy.com

*For information on accreditation and programs, contact*
> **Commission on Massage Therapy Accreditation**
> 5335 Wisconsin Avenue, NW, Suite 440
> Washington, DC 20015-2030
> Tel: 202-895-1518
> Email: info@comta.org
> http://www.comta.org

*For information about state certification and education require-ments, contact*
> **National Certification Board for Therapeutic Massage and Bodywork**
> 1901 South Meyers Road, Suite 240
> Oakbrook Terrace, IL 60181-5243
> Tel: 800-296-0664
> Email: info@ncbtmb.com
> http://www.ncbtmb.com

## INTERVIEW

*Wendy Keller has been a certified clinical massage therapist since 2004, and is the owner of Wendy Keller Massage. (Visit http://www. kellermassage.com to learn more about her practice.) Wendy discussed her career with the editors of* Careers in Focus: Complementay and Alternative Health Care.

**Q. Tell us about your business.**
**A.** I have a private practice within a spa-salon atmosphere and a chiropractic clinic. Also, I do chair massage at events and in private business settings.

**Q. What is one thing that people may not know about massage therapy?**

**A.** Massage can be about more than relaxation. I treat more than 30 specific medical conditions [and injuries] such as carpal tunnel, sciatica, herniated discs, degenerative disc disease, IT Band syndrome, plantar fasciitis, rotator cuff injuries, torn and damaged muscles, tendons, and ligaments, etc. There are also different ways to specialize such as clinical therapy, which is what I do, energy therapies, reflexology, craniosacral therapy, stone therapies, lomi-lomi, and many more.

**Q. Why did you decide to become a massage therapist?**

**A.** My mother suffers from a chronic pain disease. I wanted to be in a position to help people like her.

**Q. What do you like most and least about your job?**

**A.** I enjoy the difference between when a client comes to me in pain and when they leave with a sense of hope and relief.

The most frustrating part of being in the massage industry are the misconceptions the general public has of what massage therapy is.

**Q. What are the most important professional qualities for massage therapists?**

**A.** The most important qualities to possess are professionalism, communication, and competence. As massage therapy receives more recognition and regulation, the industry is establishing higher standards. Massage therapy directly affects people's blood and lymphatic systems, while relaxing and stimulating certain musculature to reduce pain and enhance healing. Without the proper training, there are certain situations (a client's medical history and medications combined with certain massage techniques and other contraindications) that can harm a client. The difference between seeing a client and gaining a clientele, is how well you know your stuff, how you treat people, how they perceive you, how well you listen to their needs, and your ability to explain a progressive treatment session or plan.

**Q. What is the future employment outlook for massage therapists?**

**A.** As awareness is more developed within the medical field and people become more accepting of massage as an alternative therapy, the industry will continue to grow.

# Myotherapists

## OVERVIEW

Myotherapy is a method of relieving muscle pain and spasms and improving overall circulation through applied pressure to trigger points. Pressure is applied using fingers, knuckles, and elbows. Those who practice myotherapy are called *myotherapists*.

## HISTORY

Bonnie Prudden, a fitness and exercise enthusiast, first developed myotherapy in 1976. During the 1970s, Prudden worked for Dr. Janet Travell, the former personal physician to President Kennedy. Together they treated chronic pain using trigger point injection therapy. Prudden would identify the trigger points on the patient's body with ink, then Dr. Travell would inject the sites with a solution of procaine (a type of local anesthetic) and saline. Afterwards, Prudden would conduct muscle exercises and teach patients stretching exercises to do at home in order to keep the muscle strong and relaxed. By chance, while working on a patient, Prudden found that by holding the pressure to trigger points for a longer period of time, the same relief was achieved without the use of invasive needles and solutions. In 1979, the Bonnie Prudden School of Physical Fitness and Myotherapy was established in Tucson, Arizona.

### QUICK FACTS

**School Subjects**
Biology
Business
Health

**Personal Skills**
Communication/ideas
Helping/teaching

**Work Environment**
Primarily indoors
Primarily one location

**Salary Range**
$16,000 to $34,870 to $70,840+

**Minimum Education Level**
Some postsecondary training

**Certification or Licensing**
Voluntary (certification)
Required by certain states (licensing)

**Outlook**
Faster than the average

**DOT**
N/A

**GOE**
N/A

**NOC**
N/A

**O*NET-SOC**
N/A

## THE JOB

Myotherapy, also called trigger point therapy or neuromuscular massage therapy, is a method of relieving pain, improving circulation, and alleviating muscle spasms. Myotherapists identify the source of pain, called a trigger point, and erase it by the use of applied pressure to these tender spots.

Through the Bonnie Prudden School of Physical Fitness and Myotherapy, students are taught the Prudden method of myotherapy, in addition to anatomy, physiology, exercise, and physical fitness. Classes such as modern dance, drawing, and live sculpture are also offered to encourage students to analyze how the human body moves. After completion of the program, students are given an exam and are required to undergo recertification at the school every two years. (See the "Certification or Licensing" section for more information.)

A first-time consultation begins with a thorough history of the patient. "Many times pain is the result of an old injury or accident," says Janice Stroughton, a certified myotherapist. "It could also occur as the result of the patient's background and lifestyle." Stroughton explains that weakness and muscle injury is accumulated throughout a lifetime. The average age of patients is between 35 and 55 years—"about the time a person's bucket of accumulated trigger points starts to overflow." Once weak spots are created in the muscle, both physical and emotional stress can cause the spots to go into painful spasms. Myotherapists get rid of spasms by using their fingers, knuckles, or elbows to apply pressure to these trigger points. As muscles relax, the patient is relieved of pain. Afterwards the muscle is taught to remain loose and lengthened through the use of exercises. Myotherapists also teach the patient several corrective exercises to do at home.

Myotherapy works on pain as long as the source is muscular, not systemic. It has shown to be effective for alleviating pain caused by arthritis, bursitis, scoliosis, sciatica, and even pain associated with lupus, AIDS, and muscular dystrophy.

Stroughton collected her own trigger points from years of playing tennis. Complications from scoliosis gave her more pain than she could endure. "I first learned about myotherapy from a tennis instructor who had undergone treatments and persuaded me to give the method a try." Stroughton was so convinced of the benefits of myotherapy that she became a myotherapist. Today, Stroughton is a certified myotherapist at the Myotherapy Pain Control Center in Maryland.

Patients are referred to the Pain Control Center by a medical physician, osteopath, chiropractor, or acupuncturist. Usually, patients have already undergone the battery of X rays, tests, and procedures to ensure pain is not structural in origin. For new patients, history and assessment is taken. "Many times chronic pain is caused by occupation, disease, past accident, surgeries, or participation in sports," says Stroughton. Patients then take the Kraus-Weber Minimum Muscular Fitness Test for Key Posture Muscles. Divided into six tests for different muscle masses, it gauges the flexibility and strength of a person's muscles.

Myotherapists use a trigger point pain chart to mark down the sources of a patient's pain. Once a trigger point is found, the patient identifies its intensity by grading it on a scale of one to 10—one being mild, and 10 almost unbearable. Each location is color marked on the paper chart to indicate the type of pain and the date it is erased.

Patients arrive for treatments barefooted and wearing loose clothing. "Patients are encouraged to bring a friend or family member to observe how treatments and exercises are done," explains Stroughton. "That way, the exercises may be repeated correctly at home. Treatments are 50 percent myotherapy and 50 percent corrective exercises." Using the completed pain chart, trigger points are identified and erased. The location of a trigger point determines the amount and length of pressure applied—on the average seven seconds for most body areas and four to five seconds for the face and head. Tools such as the crook (a metal rod shaped like a shepherd's hook) and the bodo (a wooden dowel) are used to give the myotherapist greater extension and also to help fight fatigue. Small bodos are used to work the hands and feet, while larger bodos are helpful in working larger muscle masses such as the quadriceps and gluteus.

Once the muscles are relaxed, they need to be maintained with exercises specially designed for the patient's problem areas. Patients and their helpers are instructed in the proper way to conduct maintenance exercises to help keep the muscles strong and flexible. These exercises also help improve coordination, strength, and posture.

Stroughton's work schedule varies. Phone consultations with patients take up a large part of the day, as does paperwork. She limits herself to two or three patient treatments a day. Myotherapy is physically taxing on the practitioner. "You always risk injuring yourself," says Stroughton. "You need to be aware of how you use your own body."

## REQUIREMENTS

### High School

Enid Whittaker, a certified myotherapist and instructor, suggests taking anatomy and physiology classes if you are interested in a career in myotherapy. This will help you understand how the human body works. Also, creative classes such as drawing and sculpture, especially of the human body, will foster good hand coordination skills. Physical fitness classes and dance classes are helpful in developing a strong and flexible body. This is important because myotherapy is physically demanding on the therapist. If you are interested in setting up a private practice, Whittaker also suggests taking business classes, such as marketing, accounting, bookkeeping, and computer science.

### Certification or Licensing
There are other schools offering classes in myotherapy, but the Bonnie Prudden Myotherapy School is considered the most reputable program available. The school offers a nine-and-a-half month certification program for its graduates. A total of 1,300 hours of program work is completed at the school, after which you may sit for the board exam. For recertification every two years, you are required to take continuing education classes (about 45 hours total) covering new techniques.

Certification is also available from other massage therapy schools, usually requiring completion of a series of workshops or seminars. In some states, you must also become a licensed massage therapist before practicing myotherapy.

### Other Requirements
"Working with people in pain can sometimes be unpleasant," says Janice Stroughton. "Don't expect cheery faces and pleasant conversation." Patients, many of whom have been suffering pain for some time, will be grouchy and in a foul mood. Sometimes a good sense of humor is enough to erase a patient's crankiness. Despite having to deal with bad tempers, Stroughton finds reward in helping patients with their problems and offering them relief from pain. "The best part of my job is knowing I made a difference in someone's life, in regards to pain. It is like giving someone new hope." Stroughton quotes her mentor, Bonnie Prudden, when she says, "Pain, not death, is the enemy."

Questions arise during treatment, such as, Should pressure be kept a few seconds longer? Is the patient ready to end his or her sessions? Are these exercises challenging enough? Good intuition is another important quality you will need in order to answer such questions on the spot. While you will learn the basics of myotherapy in school, you'll need instincts and intuition to help you in actual practice.

Because of the repetitive movements used in myotherapy, many practitioners often run the risk of self-injury. It's important to be aware of your body's limitation and not overuse your own muscles and joints. Sometimes, myotherapists need treatment for their own repetitive stress problems.

## EXPLORING
If you can afford it, consider going to several different massage therapists who offer different types of massage. Ask if you can set up

an information interview with various kinds of massage therapists, including myotherapists. Explain that you are interested in pursuing this career and come to the interview prepared to ask questions. What is your educational background? Why were you drawn to the job? What is the best part of this work?

A less costly approach is to find books on massage instruction at a local public library or bookstore. Massage techniques can then be practiced at home. Books on self-massage are available. Many books discuss in detail the theoretical basis for the techniques. Videos that demonstrate massage techniques are available as well.

Consider volunteering at a hospice, nursing home, or shelter. This work will give you experience in caring for others and help you develop good listening skills. As a myotherapist, it is important for you to listen well and respond appropriately to your clients' needs. The therapist must make clients feel comfortable, and volunteer work can help you learn the skills necessary to achieve this.

## EMPLOYERS

Myotherapists are employed in a number of health care settings. They may work at a physician's clinic, especially one that treats patients with nerve damage or arthritic pain. Others choose to open up their own practice. Remember, though, that in addition to giving treatments, myotherapists are also responsible for all duties associated with running a business, handling tax concerns, organizing the office space and supplies, and hiring support staff. The reward is having the freedom to determine their own workdays and hours.

Myotherapists can also join an established clinic. Because of the growing interest and acceptance in myotherapy, many clinics have found it necessary to hire more therapists.

Another option is to combine myotherapy training with other disciplines, such as acupuncture, chiropractic, or massage therapy. These therapists can work for massage clinics, day spas, and alternative medicine practices.

## STARTING OUT

It may be difficult for new myotherapists to immediately set up their own businesses. Consider applying to clinics or physician's group practices to see if they might be interested in offering myotherapy as part of their services. Your chances of finding opportunities are better at organizations that concentrate on alternative and integrative medicine. Working in an established clinic or practice will give you experience, help you build a clientele, and generate publicity for your services.

## ADVANCEMENT

Career advancement depends on how myotherapists choose to practice. If they opt to open a private practice, then the obvious advancements would be a larger office, a bigger client base, and perhaps having a staff of myotherapists working for them. Those who choose to join an existing practice advance by growing their client base, gaining seniority, or perhaps establishing their own pain clinic. Myotherapists who join a medical practice advance in the form of more responsibilities, a larger salary, or better benefits. Experienced myotherapists may go on to become instructors in massage therapy schools.

## EARNINGS

Salaries for this occupation vary depending on the work setting. Enid Whittaker sees four to seven patients per day. The average patient, depending on the type of pain, needs about four to eight visits, with each treatment costing an average of $75. On the high end, a patient may spend up to $600 to finish pain treatment. Of course, some myotherapists opt to schedule more patients daily and may work with different treatment fees. Because of the physical demands of the job, myotherapists often work less than 40 hours a week. A large percentage of practitioners practice part time, from 10 to 20 hours a week.

The U.S. Department of Labor reports that the median annual salary for massage therapists was $34,870 in 2007, and salaries ranged from less than $16,000 to $70,840 or more annually.

Myotherapists in private practice must also be responsible for overhead costs, in addition to acquiring health insurance and other benefits. A myotherapist employed full time at a hospital or other clinical setting may enjoy benefits such as health insurance and paid vacation and sick time. Though employed myotherapists may have greater job security and better benefits, they do not have the option of setting their own work schedules and hours that independent myotherapists enjoy.

Enid Whittaker sums it up best when she stresses, "One becomes a myotherapist because of a desire to help others, not to get rich."

## WORK ENVIRONMENT

Massage therapists, including myotherapists, work in clean, comfortable settings. It is important to maintain a hygienic working area. This involves changing sheets on the massage table after each client, as well as cleaning and sterilizing any implements used, and washing hands frequently. Myotherapists use massage tables and a variety of tools to manipulate muscles. Their offices have adequate space for teaching exercises and simple exercise equipment.

Since the physical work is sometimes demanding, myotherapists need to take measures to prevent repetitive stress disorders, such as carpal tunnel syndrome. The workweek of a myotherapist is typically 35 to 40 hours, which may include evenings and weekends to accommodate working clients.

## OUTLOOK

Even though there are no official figures, the field of myotherapy has grown. The public, especially in the past few decades, has become more proactive when it comes to their bodies and health. Many people are tired of the dependence on traditional medicine and are looking for alternative methods of pain relief. There is a growing acceptance of myotherapy from the public and the medical field. Many physicians, especially those specializing in neurology and rheumatology, are referring patients for myotherapy treatments more and more. Insurance companies, though slowly, are beginning to cover myotherapy treatments.

About 85 percent of the population experiences some sort of pain, most commonly back pain and headaches. Many people's work involves developed movements that are highly repetitive, with little flexibility. A fairly sedentary occupation such as computer programming will usually result in trigger points to the upper and lower back. Construction work, a highly strenuous occupation, will gather trigger points in the back and torso. Chronic pain can also be sports-related. Beside traditional activities like tennis and golf, some people are fascinated with extreme sports such as mountain and rock climbing and snowboarding. Many athletes turn to the benefits of myotherapy as a form of injury prevention and maintenance.

## FOR MORE INFORMATION

*For more information on myotherapy, contact*
**Bonnie Prudden Myotherapy**
PO Box 65240
Tucson, AZ 85728-5240
Tel: 800-221-4634
Email: info@bonnieprudden.com
http://www.bonnieprudden.com

*For information and a directory of certified myotherapists, visit the following Web site:*
**International Myotherapy Association**
Email: info@myotherapy.org
http://www.myotherapy.org

# Naturopaths

## QUICK FACTS

**School Subjects**
Biology
Business
Chemistry

**Personal Skills**
Helping/teaching
Technical/scientific

**Work Environment**
Primarily indoors
Primarily one location

**Minimum Education Level**
Medical degree

**Salary Range**
$25,000 to $40,000 to
$90,000+

**Certification or Licensing**
Required by certain states

**Outlook**
Faster than the average

**DOT**
N/A

**GOE**
N/A

**NOC**
3123

**O*NET-SOC**
N/A

## OVERVIEW

*Naturopaths* (pronounced "nature-o-paths")—also called *naturopathic physicians, naturopathic doctors,* and *NDs*—are licensed health professionals who practice an approach to health care called naturopathic medicine. Naturopathic medicine (also called naturopathy) is a distinct system of health care that uses a variety of natural approaches to health and healing, including clinical nutrition, counseling, herbal medicine, homeopathy, and physical therapy. Naturopaths recognize the integrity of the whole person, and they emphasize the individual's inherent capacity for self-healing. Some naturopaths are not licensed health professionals but have studied the field of naturopathy through correspondence programs, under the supervision of other naturopaths, or completed some other type of certificate-granting program. This article, however, focuses primarily on the career of naturopathic doctors. There are more than 3,000 naturopathic doctors employed in the United States.

## HISTORY

The therapies and philosophy on which naturopathic medicine is based can be traced back to the ancient healing arts of early civilizations. Healers in ancient times used natural treatments that relied on the body's innate ability to heal itself. They made use of foods, herbs, water, massage, and fasting.

Hippocrates, who is thought by many to be the fouding figure of modern medicine, is also often considered to be the earliest predecessor of naturopathic physicians. He used many natural approaches to health care. He is reported to have told his followers, "Let your food be your medicine and your medicine be your food."

During the 18th and 19th centuries, an alternative healing movement in Europe contributed to the development of naturopathic medicine. The German homeopathic practitioner John H. Scheel is credited with first using the term "naturopath" in 1895.

Dr. Benedict Lust introduced naturopathy to the United States. He founded the American School of Naturopathy, which graduated its first class in 1902. In 1909, California became the first state to regulate legally the practice of naturopathy. Early naturopaths, including Dr. John Kellogg, his brother Will Kellogg, and C. W. Post, helped popularize naturopathy.

Naturopathy flourished in the early part of the 20th century. By 1930, there were more than 20 naturopathic schools and 10,000 practitioners nationwide. With the rise of modern pharmaceuticals and allopathic (conventional) medicine, naturopathic medicine experienced a decline during the 1940s and 1950s. The latter part of the 20th century, however, saw a strong revival in the field of naturopathy due to rapidly growing public interest in alternative health care approaches. One sign of the importance of alternative medicine was the founding in 1992 of the Office of Alternative Medicine (OAM) as part of the National Institutes of Health. The OAM's responsibilities included evaluating treatments and providing information to the public about them. In 1999 the OAM became the National Center for Complementary and Alternative Medicine (NCCAM), with greater access to resources for initiating and funding additional research projects.

Today, the NCCAM provides funding to numerous research centers evaluating alternative treatments in a wide variety of areas including addiction, cancer, cardiovascular diseases, pediatrics, and arthritis. The OAM began with an annual budget of $2 million. As officials realized the importance of this work, more money has been dedicated to the study of alternative medicine, and today the NCCAM's annual budget has increased to more than $121 million.

## THE JOB

In states where naturopathic doctors are licensed medical professionals, they provide complete diagnostic and therapeutic services. They are consulted as primary care physicians, and they receive referrals from other physicians. Patients consult naturopaths for a variety of health problems, including digestive disorders, chronic fatigue, asthma, depression, infections, obesity, colds, and flu.

When seeing a new patient, licensed NDs first take a careful medical history to understand the state of health of the whole individual—body, mind, and spirit. They consider the patient as a whole person who has something out of balance, and they don't just focus on the symptoms of illness. Naturopathic doctors ask many questions about lifestyle, eating habits, stress, and many other issues. They listen carefully to determine what imbalance may be causing illness or preventing recovery. They may spend an hour to an hour and a half with a new patient.

Naturopathic doctors take a holistic approach to health care. They recognize the connection between the health of the mind and the health of the body. Depression, stress, and fear all can have an impact on physical health. Naturopaths listen carefully to their patients to learn about the outside forces, such as a stressful work environment or family situation, that may be contributing to the illness.

Once they make a diagnosis, NDs prescribe a course of treatment. Naturopathic doctors practice health care that supports the body's self-healing processes. They recognize that the human body has a natural capability to heal itself, so they use methods of care that will work with these processes. Naturopathic doctors use many natural and noninvasive healing techniques. They are trained in counseling, herbal medicine, clinical nutrition, homeopathy, hydrotherapy, massage, and other types of physical medicine.

Naturopathic doctors believe that most conventional doctors treat only the illness, not the patient. In treating the patient, NDs recommend methods that have more lasting effects. They recommend changes in diet, prescribe botanical medicine (herbs), and recommend vitamins. They may even offer counseling to help the patient make lifestyle changes.

Naturopathic medicine is most effective in treating chronic illness. Like many other alternative health care approaches, naturopathy is not usually used for acute, life-threatening illnesses. Some NDs are trained in techniques of minor surgery. They do not perform major surgery, but they may be involved in the recovery process after surgery. For some conditions, naturopaths may refer a patient to a specialist, such as a cardiologist or oncologist. Even while a patient is seeing a specialist, the naturopath continues to work with the individual and the self-healing process. This can result in a team-care approach.

Only 14 states currently license naturopathic physicians to provide medical care. Those who are licensed can maintain their licenses even if they practice in a state other than the license-granting one. (That is, a doctor licensed by Arizona, for example, can maintain that license even if he or she ends up moving and practices in another state.) However, NDs who practice in states that do not offer licensing must restrict the scope of their practices to areas such as homeopathy (a form of therapy that emphasizes natural remedies and treatments) and nutrition counseling.

The majority of naturopaths are in private practice. That means that they must have the skills to run a business on a day-to-day basis. They interview, hire, and train staff and oversee the functioning of an office. More and more insurance companies are covering naturopathic medicine in states that offer licenses, and NDs must be able to oversee complicated insurance billing procedures in order to be paid for their services.

## REQUIREMENTS

### High School

If you want to pursue a career in naturopathy, you'll be entering a premed program in college, so take high school science courses, such as biology and chemistry. The physical education courses of some high schools offer instruction in health, nutrition, and exercise that would help prepare you for important aspects of work as a naturopath.

English, psychology, and sociology courses will help you sharpen your communication and people skills. As a naturopath, you will need to be an excellent listener and communicator. Much of a naturopathic physician's work involves listening to and counseling clients. Business, math, and computer classes will prepare you to run a business.

### Postsecondary Training

To become a naturopathic physician, you must first complete a premed undergraduate program before pursuing the graduate degree Doctor of Naturopathic Medicine (ND, or sometimes NMD). Your undergraduate courses should include those of a typical premed curriculum, including biology, inorganic chemistry, and organic chemistry. Courses in nutrition and psychology are also important. You should contact the accredited naturopathic colleges as early as possible to ensure that you complete the courses required by the school of your choice.

When you're searching for a naturopathic medical school, find one that's accredited and offers the Doctor of Naturopathic Medicine degree. Schools without accreditation offer correspondence courses and may offer certificates. Only a degree from an accredited school, however, will prepare you to become a licensed naturopath. There are only six naturopathic schools in the United States and Canada accredited by the Council on Naturopathic Medical Education. They are Bastyr University, Kenmore, Washington (http://www.bastyr. edu); the National College of Natural Medicine, Portland, Oregon (http://www.ncnm.edu); the Southwest College of Naturopathic Medicine and Health Sciences, Tempe, Arizona (http://www.scnm.edu); the University of Bridgeport College of Naturopathic Medicine, Bridgeport, Connecticut (http://www.bridgeport.edu/naturopathy); the Canadian College of Naturopathic Medicine, Toronto, Ontario, Canada (http://www.ccnm.edu); the Boucher Institute of Naturopathic Medicine, New Westminster, British Columbia, Canada (http://www.binm.org). The National University of Health Sciences, Lombard, Illinois (http://www.nuhs.edu) has been granted candidacy status. Candidacy status does not ensure accreditation, but it is an important initial step toward it.

The naturopathic doctoral degree is a four-year program requiring courses in anatomy, physiology, biochemistry, and other basic medical sciences. Students must also take courses in nutrition, botanical medicine, homeopathy, naturopathic obstetrics, psychological medicine, and minor surgery. In addition to course instruction, students receive extensive clinical training.

If you are not interested in completing the ND or NMD degree, other postsecondary training is available. The American Naturopathic Medical Accreditation Board's Web site (http://www.anmab.org) can provide you with information on correspondence and resident programs. These programs, however, do not typically have the broad medical background of ND programs, and those educated in this way do not meet requirements in states with licensing regulations.

## Certification or Licensing

To practice medicine as a naturopathic physician, you must be licensed in the state in which you practice. Currently licensing is available in 14 states—Alaska, Arizona, California, Connecticut, Hawaii, Idaho, Kansas, Maine, Montana, New Hampshire, Oregon, Utah, Vermont, and Washington—as well as in Puerto Rico, the Virgin Islands, and the District of Columbia. Minnesota will begin licensing in June 2009. While Florida does have a few licensed naturopaths, the state stopped granting new licenses in the 1960s. As the public's awareness of this field grows and as it becomes more popular, more and more states are considering setting licensing requirements. The AANP also promotes licensure and is working to have statutes regulating the profession in all 50 states by 2010. All state licenses are contingent upon passing the Naturopathic Physicians Licensing Examinations (NPLEX), a standardized test for all naturopathic physicians in North America. As this field of health care continues to gain wide acceptance, the number of licensed states is expected to grow. To maintain their licenses in naturopathic medicine, NDs are required to complete a certain amount of continuing education throughout their professional lives.

Naturopathic physicians who practice in unlicensed states are not allowed to practice as physicians. They can still use their skills and knowledge to help people improve their lives, but they usually limit their practices to homeopathy or nutritional counseling.

The American Naturopathic Medical Association (ANMA) is not in favor of licensure. This group is composed of a broader range of naturopaths, including those who do not hold ND degrees, those who have gotten their education through correspondence programs, and those who believe naturopathy treatments should involve only natural methods and nonprescription substances. Instead of licensure, the ANMA offers and promotes certification through its American Naturopathic Certification Board. Certification is available at two levels, based on education and experience, and it requires passing a written examination. Continuing education is needed to keep current certification.

## Other Requirements

A primary requirement for a successful naturopath is a strong desire to help people improve their lives. You must also have a fundamental belief in the whole-person approach to healing. Because counseling plays such an important role in treatment, naturopathic physicians need excellent listening and communication skills. Keen powers of observation and good decision-making abilities are essential to accurate medical assessment. Like other medical professions, naturopathy

## Potential Career Paths

After graduating from accredited training programs, naturopaths have a variety of career paths available to them, including the following:

- Primary care physician
- Research scientist
- College professor
- Natural pharmacist
- Wellness educator
- Public health administrator
- Research and development scientist
- Consultant to industry, public service, insurance companies, political, and other organizations

Source: Association of Accredited Naturopathic Medical Colleges

requires a commitment to lifelong learning. Idealism and a firm belief in the efficacy of natural approaches to medicine are important. You must have the courage of your convictions and be willing to stand up for your beliefs. Naturopathy has become much more respected within the medical profession in recent years, but it is still not accepted by some conventional doctors.

## EXPLORING

Do some reading on the history and practice of naturopathy. You can visit the National Center for Complementary and Alternative Medicine's Web site (http://nccam.nih.gov) to learn about developments in the field of naturopathy and other alternative medicines.

Make an appointment for a medical checkup with a naturopathic physician. Find out what the practice of naturopathy is like, and think about whether you would like to practice medicine this way. Ask a naturopath to talk with you about the field. Perhaps that person will be willing to be a mentor for you.

Visit the naturopathic colleges that interest you. Sit in on classes. Talk to students about their experiences. Find out what they like and what they don't like. Talk to the faculty and learn about their approaches to teaching. Ask what they see as the best opportunities in the field.

## EMPLOYERS

More than 3,000 naturopathic doctors are employed in the United States. Most naturopaths go into private or group practice. A few NDs find positions in natural health clinics. Due to the small number of accredited doctoral programs, only a very small percentage of naturopaths become teachers. The federal government is encouraging research into the efficacy of alternative health care approaches. More research opportunities are becoming available, and an increasing number of naturopaths are pursuing this aspect of the profession. The thriving natural food industry is providing more opportunities for naturopaths as consultants. The majority of NDs work in the states that license them; however, naturopathic physicians can be found throughout the country.

## STARTING OUT

The career services office of the naturopathic college you attend can help you in searching for that first job. Join professional organizations, attend meetings, and get to know people in your field. Networking is one of the most powerful ways of finding a new position. Get to know professionals in other areas of alternative health care. As other alternative health care modalities expand, they will be more likely to include naturopaths in alternative clinics.

As a newly licensed naturopathic physician, you might begin working on a salary or income-sharing basis in a clinic or in an established practice with another naturopath or other health care professional. This would allow you to start practicing without the major financial investment of equipping an office. You might be able to purchase the practice of an ND who is retiring or moving. This is usually easier than starting a new solo practice because the practice will already have patients. However, some newly licensed practitioners do start immediately in private practice.

## ADVANCEMENT

Because most naturopaths work in private or group practice, advancement frequently depends on the physician's dedication to building a patient base. NDs in private practice need a general sense of how to run a successful business. They must promote their practices within the community and develop a network of contacts with conventional medical doctors or other alternative practitioners who may refer patients to them.

Some naturopaths advance by starting their own clinics with other naturopaths or with other alternative health practitioners. In any medical field, learning is lifelong, and many naturopaths derive a sense of professional satisfaction from keeping up on changes in allopathic medicine and in natural health research. A few very experienced NDs write textbooks or become professors at the accredited universities. With the growing government interest in research into natural health care, more naturopathic physicians will find opportunities for advancement as researchers.

## EARNINGS

Most naturopaths can make a comfortable living in private practice, but generally naturopathic medicine is not as financially rewarding as some other branches of medicine. Financial success as a naturopath requires dedication to building a practice and promoting natural health treatment. Although a well-established naturopath in an urban area may make about $200,000 a year, most earn less. A beginning naturopath may have an annual income of around $20,000 to $30,000. After some years of practice, NDs generally earn between $60,000 and $80,000 per year, according to the Association of Accredited

Naturopathic Medical Colleges. NDs who run their own practices take their earnings once expenses such as rent or mortgages, insurance premiums, equipment costs, and staff salaries have been paid. For an example of the difference between a clinic's income and that of the ND, consider an established practice in Seattle, Washington, advertised for sale on the Canadian College of Naturopathic Medicine Web site (http://www.ccnm.edu). The clinic's gross receipts were listed as $250,000+, but the ND could expect to earn much less, with a net income listed as $90,000 per year.

Income also depends on such factors as the size and geographic location of a practice. In states that license NDs, the population is typically more interested in natural health. In those states, naturopaths may have larger practices than in states that do not license, and thus they have higher incomes.

Since most naturopathic physicians are in private practice, they must provide their own benefits. Those who are employed by universities, research institutes, or clinics run by others may receive benefits, such as vacation and sick pay, insurance, and contributions to retirement accounts.

## WORK ENVIRONMENT

Naturopathic physicians work in clean, quiet, comfortable offices. Most solo practitioners and group practices have an office suite. The suite generally has a reception area. In clinics, several professionals may share this area. The suite also contains examining rooms and treatment rooms. In a clinic where several professionals work, there sometimes are separate offices for the individual professionals. Many naturopaths have an assistant or office staff. Those who are in private practices or partnerships need to have good business skills and self-discipline to be successful.

Naturopaths who work in clinics, research settings, or universities need to work well in a group environment. They frequently work under supervision or in a team with other professionals. They may have offices of their own, or they may share offices with team members, depending on the facility. In these organizations, the physical work environment varies, but it will generally be clean and comfortable. Because they are larger, these settings may be noisier than the smaller practices.

Most naturopathic physicians work about 42 hours per week, although many put in longer hours. Larger organizations may determine the hours of work, but NDs in private practice can set their own hours. Evening and weekend hours are sometimes scheduled to accommodate patients' needs.

# OUTLOOK

While the U.S. Bureau of Labor Statistics does not provide specific information on the employment outlook for naturopathic physicians, it does project overall employment in the field of health care occupations to grow much faster than the average for all industries over the next several years.

As public interest in alternative health care grows, many health-conscious individuals are attracted to naturopathy because of its natural, holistic, preventive approach. Additionally, the average life span is increasing. As a result, the number of older people is also increasing. The elderly frequently have more health care needs, and the growth of this segment of the population is likely to increase the demand for NDs who provide personalized and attentive care. Another sign that the future is bright for naturopaths is the growing number of insurance policies that provide coverage for alternative health care services. Coverage still varies according to the insurer, but in states where NDs are licensed, more companies are paying for their services.

All of these factors should contribute to the employment of naturopathic physicians to grow faster than the average in the 21st century. According to Robert Lofft, former executive director of the Council on Naturopathic Medical Education, "NDs are in great demand. Many cannot accept any more patients. The demand is outpacing the supply." While the demand for naturopathy is increasing, college enrollments are also growing. New NDs may find increasing competition in geographic areas where other practitioners are already located.

# FOR MORE INFORMATION

*For information about naturopathic medicine, accredited schools, and state licensing status, contact*

**American Association of Naturopathic Physicians**
4435 Wisconsin Avenue, NW, Suite 403
Washington, DC 20016-1851
Tel: 202-237-8150
Email: member.services@naturopathic.org
http://www.naturopathic.org

*For information on certification, contact*

**American Naturopathic Certification Board**
101 East Broadway, Suite 415
Missoula, MT 59802-4510
Tel: 406-543-6154
Email: info@ancb.net
http://www.ancb.net

*For information on accredited programs and education, contact*
**American Naturopathic Medical Accreditation Board**
2035 East Windmill Lane, Suite B
Las Vegas, NV 89123-2077
Tel: 702-914-5770
Email: info@anmab.org
http://www.anmab.org

*For more information on the ANMA, approved schools, and certification, contact*
**American Naturopathic Medical Association (ANMA)**
PO Box 96273
Las Vegas, NV 89193-6273
Tel: 702-897-7053
http://www.anma.org

*For information on accredited educational programs, contact*
**Association of Naturopathic Medical Colleges**
4435 Wisconsin Avenue, NW, Suite 403
Washington, DC 20016-1851
Tel: 866-538-2267
Email: info@aanmc.org
http://www.aanmc.org

*For general information and information on accreditation of naturopathic colleges, contact*
**Council on Naturopathic Medical Education**
PO Box 178
Great Barrington, MA 01230-0178
Tel: 413-528-8877
Email: staff@cnme.org
http://www.cnme.org

*For more information on alternative medicines, contact*
**National Center for Complementary and Alternative Medicine**
9000 Rockville Pike
Bethesda, MD 20892-0001
Email: info@nccam.nih.gov
http://nccam.nih.gov

*For comprehensive Internet information on alternative and conventional health care and extensive links, visit*
**HealthWorld Online**
http://www.healthy.net

# INTERVIEW

*Kristina Conner, ND, is an instructor in naturopathic medicine at the National University of Health Sciences (http://www.nuhs.edu) in Lombard, Illinois. She discussed her career with the editors of* Careers in Focus: Complementary and Alternative Health Care.

**Q. How long have you worked as an ND? Please tell us about your practice and your work as an educator.**

**A.** I graduated from naturopathic school seven years ago. Since then, I have been working as a naturopathic physician in private practice or academics. I completed a residency at the University of Bridgeport College of Naturopathic Medicine, then continued to work there as clinic coordinator and clinical faculty. I spent some time in private practice before starting my current position. I am a faculty member at the National University of Health Sciences—the newest accredited program for naturopathic medicine. I teach in the subject areas of naturopathic counseling, hydrotherapy, homeopathy, primary care, nutrition, and naturopathic foundations.

**Q. What is one thing that young people may not know about a career in naturopathy?**

**A.** One thing young people may not realize are all of the options possible in the field of naturopathic medicine. A big misconception among the public is that we are not "real" doctors, only useful to certain people or conditions. Despite the fact that we are licensed as physicians in only 14 states, the District of Columbia, Puerto Rico, and the U.S. Virgin Islands, all naturopathic training is comprehensive and rigorous. And naturopathic medicine is a very diverse field, and becoming more so every day. Naturopathic physicians treat a wide range of patients who have all types of conditions. Although naturopathic medicine by itself is not always curative for a given condition, it can always play a role in achieving and maintaining health.

**Q. What are some of the pros and cons of your job?**

**A.** A large pro for me in my position is the opportunity to help patients at a fundamental level, to restore health and practice true preventative medicine. Through teaching, I am able to assist students in their transition to physician-hood. By doing this, I am able to impact a large number of people, thinking of all the patients that those students will serve when they are practicing.

The biggest challenge as an ND is there are few of us in a still-developing profession. This is both frustrating and exciting to be a part of. Yet, we have made a large impact in the competitive health care world, while we rapidly grow in numbers and become more organized.

**Q. How did you train for this field?**

**A.** I have an undergraduate degree in liberal arts, which I believe is excellent training for medicine. Since I do not have a science degree, I needed to complete some science prerequisites separately. I attended Bastyr University for my doctorate degree in naturopathic medicine. Then I completed my residency in family and integrated medicine. I find that the training never really ends, though, as there is always something new to learn.

**Q. What advice would you give to young people who are interested in the field?**

**A.** First, I would commend any student interested in the field, since that shows independent thinking, something our healthcare system desperately needs. Then I would recommend that a student obtain an undergraduate degree that encourages that type of thought; a well-educated person makes an excellent naturopathic doctor. Next, I would encourage the student to learn about naturopathic medicine by becoming a patient, speaking with practitioners, and reading publications about naturopathic medicine or written by naturopathic doctors. Visit naturopathic schools and see which one is right for you. And finally, follow your heart—if you love and respect naturopathic medicine, you will be successful as a practitioner.

**Q. What is the future employment outlook for naturopathy?**

**A.** The future employment outlook is excellent for naturopathic medicine, as the public demand grows for individualized, natural approaches to reach and maintain a healthy lifestyle. This is especially true in areas where there are few NDs despite the need, like here in Illinois and many other Midwestern states. And in states with many NDs, such as Washington, Oregon, and Arizona, we are becoming an even more integral part of the health care system. The opportunities for naturopathic physicians are numerous, including private practice, integrative practice, research, academics, consultation, and public health.

# Nurse-Midwives

## OVERVIEW

*Nurse-midwives* are registered nurses with advanced training who assist in family planning, pregnancy, and childbirth. They also provide routine health care for women. Nurse-midwives work in hospitals, with physicians in private practice, in freestanding birth centers or well-woman care centers, in women's clinics, and even in the homes of clients. There are more than 11,000 nurse-midwives in the United States.

## HISTORY

Women have been giving birth by natural methods for thousands of years, since pain medication, hospitals, and medical intervention were largely unavailable until recent years. Women gave birth at home, guided by other women who were designated assistants, or midwives. *Midwife* means "with woman," and early midwives, like today's professional nurse-midwives, coached mothers-to-be through their pregnancy and labor. They helped women deliver their babies and taught new mothers how to care for their infants.

In the early 1900s, however, birth was transformed from a natural event into a technological marvel. New pain medications and medical procedures took birth into the 20th century, and childbearing moved from home to hospital. Back then, midwives practiced mainly in rural areas where doctors were unavailable, or where poorer women could not afford to deliver in a hospital.

Ironically, as these medically assisted births became more prevalent in America, professional midwifery became more regulated than it had been in the past. In the early 1920s, nurse Mary Breckenridge founded the Frontier Nursing Service in eastern Kentucky to bring medical services to people in areas too poor for hospitals, as well as to women who could not afford to have their babies delivered by a high-priced doctor. After completing her midwifery training in England, Breckenridge made prenatal care an additional focus of her service.

Midwife care around the world was proving itself to be both low in cost and high in quality. The Maternity Association and the Lobenstine Clinic (both in New York) established the first U.S. midwifery school and graduated its first class in 1933. In the mid-1930s, the Frontier Nursing Service opened its own nurse-midwifery school, and it remains today the oldest continuing U.S. midwifery program.

During the next few decades, most women who were able to deliver in a hospital preferred the lull of pain medication and the perceived safety of the medical establishment, and midwifery remained a tool of poor and rural women. Pregnancy and childbirth were considered medical procedures best left in the hands of obstetricians and gynecologists. Both the medical community and the public have generally frowned upon midwifery in favor of doctors and hospitals.

Since the 1960s, however, this attitude has been changing as more women insist on more natural methods of giving birth. In 1968, the American College of Nurse-Midwives (ACNM), the premier midwife organization in the United States, was established. This creation of a nationally standardized entity to regulate midwife training and practice introduced midwifery as a positive, healthy, and safe alternative to hospital births. The nurse-midwife, officially known as a *certified nurse-midwife* (CNM), has gradually become accepted as a respected member of the health care teams involved with family planning, pregnancy, and labor.

A number of studies have indicated that babies delivered by nurse-midwives are less likely to experience low birth weights and other health complications than babies delivered by physicians. In fact, a recent study from the National Center for Health Statistics, Centers for Disease Control and Prevention, indicates that the risk of death for the baby during birth was 19 percent lower for CNM-assisted deliveries than for physician-attended births.

The proven safety standards of births attended by nurse-midwives, the cost-effectiveness of a CNM-assisted pregnancy and labor, and the personal touch that many women get from their nurse-midwives will ensure that CNMs become vital links between traditional birthing practices and the high-tech worlds of today and tomorrow.

## THE JOB

Nurse-midwives examine pregnant women and monitor the growth and development of fetuses. Typically a nurse-midwife is responsible for all phases of a normal pregnancy, including prenatal care, assisting during labor, and providing follow-up care. A nurse-midwife always works in consultation with a physician, who can be called upon should complications arise during pregnancy or childbirth. Nurse-midwives can provide emergency assistance to their patients while physicians are called. In most states, nurse-midwives are authorized to prescribe and administer medications. Many nurse-midwives provide the full spectrum of women's health care, including regular gynecological exams and well-woman care.

Not all midwives are certified nurse-midwives. Most states recognize other categories of midwives, including direct-entry (or licensed) midwives, certified professional midwives, and lay (or empirical) midwives.

*Direct-entry midwives* are not required to be nurses in order to practice as midwives. They typically assist in home births or at birthing centers and are trained through a combination of formal education, apprenticeship, and self-education. Direct-entry midwives are legally recognized in 29 states that offer licensing, certification, or registration programs, and they perform most of the services of CNMs. Although they generally have professional relationships with physicians, hospitals, and laboratories to provide support and emergency services, few direct-entry midwives actually practice in medical centers. Direct-entry midwives can receive the certified midwife designation from the American College of Nurse-Midwives in recognition of their professional abilities.

*Certified professional midwives* (CPMs) must meet the basic requirements of the North American Registry of Midwives (NARM). Potential CPMs must pass a written examination and an assessment of their skills, and they must have proven training assisting in out-of-hospital births. The NARM accepts various midwifery programs and practical apprenticeship as a basis for certification.

*Lay midwives* usually train by apprenticing with established midwives, although some may acquire formal education as well. Lay midwives are not certified or licensed, either because they lack the necessary experience and education or because they pursue nontraditional childbirth techniques. Many lay midwives practice only as part of religious communities or specific ethnic groups, and they typically assist only in home birth situations. Some states have made it illegal for lay midwives to charge for their services.

Since the education and certification standards for direct-entry midwives, certified professional midwives, and lay midwives vary from state to state, the rest of this article will deal only with certified nurse-midwives, who must complete a core nursing curriculum—as well as midwifery training—to become midwives. When the terms "nurse-midwife" and "midwife" are used in this article, certified nurse-midwife is implied.

Deborah Woolley has been a registered nurse since 1975 and has been practicing as a nurse-midwife since 1983. For Woolley, midwifery offered her the opportunity to have a positive impact on women's health care and childbirth experiences. "I started out as a nurse assigned to the labor and delivery unit. But I became frustrated with the type of care the women were getting," Woolley says. "You'll find that a lot among midwives. Most of the midwives I talk to can point to an event that was the straw that broke the camel's back, as it were—when they realized that they wanted to have more influence over the experience the woman is having. Midwifery's focus is on improving conditions for women and their families. In a way, midwifery is a radical departure from the old way of looking at pregnancy."

Woolley typically arrives at the hospital at 7:00 A.M. and spends the first hour or more seeing patients in postpartum—that is, women who have given birth the day or night before. At about 8:30 A.M., Woolley goes down to the clinic to begin seeing other patients. "I work a combination of full days and half-days during the week. On a half-day, I'll see patients for four hours and work on paperwork for one hour. On a full day, I'll see patients for eight hours and work on paperwork for two hours," she says. "But that doesn't mean I always leave exactly at five o'clock. At the clinic, we see everyone who shows up."

After Woolley meets a new patient, she'll spend an hour or so taking the patient's medical history, examining her, and getting her scheduled into the prenatal care system. "I also ask about a patient's life. I spend time with the patient and try to get to know her and what's going on in her life. It makes a big difference in the care she's provided. I think one of the things that makes midwives so effective is that they really get to know their patients."

An important part of a nurse-midwife's work is the education of patients. Nurse-midwives teach their patients about proper nutrition and fitness for healthy pregnancies and about different techniques for labor and delivery. Nurse-midwives also counsel their patients in the postpartum period about breast-feeding, parenting, and other areas concerning the health of mother and child. Nurse-midwives provide counseling on several other issues, including sexually transmitted diseases, spousal and child abuse, and social support networks. In some cases, this counseling may extend to family members of the soon-to-be or new mother, or even to older siblings of the family's newest addition. Woolley believes that this education is one of a midwife's key responsibilities. "I spend a lot of time teaching things like nutrition, the process of fetal development, and basic parenting skills. I'll refer patients to Lamaze classes. I'll also screen patients for family problems, such as violence in the home, and teach them how to get out of abusive situations," Woolley says. "In other words, I'll teach a patient anything she needs to know if she's pregnant. I try to empower women to take charge of their own health care and their own lives."

Apart from seeing patients, Woolley is also responsible for maintaining patient records. "I have to review lab results and ultrasounds and fill out birth certificates—things like that," she says. "There's a lot of writing involved, too. I have to document everything that I do with patients, including what I've done and how and why I've done it." This may include recording patient information, filing documents and patient charts, doing research to find out why a woman is having a particular problem, and consulting with physicians and other medical personnel. Many midwives build close relationships with their patients and try to be available for their patients at any time of the day or night.

## REQUIREMENTS

### High School
In high school, you should begin preparing for a career as a nurse-midwife by taking a broad range of college preparatory courses, with a focus on science classes. Anatomy, biology, and chemistry will give you solid background information for what you will be studying in college. Additional classes in sociology and psychology will help you learn how to deal with a variety of patients from different ethnic and economic groups. English and business classes will teach you how to deal with the paperwork involved in any profession. Finally, you should consider learning foreign languages if you want to serve as a midwife to immigrant communities.

### Postsecondary Training
All CNMs begin their careers as registered nurses. The two most common ways to become a registered nurse are to get a bachelor's degree in nursing from an accredited four-year program or to get an associate's degree in nursing from an accredited two-year program. When you are choosing an undergraduate school to attend, however, keep in mind that a bachelor's degree in nursing is required for entry into most certificate or graduate degree programs in nurse-midwifery. Bachelor's degrees are also usually required for those who want to advance into supervisory or administrative positions or hold jobs in public health agencies.

After you have completed your undergraduate education and passed the licensing exam to become a registered nurse, you can apply to nurse-midwifery programs. There are currently 39 nurse-midwifery and midwifery programs that are accredited by the American College of Nurse-Midwives (ACNM). A certificate program typically requires nine to 12 months of study. Graduate programs that result in master's degrees usually take 16–24 months to complete, and some also require one year of clinical experience in order to earn a nurse-midwife degree. In these programs, the prospective nurse-midwife is trained to provide primary care services, gynecological care, preconception and prenatal care, labor delivery and management, and postpartum and infant care. Doctorate degrees (such as a Doctor of Nursing Practice) are typically required for those who want to work in top levels of administration, in research, or in education. These degrees normally take four to five years to complete. Approximately 68 percent of CNMs have a master's degree, according to the ACNM.

By 2010, all graduates of midwifery education programs will be required to have a master's degree in order to be able to take the national certifying exam offered by the American Midwifery Certification Board.

Procedures that nurse-midwives are trained to perform include physical examinations, pap smears, and episiotomies. They may also repair incisions from cesarean sections, administer anesthesia, and prescribe medications. Nurse-midwives are trained to provide counseling on subjects such as nutrition, breast-feeding, and infant care. Nurse-midwives learn to provide both physical and emotional support to pregnant women and their families.

## Certification or Licensing

After earning either a midwifery certificate from a nationally accredited nurse-midwifery program or a master's degree in midwifery, midwives are required to take a national examination administered by the American Midwifery Certification Board. Upon passing the exam, the new midwife achieves full endorsement as a medical professional, as well as the title certified nurse-midwife. Those who have passed this examination are licensed to practice nurse-midwifery in all 50 states. Each state, however, has its own laws and regulations governing the activities and responsibilities of nurse-midwives.

Nurse-midwives must meet the same licensing requirements as registered nurses.

## Other Requirements

If you are interested in becoming a nurse-midwife, you will need skills that aren't necessarily taught in midwifery programs. Nurse-midwives need to enjoy working with people, learning about their patients' needs, and helping them through a very important life change. They should be sympathetic to the needs of their patients.

## Books to Read

Canfield, Jack, Mark Victor Hansen, and LeAnn Thieman. *Chicken Soup for the Nurse's Soul, Second Dose: More Stories to Honor and Inspire Nurses.* Santa Barbara, Calif.: Chicken Soup for the Soul, 2007.

Davis, Elizabeth, Linda Harrison, and Suzanne Arms. *Heart & Hands: A Midwife's Guide to Pregnancy & Birth.* 4th ed. Berkeley, Calif.: Celestial Arts, 2004.

Singingtree, Daphne. *Birthsong Midwifery Workbook.* 5th ed. Eugene, Oreg.: Eagletree Press, 2007.

Thibeault, Stephanie. *Stressed Out About Nursing School! An Insider's Guide to Success.* 2d ed. Marblehead, Mass.: HCPro Inc., 2006.

Varney Burst, Helen. *Varney's Midwifery.* 4th ed. Sudbury, Mass.: Jones and Bartlett Publishers, 2004.

They need to be independent and able to accept responsibility for their actions and decisions. Strong observation skills are key, as nurse-midwives must be tuned into their patients' needs during pregnancy and labor. Nurse-midwives also need to listen well and respond appropriately. They must communicate effectively with patients, family members, physicians, and other hospital staff, as well as insurance company personnel. Finally, nurse-midwives should be confident and composed, responding well in an emergency and keeping their patients calm.

## EXPLORING

Volunteer work at your local hospital or clinic may put you in contact with nurse-midwives who can help you learn more about midwifery. You might also volunteer to visit and offer emotional support to laboring mothers-to-be at a hospital or birth center.

You may wish to contact a professional midwifery organization for more information about the field. These associations often publish journals or newsletters to keep members informed of new issues in midwifery. The better-known organizations may have Web sites that can give you more information about midwifery in your area. A list of some organizations is provided at the end of this article.

Finally, young women may wish to see a nurse-midwife in lieu of a physician for their well-woman care. Although nurse-midwives are usually thought of in conjunction with pregnancy, many women use

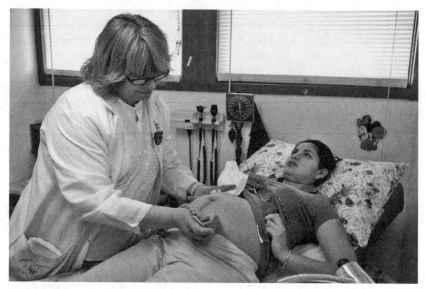

A certified nurse-midwife performs an abdominal exam on a patient.
(Matt Rourke, AP Photo)

nurse-midwives as their primary medical contact from their teenage years through menopause.

## EMPLOYERS

There are more than 11,000 nurse-midwives in the United States. More than half work primarily in an office or clinic environment, and physician practices and hospitals are the places where most CNMs are employed. At hospitals, CNMs see patients and attend deliveries on hospital grounds and use hospital-owned equipment for examinations and other procedures. Additional medical personnel are always available for emergency situations. Other nurse-midwives work in family planning clinics and other health care clinics and privately funded agencies. These nurse-midwives usually have relationships with specific hospitals and physicians in case of an emergency. Finally, some nurse-midwives operate their own clinics and birthing centers, while others work independently and specialize in home birth deliveries.

## STARTING OUT

Deborah Woolley earned a bachelor's degree in nursing and then began her career as a nurse at a labor and delivery unit in a Texas hospital. While working, she attended graduate school and earned a master's degree in maternal child nursing. She then went to Chicago, where she began training as a nurse-midwife. "After earning my nurse-midwifery degree," Woolley says, "I heard there were openings at Cook County Hospital [now known as John H. Stroger Jr. Hospital of Cook County] here in Chicago. So I applied for a job there. What I liked about Cook County was that they continued to train me while I was working. They gave me assertiveness training and training in urban health issues."

Like Woolley, most nurse-midwives finish their formal education in nursing and midwifery before beginning work. They usually have some opportunities to work with patients as a student. Beginning midwives may also intern at a hospital or clinic to fulfill class requirements.

Nurse-midwives can begin their careers in various ways. Some may move from an internship to a full-time job when they complete their education requirements at a certain facility. Others may seek out a position through a professional midwifery organization or try for a job at a specific location that interests them. Finally, some nurse-midwives begin by working as nurses in other areas of health care and then move into midwifery as opportunities become available.

The American College of Nurse-Midwives offers an online career center for midwives (http://www.MidwifeJobs.com) that allows job candidates to post their resumes and search job listings.

## ADVANCEMENT

With experience, a nurse-midwife can advance into a supervisory role or into an administrative capacity at a hospital, family planning clinic, birthing center, or other facility. Many nurse-midwives, like Deborah Woolley, choose to continue their education and complete Ph.D. programs. With a doctorate, a nurse-midwife can do research or teaching. "I spent four-and-a-half years at Cook County while I was working on my Ph.D.," Woolley says. "From there I was recruited to Colorado to head up the midwifery unit at a hospital there. After six years as a director in Colorado, I learned that the director's position here at the University of Illinois-Chicago was open, and I jumped at the chance to come back to Chicago."

Nurse-midwives with advanced degrees may choose to move away from the day-to-day patient care and write for journals or magazines. They may also lean more toward the research aspects of prenatal care and obstetrics. Finally, nurse-midwives may prefer to apply their experience and education as a midwife toward other areas of medicine or hospital administration.

# EARNINGS

Certified nurse-midwives who work for large hospitals tend to earn more than those working for small hospitals, clinics, and birthing centers. The most experienced nurse-midwives, including those in supervisory, director, and administrative positions, have the highest earnings. Salaries also vary according to the region of the country and whether the employing facility is private or public. Because of their special training, CNMs are among the higher paying nursing professions. According to Salary.com, certified nurse-midwives earned salaries that ranged from less than $71,881 to $99,153 or more in 2008. Median annual earnings for certified nurse-midwives were $85,945.

Nurse-midwives generally enjoy a good benefits package, although these too can vary widely depending on employer. Those working in hospitals or well-established clinics or birthing centers usually receive a full complement of benefits, including medical coverage, paid sick time, and holiday and vacation pay. They may also be able to work a more flexible schedule to accommodate family or personal obligations.

# WORK ENVIRONMENT

Nurse-midwives who work in hospitals or as part of a physician's practice work indoors in clean, professional surroundings. Although most nurse-midwives perform checkups and routine visits alone with their patients, a number of other health care professionals are on hand in case the midwife has a question or needs assistance in an emergency. Nurse-midwives often consult with doctors, medical insurance representatives, and family members of their patients, as well as other midwives in order to determine the best care routine for the women they serve.

In a hospital, nurse-midwives usually wear professional clothing, a lab coat, and comfortable shoes to allow for plenty of running around during the day. They often wear hospital scrubs during delivery. In a freestanding birth center, the nurse-midwives may have a more casual dress code but still maintain a professional demeanor.

Midwives try to make their offices and birthing areas as calm and as reassuring as possible so their patients feel comfortable during checkups and delivery. Soft music may play in the background, or the waiting area may be decorated like a nursery and filled with parenting magazines.

Although most nurse-midwives work a 40-hour week, these hours may not reflect the typical nine-to-five day, since babies are delivered at all hours of the day and night. Many hospitals or clinics offer nurse-midwives a more flexible schedule in exchange for having them "on-call" for births.

Finally, although there are no gender requirements in the profession, nurse-midwifery is a field dominated by women. Approximately 98 percent of nurse-midwives in the United States are female. Women have traditionally helped each other through pregnancy and delivery. Just as women who became doctors 100 years ago had to overcome many barriers, men considering entering midwifery should be prepared for hurdles of their own.

## OUTLOOK

The U.S. Department of Labor predicts employment for all registered nurses to grow much faster than the average for all careers through 2016, and this should be especially true for specialists. As certified nurse-midwives gain a reputation as highly trained and compassionate professionals, they will become an integral part of the health care community. According to the ACNM, the number of births in the United States attended by midwives rose from 4 percent in 1986 to 11.2 percent in 2005. Currently, there are more positions than there are nurse-midwives to fill them.

There are two factors driving the demand for nurse-midwives. The first element is the growth of interest in natural childbearing techniques among women. The number of midwife-assisted births has risen dramatically since the 1970s. Some women have been attracted to midwifery because of studies that indicate natural childbirth is more healthful for mother and child than doctor-assisted childbirth. Other women have been attracted to midwifery because it emphasizes the participation of the entire family in prenatal care and labor.

The second factor in the growing demand for nurse-midwives is economic. As society moves toward managed care programs and the health care community emphasizes cost-effectiveness, midwifery should increase in popularity. This is because the care provided by nurse-midwives costs substantially less than the care provided by obstetricians and gynecologists. If the cost advantage of midwifery continues, more insurers and health maintenance organizations will probably direct patients to nurse-midwives for care.

## FOR MORE INFORMATION

*For a listing of accredited nursing programs, contact*
**American Association of Colleges of Nursing**
One Dupont Circle, NW, Suite 530
Washington, DC 20036-1135

Tel: 202-463-6930
Email: ccrowell@aacn.nche.edu
http://www.aacn.nche.edu

*This organization is the largest and most widely known midwifery organization in the United States. The ACNM accredits midwifery programs. For more information on the career and education of nurse-midwives, visit the ACNM's Web site.*
**American College of Nurse-Midwives (ACNM)**
8403 Colesville Road, Suite 1550
Silver Spring, MD 20910-6374
Tel: 240-485-1800
http://www.acnm.org

*The AMCB is the national certifying body for nurse-midwives. For more information on the certification process, contact*
**American Midwifery Certification Board (AMCB)**
849 International Drive, Suite 205
Linthicum, MD 21090-2228
Tel: 866-366-9632
http://www.amebmidwife.org

*The following organization can provide information about all types of midwifery:*
**Midwives Alliance of North America**
611 Pennsylvania Avenue, SE, #1700
Washington, DC 20003-4303
Tel: 888-923-6262
Email: info@mana.org
http://www.mana.org

# Oriental Medicine Practitioners

## OVERVIEW

*Oriental medicine practitioners,* or *OM practitioners,* are health care professionals who practice a variety of health care therapies that are part of the ancient healing system of Oriental medicine. Oriental medicine is a comprehensive system of health care. It includes several major modalities: acupuncture, Chinese herbology, Oriental bodywork or massage, exercise, and dietary therapy. Each of these major areas has numerous variations, but all forms are based on traditional Oriental medicine principles. A practitioner may practice one or many of the therapies of Oriental medicine.

More than one-third of the world's population relies on Oriental medicine practitioners for the enhancement of health and for prevention and treatment of disease. In the West, Oriental medicine is rapidly growing in popularity as an alternative health care system. There are more than 14,000 Oriental medicine/acupuncture practitioners in the United States.

## HISTORY

Traditional Chinese medicine (TCM) has more than 3,000 years of clinical history. The basic principles of TCM were first recorded in the Yellow Emperor's *Classic of Internal Medicine (Huang Di Nei Ching)* in China approximately 2,300 years ago. Traditional Chinese medicine practitioners continually applied, developed, and refined those principles for centuries.

Oriental medicine is based on an energetic model of health that is fundamentally different from the biochemical model of Western medi-

## QUICK FACTS

**School Subjects**
Biology
Business
Psychology

**Personal Skills**
Helping/teaching
Technical/scientific

**Work Environment**
Primarily indoors
Primarily one location

**Minimum Education Level**
Some postsecondary training

**Salary Range**
$15,000 to $45,000 to
$200,000+

**Certification or Licensing**
Required by certain states

**Outlook**
Faster than the average

**DOT**
N/A

**GOE**
N/A

**NOC**
3232

**O*NET-SOC**
N/A

cine. The ancient Chinese recognized a vital energy that they believed to be the animating force behind all life. They called this life force *qi* (pronounced "chee"). They discovered that the body's qi flows along specific channels—called meridians—in the body. Each meridian is related to a particular physiological system and internal organ. When the body's qi is unbalanced, or when the flow of qi along the channels is blocked or disrupted, disease, pain, and other physical and emotional conditions result. The fundamental purpose of all forms of Oriental medicine is to restore and maintain balance in the body's qi.

As traditional Chinese medicine spread gradually throughout Southeast Asia, each culture adapted the principles of TCM to its own healing methods. The Japanese, Koreans, and other Asian peoples contributed to the development of the ancient Chinese principles and developed their own variations. In recognition of the contributions of many Asian cultures, TCM is now referred to as traditional Oriental medicine (TOM), or simply Oriental medicine (OM).

Since the advent of quantum physics, the Western world has developed a new interest in and appreciation for the bioenergetic model of health of the Oriental world. Western physics is generating a new science of resonance and energy fields that proposes that a person is more a "resonating field" than a substance. Oriental medicine is completely consistent with this concept.

Oriental medicine practitioners are increasingly consulted in Europe, North America, and Russia for general maintenance of health, treatment of disease, and relief of pain. Since the 1970s, acupuncture and Oriental medicine have been among the fastest growing forms of health care in the United States. During the last decade of the 20th century, the increasing interest in alternative medicine in the United States and throughout the world brought Oriental medicine practitioners to the forefront of the field of alternative health care.

## THE JOB

Oriental medicine practitioners usually specialize in one or more of the healing modalities that make up Oriental medicine. In the United States, the educational career paths for OM practitioners are currently organized around acupuncture, Oriental medicine (acupuncture and Chinese herbology), and Oriental bodywork. Not all disciplines are licensed or recognized in every state. However, each specialty is based on the fundamental OM principle of diagnosing and seeking to balance disturbances of *qi*.

Oriental medicine practitioners begin a new relationship with a client by taking a careful history. Next, they use the traditional Chinese approach called the "four examinations" for evaluation and diagnosis.

These include asking questions, looking, listening/smelling, and touching. OM practitioners use the four examinations to identify signs and symptoms. They synthesize all they learn about the individual into a vivid profile of the whole person, which includes the mind, body, and spirit. The first appointment generally lasts an hour or more.

While examining a patient, the practitioner looks for any sign of disharmony. The results of the evaluation and diagnosis determine the course of therapy. Depending on a practitioner's training and on the needs of the individual client, the OM practitioner may recommend one or more of the major modalities: acupuncture, Chinese herbology, Oriental bodywork, exercise, or dietary therapy.

In the West, acupuncture is the best-known form of traditional Oriental medicine, and it is sometimes considered synonymous with Oriental medicine. Acupuncture is a complete medical system that encourages the body to improve functioning and promote natural healing. *Acupuncturists* help clients maintain good health and also treat symptoms and disorders. They insert very thin needles into precise points on the skin that stimulate the area and work to balance the circulation of energy. For more detailed information, see the article "Acupuncturists."

In the United States, most of the modalities of traditional Chinese medicine are now frequently considered under the more general term of Oriental medicine. However, even practitioners from Japan, Korea, and other Asian countries still consider Chinese herbology to be uniquely Chinese. Chinese herbology (also known as the Chinese herbal sciences) studies the properties of herbs, their energetics, and their therapeutic qualities. It has a 2,000-year history as a distinct body of knowledge, independent of acupuncture. *Chinese herbalists* practice herbal science according to the principles of Oriental medicine. After performing a careful evaluation and diagnosis, they determine which herbs can be used to help restore the balance of a patient's qi. Chinese herbalists develop formulas based on the unique combination of the individual's characteristics, symptoms, and primary complaints.

Tuina, or Tui Na (both pronounced "twee nah"), is a form of Oriental bodywork or massage that has been used in China for 2,000 years. It is sometimes referred to as Oriental physical therapy. *Tuina practitioners* seek to establish a more harmonious flow of qi through the channels (meridians) of the body. They accomplish this through a variety of different systems: massage, acupressure (similar to acupuncture, but using pressure from fingers and hands instead of needles), energy generation exercises, and manipulation. The tuina practitioner evaluates the individual's specific problems and develops a treatment plan that emphasizes acupressure points and energy meridians as well as pain sites, muscles, and joints. Unlike traditional Western types of massage that involve a more general-ized treatment, tuina focuses on specific problem areas. Treatments usually last half an hour to an hour. The number of sessions depends on the needs of the client. Some Oriental bodywork practitioners use Chinese herbs to assist the healing process.

Qigong, also spelled *Qi Gong* or *Chi Kung* (all pronounced "chee goong"), is a Chinese system of exercise, philosophy, and health care. It is a healing art that combines movement and meditation. The Chi-nese character "qi" means life force; the character "gong" means to cultivate or engage. Hence, qigong literally means to cultivate one's life force or vital energy. Qigong has five major traditions: Taoist, Bud-dhist, Confucian, martial arts, and medical. It has more than a thou-sand forms. Kung fu is an example of a martial arts qigong. *T'ai qi* (t'ai chi) has Taoist, martial arts, and self-healing forms. Medical qigong combines meditation with breathing exercises. Through the regular practice of qigong, the circulation of the qi is stimulated. Qigong can help body functions return to normal for those who are sick and can increase the sense of well-being for those who are already healthy.

Oriental dietary therapy helps to restore harmony to the qi through balancing what the individual eats. When the diet becomes unbal-anced, it can trigger disharmony. The Oriental medicine practitio-ner recommends adjustments in the diet that will restore balance. The therapeutic basis for dietary therapy is the same as for Chinese herbology. The practitioner considers the energetics and therapeutic qualities of each kind of food in order to select precisely the right foods to restore balance to the individual's qi.

In addition to working to help their clients achieve a more balanced state, Oriental medicine practitioners usually have many other duties. Most are self-employed, so they have all of the obligations of running their own businesses. They must keep records of their clients' histories and progress and manage billing and receiving payments. If services are covered by insurance, OM practitioners bill the client's insurance company. Practitioners also must work hard to build their clientele. A career in Oriental medicine requires lifelong learning, and practitio-ners continually study and increase their knowledge of their field.

## REQUIREMENTS

### High School

To prepare yourself for a career as an Oriental medicine practitioner, you need to learn to understand the human body, mind, and spirit. Courses in science, particularly biology, will help you prepare for medical courses ahead. Psychology, philosophy, sociology, and com-parative religion classes can help you learn about the mind and spirit.

Physical education and sports training will help you prepare for the exercise and massage aspects of Oriental medicine. English, drama, debate, and speech can help you develop the communication skills you will need to relate to your clients and to build your business. Most Oriental medicine practitioners are self-employed, so you will also need business, math, and computer skills.

### Postsecondary Training

In the United States, there are presently three defined career paths for Oriental medicine practitioners: acupuncture, Oriental medicine (acupuncture and Chinese herbology), and Oriental bodywork. More than 60 schools in the United States have courses in Oriental medicine and acupuncture. The duration of programs will vary, but most students choose to attend a program at the master's level. For admission to a master's level program, almost every school requires at least two years of undergraduate study. Others require a bachelor's degree in a related field, such as science, nursing, or premed. Most Oriental medicine programs provide a thorough education in Western sciences as well as Chinese herbology, acupuncture techniques, and all aspects of traditional Oriental medicine.

Choosing a school for Oriental medicine can be complex. An important consideration is where you want to live and practice. State requirements to practice Oriental medicine vary greatly, so be sure to choose a school that will prepare you to practice in your desired location.

If you plan to apply for federal financial assistance, look for a college accredited by the Council of Colleges of Acupuncture and Oriental Medicine's Accreditation Commission for Acupuncture and Oriental Medicine (http://www.acaom.org), because these programs are recognized by the U.S. Department of Education.

Oriental bodywork therapy is not taught as a separate discipline in schools of Oriental medicine. To become an Oriental bodywork therapist, you must first meet the requirements of your state to become a massage therapist. Most massage therapy schools require a high school diploma for entrance. Postsecondary or previous study of science, psychology, and business can be helpful. Some schools require a personal interview. Accredited massage schools generally offer a minimum of 500 hours of training, which includes the study of anatomy, physiology, kinesiology (the study of human movement), ethics, and business practices. In addition, the school should provide courses in the theory and practice of massage therapy and supervised hands-on training. For an in-depth discussion of massage therapy, be sure to see the article "Massage Therapists."

Once you complete a program in general massage therapy, you can specialize in Oriental bodywork. Some massage schools offer courses in Oriental bodywork. A specialty in Oriental bodywork requires 150 to 500 hours of additional training. The American Organization for Bodywork Therapies of Asia can supply you with information about schools that offer training.

## Certification or Licensing

The National Certification Commission for Acupuncture and Oriental Medicine (NCCAOM) promotes nationally recognized standards for acupuncture and Oriental medicine. In order to qualify to take the NCCAOM exam, students must complete a three-year accredited master's level or candidate program. Four designations are available: Diplomate in Oriental Medicine (Dipl. O.M.), Diplomate in Acupuncture (Dipl. Ac.), Diplomate in Chinese Herbology (Dipl. C.H.), and Diplomate in Asian Bodywork Therapy (Dipl. A.B.T.).

Licensing requirements vary widely from state to state, and they are changing rapidly. Most states use the NCCAOM certification as their standard for licensure. Other states seek certification and additional educational requirements. Check with the licensing board of the state in which you intend to practice.

The nationwide trend in acupuncture and Oriental medicine is toward more education and universal certification and licensing requirements. A recent development is the Doctor of Oriental Medicine (D.O.M.) designation. See the Web sites of the American Association of Acupuncture and Oriental Medicine (http://www.aaom. org) and the National Oriental Medicine Accreditation Agency (http://www.nomaa.org) for more information.

Individual states regulate Oriental bodywork practitioners as they do general massage therapists. Currently, 38 states and the District of Columbia regulate the practice of massage therapy, requiring licensure, certification, or registration. They generally require completion of a 500-hour program and the National Certification Exam for Therapeutic Massage and Bodywork or the National Certification Examination for Therapeutic Massage. The National Certification Board for Therapeutic Massage and Bodywork provides more information about each exam at its Web site, http://www.ncbtmb.com. The American Massage Therapy Association can give you information regarding the laws of your state. If your state does not have licensing requirements, check with your county or municipality for regulations governing massage therapy.

## Other Requirements

Oriental medicine practitioners work with people who may be ill or in pain, so they need to be compassionate and understanding. Listening skills, strong intuition, careful observation, and problem-solving skills are also valuable.

Oriental medicine is a science of understanding energetics in the body, and it is a healing art. Whether you pursue a career as an Oriental bodywork therapist or as an acupuncturist, you need to be successful at understanding and learning this unique approach to health care. Acupuncturists need sensitive hands and keen vision. Oriental bodywork practitioners need strong hands and physical stamina.

## EXPLORING

Study Oriental history and philosophy to help you learn to understand Oriental medicine's approach to healing. Watch videos, read, or take courses in *t'ai qi*, kung fu, or other forms of *qigong*. These ancient methods for achieving control of the mind and body will be part of your studies in Oriental medicine. Health food stores have books on acupuncture, Chinese herbology, and perhaps Oriental bodywork.

Talk with people who have experienced acupuncture, Chinese herbal therapy, or Oriental bodywork therapy. Ask them what it was like and if they were happy with the results of the alternative treatment. You may even want to make an appointment to see an Oriental medicine practitioner. By experiencing acupuncture or massage therapy firsthand, you can better determine if you'd like to practice it yourself.

Visit colleges of Oriental medicine or massage schools and ask an admissions counselor if you could sit in on a class. Try to talk to the students after class and ask what they like or dislike about their school, class schedule, or choice in career.

Investigate the national and state professional associations. Many of them are listed at the end of this article and have excellent Web sites. Some associations offer student memberships. See if you can attend a meeting to learn about the current issues in OM and introduce yourself to some of the members. Networking with experienced practitioners can help you learn more about Oriental medicine, find a school, and perhaps even find a job.

## EMPLOYERS

More than 14,000 Oriental medicine and acupuncture practitioners are currently employed in the United States. Most Oriental medicine practitioners who specialize in acupuncture, Chinese herbology, or other forms of Oriental medicine operate private practices. Some form or join partnerships with other OM or other alternative health care practitioners. Professionals such as chiropractors, osteopaths, and other licensed physicians increasingly include Oriental medicine practitioners in their practices.

As Oriental medicine and acupuncture become more accepted, there are growing opportunities for practitioners in hospitals and university medical schools. A few are engaged in medical research. They conduct studies on the effectiveness of Oriental medicine in treating various health conditions. There is a growing emphasis on research in acupuncture, and this area is likely to employ more people in the future. A few Oriental medicine practitioners work for government agencies, such as the National Institutes of Health.

Oriental bodywork therapists practice in clinics with acupuncturists, other OM practitioners, or other alternative health practitioners. They also work in many of the locations where conventional massage therapists practice, such as conventional doctors' offices, hotels, spas, cruise ships, fitness centers, nursing homes, and hospitals. Some establish private practices or run their own clinics. A few teach Oriental bodywork in massage schools or in programs that specialize in Oriental bodywork.

## STARTING OUT

When you start out as an Oriental medicine practitioner, one of the most important considerations is having the proper certification and licensing for your geographical area. This is essential because the requirements for the professions and for each state are changing rapidly.

When starting out, acupuncturists sometimes find jobs in clinics with alternative health care practitioners or chiropractors or in wellness centers. This gives them a chance to start practicing in a setting where they can work with and learn from others. Some begin working with more experienced practitioners and then later go into private practice. When starting their new practices, they often keep their full-time jobs and begin their practices part time.

Oriental bodywork therapists may also find work in clinics with chiropractors or other complementary health care practitioners. In addition, they might find job opportunities in local health clubs, spas, nursing homes, hospitals, or wellness centers.

Networking with professionals in local and national organizations is always a good way to learn about job opportunities. Join the organizations that interest you, attend meetings, and get to know people in the field.

## ADVANCEMENT

Oriental medicine practitioners who specialize in acupuncture or Chinese herbology advance in their careers by establishing their own practices, building large bases of patients, or starting their own clinics. Because they receive referrals from physicians and other alternative health care practitioners, relationships with other members of the medical community are very helpful in building a patient base.

Experienced acupuncturists may teach at a school of Oriental medicine. After much experience, an individual may achieve a supervisory or directorship position in a school. The growing acceptance of acupuncture and Oriental medicine by the American public and the medical community will lead to an increasing need for research in university medical hospitals or government agencies.

For OM practitioners who specialize in Oriental bodywork, advancement can come in the form of promotions within the facility where they work. They can take more advanced courses and pursue a higher degree in Oriental bodywork. They can also become teachers or start their own practice.

## EARNINGS

Starting pay for a private practitioner specializing in acupuncture and Oriental medicine may be $15,000–$20,000 until the practice expands. Income is directly related to the number of hours worked and the rate charged per hour, which generally increases with experience. Average income for full-time acupuncturists is $30,000–$60,000. Experienced Oriental medicine practitioners with well-established practices can net $200,000 or more.

Oriental bodywork therapists' earnings depend upon the setting in which they work. Those who work with conventional massage therapists may have similar incomes. According to the U.S. Department of Labor, massage therapists earned salaries in 2007 that ranged from less than $16,000 for entry level positions, to $34,870 for mid-level, to more than $70,840 for the very experienced. Oriental bodywork therapists who are starting out can charge $40 per hour. Mid-level therapists can charge $65, and very experienced therapists may earn as much as $125 per hour. Most Oriental bodywork sessions last a full hour, so therapists' incomes are limited by the number of sessions they schedule.

Oriental medicine practitioners who work for hospitals and university medical schools usually receive benefits such as vacation days, sick leave, health and life insurance, and a savings and pension program. Self-employed practitioners must provide their own benefits.

## WORK ENVIRONMENT

Oriental bodywork therapists work in a variety of settings, and the work environment can vary greatly. In most locations, they work indoors in clean, comfortable surroundings. Solo practitioners may set up their own offices or travel to their clients' homes or places of business. If they have to travel, they frequently charge a travel fee. They have flexible schedules and can set their own hours. Those who are self-employed must provide their own benefits.

Bodywork therapists who work in doctors' offices, hospitals, fitness centers, spas, or on cruise ships usually work more regular hours, depending on their employers' demands. Depending on the employer and their working hours, therapists may receive benefits. Weekend and evening hours may be required to meet the needs of clients.

Oriental medicine practitioners who specialize in acupuncture usually work indoors in clean, quiet, comfortable offices. Since most are in private practice, they define their own surroundings. Private practitioners set their own hours, but many work some evenings or weekends to accommodate their patients' schedules. They usually work without supervision, thus they must have self-discipline. Acupuncturists who own practices must provide their own insurance, vacation, and retirement benefits.

For acupuncturists who work in clinics, hospitals, universities, and research settings, the surroundings vary. They may work in large hospitals or small colleges. However, wherever they work, health care practitioners need clean, quiet offices. In these larger settings, practitioners need to be team players. They may also need to be able to work well under supervision. Those employed by large organizations usually receive salaries and benefits, but have to follow hours set by their employer.

## OUTLOOK

The national emphasis on wellness and natural health care is expected to keep up the demand for Oriental bodywork therapists and other OM practitioners. Interest from the mainstream medical community, recent advances in research, and favorable changes in government policy are strong indicators that the field will continue to expand. As insurance, health maintenance organizations, and other third-party reimbursements increase, Oriental medicine is expected to grow. According to the American Association of Acupuncture and Oriental Medicine, the number of certified and licensed acupuncturists has nearly tripled in the last decade and should continue to grow as additional states establish legal guidelines.

The number of people who seek Oriental medicine practitioners of acupuncture for their health care needs is growing annually. Oriental medicine is used to relieve a wide range of common ailments, including asthma, high blood pressure, headache, and back pain. Many people turn to Oriental medicine practitioners for internal medicine, oncology, obstetrics/gynecology, pediatrics, urology, geriatrics, sports medicine, immunology, infectious diseases, and psychiatric disorders.

As an important part of Oriental medicine, Oriental bodywork therapy also has a bright future. As more alternative health care practitioners enter practice in response to public demand, positions for Oriental bodywork therapy will increase. Alternative health care practitioners, such as chiropractors and holistic physicians, are good sources of employment and referrals for Oriental bodywork therapists.

## FOR MORE INFORMATION

*For information on accredited programs, contact*
> **Accreditation Commission for Acupuncture and Oriental Medicine**
> Maryland Trade Center #3
> 7501 Greenway Center Drive, Suite 760
> Greenbelt, MD 20770-3580
> Tel: 301-313-0855
> Email: coordinator@acaom.org
> http://www.acaom.org

*For general information on Oriental medicine and acupuncture, listings of schools offering programs, and sources for additional resources, contact*
> **American Association of Acupuncture and Oriental Medicine**
> PO Box 162340
> Sacramento, CA 95816-2340
> Tel: 866-455-7999
> http://www.aaaomonline.org

*For information regarding state regulations for massage therapists and general information on therapeutic massage, contact*
> **American Massage Therapy Association**
> 500 Davis Street, Suite 900
> Evanston, IL 60201-4695
> Tel: 877-905-2700
> Email: info@amtamassage.org
> http://www.amtamassage.org

*To learn more about acupressure, massage therapy, national and regional workshops, and programs providing professional training, contact*
**American Organization for Bodywork Therapies of Asia**
1010 Haddonfield-Berlin Road, Suite 408
Voorhees, NJ 08043-3514
Tel: 856-782-1616
Email: office@aobta.org
http://www.aobta.org

*For information on accredited colleges, contact*
**Council of Colleges of Acupuncture and Oriental Medicine**
3909 National Drive, Suite 125
Burtonsville, MD 20866-6110
Tel: 301-476-7790
http://www.ccaom.org

*To learn about the national center that specializes in alternative medicine and for excellent resources on alternative health care approaches, visit*
**National Center for Complementary and Alternative Medicine**
9000 Rockville Pike
Bethesda, MD 20892-0001
Email: info@nccam.nih.gov
http://nccam.nih.gov

*For information on certification, contact*
**National Certification Commission for Acupuncture and Oriental Medicine**
76 South Laura Street, Suite 1290
Jacksonville, FL 32202-5410
Tel: 904-598-1005
Email: info@nccaom.org
http://www.nccaom.org

*Visit this Web site for articles on the history and practice of acupuncture.*
**Acupuncture.com**
http://acupuncture.com

# Osteopaths

## OVERVIEW

*Doctors of Osteopathic Medicine* (DOs), sometimes referred to as *osteopathic physicians* or *osteopaths*, practice a medical discipline that uses refined and sophisticated manipulative therapy based on the late 19th–century teachings of American Dr. Andrew Taylor Still. It embraces the idea of "whole person" medicine and looks upon the system of muscles, bones, and joints—particularly the spine—as reflecting the body's diseases and being partially responsible for initiating disease processes. Osteopathic physicians are medical doctors with additional specialized training in this unique approach. They practice in a wide range of fields, from environmental medicine, geriatrics, and nutrition to sports medicine and neurology, among others. More than 61,000 osteopathic physicians are members of the American Osteopathic Association.

## HISTORY

Osteopathic medicine has its roots in the hardships and challenges of 19th-century America. Its developer, Dr. Andrew Taylor Still, was born in 1828 in Virginia, the son of a Methodist minister and physician. There were few medical schools in the United States, so Still received his early medical training largely from his father. As the Civil War began, he attended the College of Physicians and Surgeons in Kansas City, but he enlisted in the army before completing the course.

In 1864, an epidemic of meningitis struck the Missouri frontier. Thousands died, including Still's three children. His inability to help them underscored his growing dissatisfaction with traditional medical approaches. After much careful study of anatomy, physiology, and the general nature of health, he became convinced that cultivating a deep understanding of the structure-function relationship between the parts of the body was the only path to a true understanding of disease. Eventually, Still came to believe in three basic principles that would form the core of his osteopathic approach to the practice of medicine. First, he saw the body as capable of self-healing, producing its own healing substances. Second, he felt health was dependent upon the structural integrity of the body. And, finally, because of these beliefs, he considered distorted structure a fundamental cause of disease.

A system of physical manipulation was an integral component of Still's new practice. He began to compare manipulative therapy with other methods then used by doctors, such as drugs and surgery. Often, he found the use of manipulative methods made drugs and operations unnecessary. Instead, he focused on the musculoskeletal system—the muscles, bones, nerves, and ligaments. Recognizing that structural misalignments often occurred in these areas, he emphasized the system's importance as a major potential factor in disease, ripe for the application of his new manipulative techniques.

Still founded the first college of osteopathic medicine in Kirksville, Missouri, in 1892, basing it upon the fundamental principles of his osteopathic concept. Fewer than 20 men and women graduated from this first osteopathic medical college in 1894. Today, there are 25 osteopathic medicine schools in the United States. Some are part of major university campuses; combined, they accept roughly 4,400 new osteopathic students annually.

Andrew Still died in 1917, leaving behind a legacy of enormous importance to the history of medicine. Medicine as we know it was in its infancy in his day, and theories, tools, and techniques we take for granted now—such as the concept of germs, the use of antiseptics, and the diagnostic possibilities presented by radiology—were just beginning. In this challenging environment, Still worked out a practical system of structural therapeutics that has withstood the pressure of later discoveries.

Although practitioners of alternative methods of healing in the United States were—and sometimes still are—seen as a threat by the medical profession, osteopathic medicine has increased in popularity. As the field grew, some students wished to use drugs as well as osteopathic techniques in treating patients. John Martin Littlejohn, for example—a Scotsman who studied with Still—widened the focus of osteopathy by concentrating not only on anatomy, but stressing physiological aspects as well. Unlike Still, Littlejohn wanted osteopathic physicians to learn all about modern medicine, along with osteopathic principles and practices. Later, Littlejohn returned to Britain, where he founded the British School of Osteopathy. Even so, the training of osteopathic physicians in the United States was, in fact, eventually to merge with the training of orthodox medical physicians.

## THE JOB

Osteopathic and orthodox medicine both use the scientific knowledge of anatomy and physiology, as well as clinical methods of investigation. In this respect, they have a similar language. The greatest differences, however, lie in the way patients are evaluated and in the approach to treatment. As a general rule, the orthodox medical approach focuses on the end result of the problem: the illness. Treatments seek to repair the imbalance presented by the illness through the prescription of drugs or by surgery. In contrast, osteopathic physicians focus on tracing the changes in a patient's ability to function that have occurred over a period of time. This is done to understand the chain of events that have altered the relationship between structure and function, resulting in the patient's present complaint. The primary aim of treatment is to remove the obstacles within a patient's body that are preventing the natural self-healing process from occurring. It's a subtle but important difference.

Like most physicians, osteopaths spend much of their day seeing patients in a clinic or hospital setting. Their specialty, of course, may take them to other venues, such as nursing homes or sports arenas.

The osteopathic physician's first task in evaluating a new patient is trying to understand the cause of the problem that the patient presents. It may sound simple, but it can be very complex. Diagnosis is a fluid art, and treatment programs are reviewed with each patient visit, changing as the patient begins to respond. To arrive at an appropriate diagnosis, osteopathic physicians record and analyze the history of prior treatment. This report will likely be greatly detailed, since osteopathic physicians consider the whole body. Since structure and function are interdependent, and all the parts of the body connect with each other, osteopaths ask questions that appear to have little relevance to the problem at hand. It is precisely that concern for seemingly irrelevant details, coupled with manipulative therapy, which distinguishes the osteopath from the more conventional Doctor of Medicine (MD).

One technique that assists in the correct evaluation of patient problems is palpation, a manual means of diagnosis and determination, whereby sensory information is received through the fingers and hands. Along with careful listening and observation, osteopathic physicians use palpitation to assess healthy tissue and identify structural problems or painful areas in a patient's body.

The osteopathic physician differs from a traditional MD, or *allopathic physician,* in one other major aspect: treatment options. For the osteopathic physicians, treatment centers on what are called osteopathic lesions, which are functional disturbances in the body that may involve muscles, joints, and other body systems. These lesions are created by mechanical and physiological reactions in the body to various types of trauma. In osteopathy, open, unhindered, and balanced movement is the most important factor in health. The lack of balance plays a major role in the onset of disease and illness. Thus, the many varied techniques employed by osteopathic physicians are concerned primarily with re-establishing normal mobility and removing or reducing the underlying lesions.

The techniques available to treat osteopathic lesions are nearly limitless. Because osteopathic physicians consider the whole body when determining the proper treatment, each application of a particular technique will be unique. Similar lesions in different patients will have different origins and will have been caused by different sorts of forces or events. Thorough evaluation of the patient help guide osteopaths in discerning what sorts of techniques will be most helpful.

## REQUIREMENTS

### High School

Students who plan a career as a physician, either as a DO or an MD, should take a college preparatory program in high school. You'll need a strong foundation in the sciences, especially biology, chemistry, and physics. In addition, take English, history, foreign languages, and all the math you can. Psychology is a helpful course in preparing you to work well with a wide variety of people coming to you for treatment. Strive to become as well-rounded an individual as possible.

### Postsecondary Training

After obtaining a bachelor's degree, prospective osteopathic physicians must apply to medical school. Students file applications along with their college transcripts and MCAT (Medical College Admission Test) scores. Admission to an osteopathic medical school, like all medical schools, is quite competitive.

The academic program leading to the Doctor of Osteopath Medicine degree involves four years of study, followed by a one-year rotating internship in areas such as internal medicine, obstetrics/gynecology, and surgery. Those interested in a specific specialty must complete an additional two to six years of residency training.

The curriculum in colleges of osteopathic medicine supports Dr. Still's osteopathic philosophy, with an emphasis on preventive, family, and community medicine. Clinical instruction stresses examining all patient characteristics (including behavioral and environmental) and how various body systems interrelate. Close attention is given to the ways in which the musculoskeletal and nervous systems influence the functioning of the entire body. An increasing emphasis on biomedical research in several of the colleges has expanded opportunities for students wishing to pursue research careers.

### Certification or Licensing

At an early point in the residency period, all physicians, both MDs and DOs, must pass a state medical board examination in order to obtain a license and enter practice. Each state sets its own requirements and issues its own licenses, although some states will accept licenses from other states.

Many osteopathic physicians belong to the American Osteopathic Association (AOA). To retain membership, physicians must complete 150 hours of continuing education every three years. Continuing education can be acquired in a variety of ways, including attending professional conferences, completing education programs sponsored by the AOA, teaching osteopathic medicine, and publishing articles in professional journals.

The AOA offers board certification, which entails passing a comprehensive written exam as a well as a practical test demonstrating osteopathic manipulative techniques. The AOA offers specialty certification in 18 areas. Some osteopathic physicians are certified by both the AOA and the American Medical Association (AMA).

### Other Requirements

The practice of osteopathic medicine usually involves a lot of personal interaction and a lot of touching, which can make some patients—and some prospective doctors—feel uncomfortable. If you plan to become an osteopathic physician, you will need excellent communication skills to tell patients what to expect and what is happening at any one moment. If patients don't understand what you are telling them, they may not pursue treatment. For this reason, good communication skills are crucial. You will also need to learn to work well with others and to be perceptive listeners.

Since a large number of osteopathic physicians go into private practice, business and management skills are useful. In addition, good manual dexterity is important. Finally, and most importantly, you must have a real commitment to caring for people in this medically specialized way.

## EXPLORING

Consider visiting an osteopathic medical college. Tours are often available and can give you extra insight into necessary training and the ways in which life at an osteopathic medical school differs from a "regular" one. If you don't live close enough to an osteopathic college to visit, write for more information or visit their Web sites.

Check into after-school or summer jobs at your local hospital or medical center. Any job that exposes you to the care of patients is a good one, even jobs you might not think of at first, or ones that aren't exactly medical, such as working with the janitorial service. Contact the American Osteopathic Association and ask for a list of osteopathic physicians in your area. Talk to as many people as you can, and don't be afraid to ask questions.

## EMPLOYERS

Osteopathic physicians can be found in virtually all medical specialties. More than one-third of all osteopathic physicians go into private practice after completing their training. They also work in hospitals, clinics, nursing homes, and other health care settings. Approximately 61,000 osteopaths are members of the American Osteopathic Association.

## STARTING OUT

Depending on the specialty in which an osteopathic physicians is interested, he or she can plan on completing a residency program of two to seven years' duration. One of the difficulties facing the profession today is that medical schools produce more students than there are available residencies at osteopathic hospitals. As a result, gaining admission to selective osteopathic medicine programs may be challenging. Graduates increasingly find residencies in traditional medical facilities. As awareness of and interest in osteopathic medicine continue to grow, this shortage of open residency positions may change. After completing a residency program, an osteopathic physician can choose to go into private practice or explore positions with a variety of health care employers.

## ADVANCEMENT

Advancement in the medical professions is dependent on the specific field. Osteopathic physicians in private practice will follow a different career path than those working in a purely clinical setting or in a research position at an academic medical center. As noted earlier, a large percentage of osteopathic physicians go into private or small-group practice. Advancement in private practice comes with increased reputation; mainly through word of mouth, a practice grows with positive referrals.

In contrast, osteopathic physicians in employee positions are more limited in their methods of advancement. Those in an academic setting face the challenge of obtaining tenure to advance from instructor to assistant professor to associate professor to professor. Becoming tenured is an arduous process, involving a combination of patient care, research, publication, and administrative responsibilities. Those who love the academic environment, however, and also want to be a practicing physician usually find their niche in academia.

## Did You Know?

- Approximately 100,000 osteopathic physicians will be in practice by 2020.
- Slightly more than 14,400 students were enrolled in osteopathic medical schools in 2006–07, an increase of nearly 18 percent since 2003–04.
- In 2007, nearly 29 percent of osteopaths were women, and females made up nearly 50 percent of students at osteopathic medical schools.
- In 2006–07, Whites made up 69 percent of osteopathic medical students; Asian Americans, 17 percent; African Americans, 4 percent; Hispanic Americans, 4 percent; and Native Americans, 1 percent.
- The states with the largest number of osteopaths in 2006 were (in descending order): Pennsylvania, Michigan, Florida, Ohio, New York, and California.
- In 2007, nearly 44.6 percent of osteopaths specialized in family and general practice; 9.5 percent in general internal medicine; 4.2 percent in general pediatrics and adolescent medicine; 3.9 percent in obstetrics; 1.4 percent in osteopathic manipulative medicine or osteopathic manipulative treatment; and 0.9 percent in pediatric specialties.

Sources: American Osteopathic Association, American Association of Colleges of Osteopathic Medicine

# EARNINGS

Osteopathic physicians earn incomes comparable to their MD counterparts. The potentially high income that comes with becoming established as a physician can be an enticing perk. According to the American Medical Association (AMA), the median net income for all physicians is $160,000. The middle 50 percent earn between $120,000 and $240,000 a year. There are a number of other factors to keep in mind, however, as described in a recent survey by the AMA. Counting postgraduate education, most physicians are in their early 30s before starting to practice. Residency pay is low (medical residents averaged $44,747 a year in 2006–07), yet residents work up to 80 hours per week. Most physicians incur high educational debt by the time they begin to practice.

Benefits for osteopathic physicians vary, depending on whether they work in private practice or for an employer. The AMA survey indicates that median net income for self-employed physicians is approximately 40 percent higher than that of employee physicians. Many factors contribute to the difference. Self-employed physicians tend to be older, have more years of experience, work more hours, and more likely to be board certified, all of which are associated with higher earnings. On the other hand, 75 percent of employee physicians receive noncash benefits in addition to their reported income, whereas some self-employed physicians do not. These benefits represent approximately 5 percent of income for employees.

# WORK ENVIRONMENT

As with the benefits earned, the environment in which an osteopathic physician works can vary. In private practice and employer-based situations, osteopathic physicians work both alone (directly with a patient) and as part of a team. Osteopathic medicine, like all medical professions, is a field of contrasts, requiring both collaboration and personal insight. The primary obstacle to be aware of going into almost any field of medicine is long hours and erratic schedules, particularly during training.

# OUTLOOK

According to the American Association of Colleges of Osteopathic Medicine (AACOM), the number of osteopathic medicine graduates has increased approximately 37 percent since 1998, making osteopathic medicine one of the fastest-growing health professions in the country. Nearly one in five medical students in the U.S. attend an osteopathic medical school, according to the AACOM. To meet the growing demand, more than a dozen new osteopathic medical colleges have opened their doors since the mid-1970s. Together, all 25 institutions currently enroll more than 15,000 students annually, of whom nearly 50 percent are women.

Although osteopathic medicine is not strictly an "alternative" approach, the field is benefiting from the current interest in these kinds of therapy. Excellent job opportunities will continue to become available for skilled osteopathic physicians. In addition to specialized practices in areas such as family medicine, increasing interest in biomedical research at the osteopathic colleges also is expanding opportunities for candidates interested in careers in medical research.

## FOR MORE INFORMATION

*To read the* Osteopathic Medical College Information Book *and for information on financial aid, visit the Web site of the AACOM.*
    **American Association of Colleges of Osteopathic Medicine (AACOM)**
    5550 Friendship Boulevard, Suite 310
    Chevy Chase, MD 20815-7231
    Tel: 301-968-4100
    http://www.aacom.org

*For information on osteopathic medicine, visit the AOA's Web site.*
    **American Osteopathic Association (AOA)**
    142 East Ontario Street
    Chicago, IL 60611-2874
    Tel: 800-621-1773
    Email: info@osteopathic.org
    http://do-online.osteotech.org

# Reflexologists

## QUICK FACTS

**School Subjects**
Biology
Health
Psychology

**Personal Skills**
Communication/ideas
Helping/teaching

**Work Environment**
Primarily indoors
Primarily one location

**Minimum Education Level**
Some postsecondary training

**Salary Range**
$7,000 to $35,000 to
$100,000+

**Certification or Licensing**
Recommended

**Outlook**
Faster than the average

**DOT**
N/A

**GOE**
N/A

**NOC**
3232

**O*NET-SOC**
N/A

## OVERVIEW

*Reflexologists* base their work on the theory that *reflexes*, specific points on the hands and feet, correspond to specific points on other parts of the body. They apply pressure to the feet or hands of their clients in order to affect the areas of the body that correspond to the areas that they are manipulating. Reflexologists believe that their work promotes overall good health, helps clients relax, and speeds the healing process.

## HISTORY

Reflexology—or something similar to it—was practiced thousands of years ago. More than 2,000 years before the common era, the Chinese learned that foot massage was a useful adjunct to the practice of acupuncture. Many modern practitioners of reflexology believe that reflexology utilizes the principles on which acupuncture and traditional Chinese medicine are based. A 4,000-year-old fresco that appears in the tomb of Ankhmahor, physician to a pharaoh, in the Egyptian city of Saqqara depicts the practice of foot massage. In North America, the Cherokee people have emphasized the importance of the feet in health, partly because it is through the feet that human beings connect with the earth. Zone theory, which provides the theoretical basis for reflexology, existed in Europe as early as the 1500s.

Although reflexology is an ancient practice, its modern form originated in the early 20th century. William Fitzgerald, a Connecticut-based physician who was an ear, nose, and throat specialist, revived the practice of reflexology in the West in 1913, when he found that applying pressure to a patient's hands or feet just before surgery decreased the level of pain experienced by the patient. In 1917, Fitzgerald wrote *Zone Therapy, or Relieving Pain at Home*, which described his work. Fitzgerald believed that "bioelectrical energy" flows from points in the feet or hands to specific points elsewhere in the body, and he thought that applying tourniquets and various instruments to the feet or hands enhanced the flow of energy. He set out to map the flow of that energy, and in the process he set up correspondences between areas on the feet or hands and areas throughout the body.

The next important figure in modern reflexology, Eunice Ingham, was a physiotherapist who had worked with Joseph Shelby Riley, a follower of William Fitzgerald. Riley had decided against using instruments to manipulate the feet and hands, opting to use his hands instead. Ingham practiced and taught extensively, mapped the correspondences between the reflexes and the parts of the body, and wrote books chronicling her work with her patients, which helped to promote the field of reflexology. She went on to found the organization now known as the International Institute of Reflexology (IIR), which continues to promote the Original Ingham Method of Reflexology. Ultimately, Ingham became known as the mother of modern reflexology. Her students have played major roles in spreading reflexology throughout the world.

## THE JOB

Reflexologists believe that the standing human body is divided vertically into 10 zones, five zones on each side of the imaginary vertical line that divides the body in two. On both sides, the zone closest to the middle is zone one, while the zone farthest from the middle is zone five. These zones also appear on the hands and feet. Reflexologists believe that by massaging a spot in a zone on the foot, they can stimulate a particular area in the corresponding zone of the body. By massaging the reflex in the middle of the big toe, for example, a reflexologist attempts to affect the pituitary gland, which is the corresponding body part.

Reflexologists also believe that their ministrations help their clients in two other ways. First, they believe that their treatments reduce the amount of lactic acid in the feet. Lactic acid is a natural waste product of the metabolic process, and its presence in large quantities is unhealthful. Second, they believe that their treatments break up calcium crystals that have built up in the nerve endings of the feet. It is their theory that the presence of these crystals inhibits the flow of energy, which is increased when the crystals are removed. Reflexologists also emphasize that their techniques improve circulation and promote relaxation.

It is worth noting that modern science has not validated the theoretical basis of reflexology, which is even less well accepted in the scientific world than are some other alternative therapies. Yet it is also worth noting that some therapies whose underlying theories have not been validated by science have been shown to be effective. Relatively few scientific studies of reflexology have been completed, but much research is underway at present, and it is likely that reflexology will be better understood in the near future.

An initial visit to a reflexologist generally begins with the practitioner asking the client questions about his or her overall health, medical problems, and the reason for the visit. The reflexologist makes the client comfortable and begins the examination and treatment.

Although most reflexologists, such as the followers of Eunice Ingham, work on their clients' feet or hands with their hands, some prefer to use instruments. In either case, the reflexologist works on the feet and looks for sore spots, which are thought to indicate illness or other problems in the corresponding part of the body. On occasion, the problem will not be manifested in the corresponding organ or part of the body but will instead be manifested elsewhere within the zone. Usually, the reflexologist will spend more time on the sore spots than on other parts of the foot. On the basis of information provided by the client and information obtained by the reflexologist during the examination, the reflexologist will recommend a course of treatment that is appropriate for the client's physical condition. In some cases, such as those of extreme illness, the reflexologist may ask the client to check with his or her physician to determine whether the treatment may be in conflict with the physician's course of treatment. Most reflexologists will not treat a client who has a fever. In addition, because reflexology treatments tend to enhance circulation, it is sometimes necessary for a client who is taking medication to decrease the dosage, on the advice of a doctor, to compensate for the increased circulation and the resulting increased effectiveness of the medication.

One of the most important aspects of the reflexologist's skill is knowing exactly how much pressure to apply to a person's feet. The pressure required for a large, healthy adult, for example, would be too much for a young child or a baby. Different foot shapes and weights may also require different levels of pressure. The practitioner must also know how long to work on the foot, since the benefits of the treatment may be offset if the treatment lasts too long. In her book *Reflexology Today*, Doreen E. Bayly, one of Ingham's students, recalled that Ingham once told her: "If you work on the reflex too long, you are undoing the good you have done." Ingham recommended 30-minute sessions, but most modern reflexologists conduct 45-minute or 60-minute sessions unless the client's condition dictates otherwise.

Most reflexologists work primarily on feet, but some work on the hands or even the ears. If a foot has been injured or amputated, it is acceptable to work on the hands. For the most part, reflexologists work on the feet because the feet are so sensitive. In addition, feet that are encased in shoes during most of the day typically require more attention than hands do. Furthermore, the feet, because of their size, are easier to manipulate. It is somewhat more difficult to find the reflexes on the hands.

## REQUIREMENTS

### High School

Because the practice of reflexology involves utilizing the correspondences between reflexes and the various parts of the body, a student who has some knowledge of medicine and anatomy will have an advantage. Study biology, chemistry, and health—anything that relates to the medical sciences. Since reflexologists must make their clients comfortable and gain their trust, some study of psychology may be useful. You might also investigate areas of bodywork and alternative medicine that are not taught in school. If you have some knowledge or practical skill in some area of massage (shiatsu or Swedish massage, for example), you will have a head start, especially since some states require reflexologists to be licensed massage therapists.

### Postsecondary Training

The single most important part of a reflexologist's training is the completion of a rigorous course of study and practice, such as that provided by the International Institute of Reflexology (IIR). There are many courses available, and they range from one-day sessions designed to train people to work on themselves or their partners to comprehensive courses that require a commitment of nine months or longer on the part of the student. Naturally, if you wish to practice professionally you should select a comprehensive course. Correspondence courses are available, but any reputable correspondence course will require you to complete a required number of hours of supervised, hands-on work. Some aspects of the technique must be demonstrated, not simply read, especially concerning the amount of pressure that the reflexologist should apply to different kinds of feet. Many reflexologists offer services other than reflexology, and you may wish to also train in other kinds of massage, aromatherapy, or another kind of bodywork. Such training may increase the likelihood that you will make a decent living, especially at the beginning of your career.

## Certification or Licensing

In two states, North Dakota and Tennessee, a reflexologist who has completed a course given by a reputable school of reflexology can be licensed or registered specifically as a reflexologist. In most states, however, reflexologists are subject to the laws that govern massage therapists. That often means that you must complete a state-certified course in massage before being licensed to practice reflexology. In many cases, reflexologists are subject to laws that are designed to regulate "massage parlors" that are fronts for prostitution. In some places, these laws require you to be subjected to disease testing and walk-in inspections by police. It is common for those who are medical doctors or licensed cosmetologists to be exempt from massage-licensing regulations. Because there is such wide variation in the law, anyone who wishes to practice reflexology should carefully study state and local regulations before setting up shop.

It is recommended that you enroll in a course that requires a substantial number of hours of training and certifies you upon graduation. If you are at least 18 years old, have a high school diploma or its equivalent, have completed a course that requires at least 110 hours of training, and have at least 90 documented postgraduate reflexology sessions, you can apply to be tested by the American Reflexology Certification Board (ARCB), which was created in 1991. The organization is designed to promote reflexology by recognizing competent practitioners. Testing is purely voluntary, but a high score from the ARCB is a good sign that a practitioner is competent.

## Other Requirements

Reflexologists work closely with their clients, so it is essential that you be friendly, open, and sensitive to the feelings of others. You must be able to gain your clients' trust, make them comfortable and relaxed, and communicate well enough with them to gather the information that they need in order to treat them effectively. It is highly unlikely that an uncommunicative person who is uncomfortable with people will be able to build a reflexology practice. In addition, you must be comfortable making decisions and working alone. Most reflexologists have their own practices, and anyone who sets up shop will need to deal with the basic tasks and problems that all business owners face: advertising, accounting, taxes, legal requirements, and so forth.

## EXPLORING

The best way to learn about the field of reflexology is to speak with reflexologists. Call practitioners and ask to interview them. Find reflexologists in your area if you can, but do not hesitate to contact people in other areas. There is no substitute for learning from those who actually do the work. Although most reflexologists run one-person practices, it may be possible to find clerical work of some kind with a successful practitioner in your area, especially if you live in a large city.

Read as much as you can on the subject. Look for information on reflexology in magazines that deal with alternative medicine and bodywork. Learn as much as you can about alternative therapies. You may find that you wish to practice a number of techniques in addition to reflexology.

## EMPLOYERS

For the most part, reflexologists work for themselves, although they may work at businesses that include reflexology as one of a number of services that they provide. It is probably wise to assume that you are going to run your own business, even if you do end up working for another organization. In most cases, organizations that use reflexologists bring them in as independent contractors rather than employees.

## STARTING OUT

You should begin by taking the best, most comprehensive course of study you can find from a school that will certify you as a practitioner. After that, if you have not found an organization that you can work for, you should begin to practice on your own. You may rent an office or set up shop at home in order to save money. You may begin by working part time, so that you can earn money by other means while you are getting your business underway. Be sure to investigate the state and local laws that may affect you.

To run your own business, you need to be well versed in basic business skills. You may want to take courses in business or seek advice from the local office of the Small Business Administration. Seek advice from people you know who run their own businesses. Your financial survival will depend on your business skills, so be sure that you know what you are doing.

## ADVANCEMENT

Because most reflexologists work for themselves, advancement in the field is directly related to the quality of treatment they provide and their business skills. Reflexologists advance by proving to the members of their community that they are skilled, honest, professional, and effective.

## EARNINGS

There are no reliable figures to indicate what reflexologists earn per year. In most cases, however, reflexologists charge between $30 and $60 per hour. Some practitioners may charge as little as $15 per hour, while a small number of well-respected reflexologists in large cities may earn $100 or even substantially more per hour. Many reflexologists do not work 40 hours per week doing reflexology exclusively. It is likely that most reflexologists earn between $7,000 and $35,000 per year, while some may earn more than $100,000 per year. Typically, it takes quite some time for new practitioners to build up a practice, so many of them rely on other sources of income in the beginning. Many reflexologists offer other holistic treatments and therapies, which means that they do not rely on reflexology to provide all their income.

Self-employed reflexologists must provide their own benefits, such as health and life insurance and a savings and pension plan.

## WORK ENVIRONMENT

Reflexologists almost always work in their homes or in their own offices. Although some reflexologists may have office help, most work alone. For this reason, practitioners must be independent enough to work effectively on schedules of their own devising. Because they must make their clients comfortable in order to provide effective treatment, they generally try to make their workplaces as pleasant and relaxing as possible. Many practitioners play soothing music while they work. Some, especially those who practice aromatherapy as well as reflexology, use scents to create a relaxed atmosphere.

## OUTLOOK

Although no official government analysis of the future of reflexology has yet been conducted, it seems safe to say that the field is expanding much more rapidly than the average for all fields. Although science still views it with skepticism, reflexology has become relatively popular in a short period of time. It has certainly benefited from the popular acceptance of alternative medicine and therapies in recent years, particularly because it is a holistic practice that aims to treat the whole person rather than the symptoms of disease or discomfort. Because reflexology treatments entail little risk to the client in most cases, they provide a safe and convenient way to improve health. The U.S. Department of Labor projects that employment of massage therapists will grow faster than the average over the next several years, and it is likely that employment in reflexology will grow similarly.

## FOR MORE INFORMATION

*For information on accredited reflexology training programs, contact*
American Commission for Accreditation of Reflexology
   Education and Training
1309 Hillcrest Drive
Anchorage, AK 99503-1746
Tel: 907-278-4646
Email: acaret@acaret.org
http://www.acaret.org

*The ARCB was created in order to promote reflexology by recognizing competent practitioners. It provides voluntary testing for working reflexologists and maintains lists of certified practitioners and educational programs.*
American Reflexology Certification Board (ARCB)
PO Box 5147
Gulfport, FL 33737-5147
Tel: 303-933-6921
Email: info@arcb.net
http://www.arcb.net

*The IIR promotes the Ingham Method of Reflexology, providing seminars worldwide as well as a thorough certification program. The institute also sells books and charts.*

**International Institute of Reflexology (IIR)**
5650 First Avenue North
PO Box 12642
St Petersburg, FL 33733-2642
Tel: 727-343-4811
Email: iir@reflexology-usa.net
http://www.reflexology-usa.net

*For information on reflexology, contact*
**Reflexology Association of America**
PO Box 207
Franklin, MA 02038-0207
Tel: 980-234-0159
Email: infoRAA@relexology-usa.org
http://www.reflexology-usa.org

# Index

Entries and page numbers in **bold** indicate major treatment of a topic.